Date Due

FEB 1 0 '98			
JUL 1 5 1999			
AUG 2 9 2000			
AUG 2 9 2000			

BRODART   Cat. No. 23 233   Printed in U.S.A

Preston
MANNING
THE ROOTS OF REFORM

FRANK DABBS

GREYSTONE BOOKS
Douglas & McIntyre
Vancouver/Toronto

Greystone Books
A division of Douglas & McIntyre Ltd.
1615 Venables Street
Vancouver, British Columbia
V5L 2H1

CANADIAN CATALOGUING IN PUBLICATION DATA

Dabbs, Frank, 1947
Preston Manning

ISBN 1-55054-602-3

1. Manning, Preston, 1942–   2. Reform Party of Canada—
Biography.   3. Politicians—Canada—Biography.   4. Canada—Politics and
government—1993   I. Title.
FC636.M36D32   1997   971.064´8´092   C97-910394-0
F1034.3.M28D32   1997

Jacket photograph by Canapress Photo Service/Tom Hanson
Jacket design by Isabelle Swiderski
Printed and bound in Canada by Friesens
Printed on acid-free paper
The publisher gratefully acknowledges the assistance of the Canada Council and of the British Columbia Ministry of Tourism, Small Business and Culture.

Excerpts from the *Globe and Mail* are reprinted with permission from *The Globe and Mail*. Excerpts from Valerie Pringle's interviews with Preston Manning and Craig Oliver are reprinted with permission from CTV and *Canada AM*.

To Dr. C. Howard Bentall

The steps of a good man are ordered by the Lord.

CONTENTS

CONTENTS

Politics is about contested ground.

—BOB WOODWARD, *The Agenda*

IN THE FEDERAL election of June 2, 1997, the Reform Party of Canada won sixty seats in the House of Commons—all from the four western provinces—and became the only third party in Canadian politics ever to sit as the Official Opposition. This is the story of the leader of the party, Preston Manning, and his central mission: bringing the West to the fore as the next great wellspring of Canadian leadership. It is the story of the constraints of practical politics and of the simple truth that a leader and a party are not one and the same.

Launched in the autumn of 1986 by a small group of like-minded western federalists, the Reform Party has taken shape through three federal elections. Reform's raison d'être was to create an alternative to western separatism, Central Canadian–focussed Liberal federalism and the failure of Brian Mulroney's Progressive Conservative government, when it had the opportunity and a large western caucus, to reform federal institutions to reflect western aspirations for an equitable place in Confederation. Preston Manning believed that he had a prescription for a new federalism that would reconcile the country's warring regions.

The Reform Party had inauspicious prospects. Third parties have been part of Western elective politics since the nonpartisan coalition of the first North-West Territories' Legislative Assembly asked Ottawa in 1888 for "full responsible government for the Territories." But these "great prairie winds," as the Winnipeg newspaper editor John Dafoe called them, never closed in on the office of the Prime Minister of Canada. Until now.

Through the twentieth century, various western parties appropriated the name populist from an American agrarian-sponsored third-party experiment at the turn of the century. More accurately, the Canadian parties were "grassroots," with differing economic and social prescriptions but a common desire to reform political institutions so that individuals rather than interests, the electorate rather than the elected, held the levers of power.

Unlike the brief moment of American populism, Canadian third parties flourished (in Quebec as well as the West) to vent their frustration with national institutions. Westerners dreamed of changing the world from their farms and labour halls through the Progressives and Farmers, Social Credit and the Canadian Commonwealth Federation. Occasionally they found common ground with politicians and voters in other regions, but never national power. Now, in three federal elections, the Reform Party has shown itself able to reach for the country's highest office.

If in the twentieth century the fulcrum of federalism was the Ottawa River, in the twenty-first century it will be the Lake of the Woods. The nation's economic centre has undergone mitosis, providing the country with two commercial-financial axes struggling for balance: one in Ontario and one in the West. Vitality, freshness and energy incline to the western side of the scale, which has the economic momentum and the political initiative. Western political discontent and desire for change has become the animating energy for a new era in Canadian politics.

The voice expressing this desire for change in Canadian public life is that of Preston Manning, scion of the West's most successful political family. The Reform Party of Canada is his personal kettle of democracy. The pillars of his life are family, faith and political change. He is born of a bloodline with a bone-marrow suspicion of authority, a deeply held view of the world as a broken place to be mended and a conviction that the principal political institutions of society need reform.

His father, Ernest, for twenty-five years the premier of Alberta, combined the common sense of prairie democrats with blue-chip management principles to become the most successful politician in Western Canadian history. Ernest was the surrogate son, protégé and successor to the great iconoclast William Aberhart, and so Preston is the third generation of Canada's most successful family of political reformers. This book traces the development of Preston Manning's ideas, from his first political experience as a young lad standing behind the curtain in his father's office.

A brilliant physicist-turned-economist, Preston Manning might have become a research scientist or academic, but the family business is politics, and so he became a politician. He first tested public life when he sought national office in 1965 as a twenty-three-year-old fresh-faced proxy for a western brand of responsible liberty. Now, in the respectable years of late middle age, he has emerged as the voice of a reforming tradition that exceeds the parochial boundaries of Aberhart's Social Credit and Ernest Manning's blue-chip western conservatism.

Preston Manning considers himself first a democrat and second a conservative. His vision of democracy is distinctively Western Canadian but is also rooted in larger history. The central idea of his politics is that an electorate with fully informed sensibilities and unfettered democratic license will do the right thing. If the will of the people seems misdirected, the appropriate response is to better inform it. He is intellectual in his approach to politics, but he is not utopian; he does not bend the world to fit a vision. Patience, not passion, is his hallmark.

Manning has synthesized old political ideologies and coupled them to a new political movement. He has wrestled with the paradox of firm leadership in an open party. Reform, however, has become an impatient, impetuous force with little apparent capacity for compromise. Manning must harness its energy to an older political culture of artisans who crafted change without conflagration.

The new energy that will carry Canada intact across the threshold of the twenty-first century and secure its democratic and economic future in the turbulent waters of globalization and international competition, crisis and conflict is coming from the experience and culture, the values and visions of the West, where the nation's best new political ideas, from social democracy to neoconservatism, have for more than half a century first been voiced and tested.

In the West nothing is taken for granted; there is no fear of trying new remedies for old problems. The West is experienced at weighing established verities against intruding realities. In leading fiscal reform—eliminating government deficit budgets and paying off debts—the West showed its willingness to conduct government innovatively in a world in which the meaning of citizenship and nationhood are changing but not the craving for liberty and responsibility.

In Preston Manning's mind, Ontario is still Canada's elder sibling from whom the others in the federation have come to expect the first word on family matters. Quebec is still the eclectic, engaging and rebellious offspring who breathes distinctiveness into the Canadian identity. But it is the West that has surprised the family. The formerly gawky, younger child—the pimply, whiny adolescent—has gone away for an education and has come home a new person, with a fresh voice.

Although it is amusing to see the contrast between the teenager and the adult, her opinions now command attention because she is no longer self-absorbed and demanding but speaks with maturity. She is as outspoken as ever, going against the grain of familial tradition, but now her opinions concern the welfare of the entire family and carry weight when family decisions are made.

As the principal political voice of this new West, Preston Manning faces a triple challenge. The first is to secure his leadership of the Reform Party. There are still extremists on its fringe who believe it can be commandeered for narrow causes. The second is to build credibility outside the West, shrugging off adversity, letting time test him in the public eye. The third is to move western-born ideas and experience into the mainstream of national life and onto centre stage in Parliament.

Can he do it all? This book provides some clues to the outcome.

ACKNOWLEDGEMENTS

THIS BOOK IS the product of the patience of my friends and colleagues. I thank, and am thankful for, Florence Erion Murphy, who provided the steady hand, wise counsel and enlightened commentary on the text that got it across the finish line. The timing and outcome of the 1997 federal election played havoc with the original schedule and pushed the production deadlines to the limit of what my editor and publisher could practically accomplish. Nancy Flight, Rob Sanders and Kelly Mitchell at Greystone Books were magnificent; I am two times lucky with this team. Avery C. Ascher contributed more than she realizes, and was gracious and good humoured about it. The late Manny Martin helped launch this book, and I wish he could have seen the landing; the best friends can never be replaced.

Preston, Sandra and Muriel Manning were accessible, candid and illuminating. They agreed to be interviewed but did not review the text; errors and omissions are the result of my research, not their memories. Ron Wood, the staff in the Calgary Southwest constituency office and the Todds—Ian, Malcolm, Robert and Ellen—did a great deal of thinking and provided extremely valuable access, background and analysis. During the 1993 and 1997 elections and in the thirty-fifth Parliament, my collaborators at *Ottawa Report*, editor and publisher Jamie Deacey and contributors Lori Winstanley, Greg Inwood, Les McIlroy, Rob

Smith, Jan Louder and Daniel Despins, greatly enhanced my understanding of the main events and players.

The professionals at the Alberta Provincial Archives, the Glenbow, Calgary, Edmonton and Casper, Wyoming, public libraries, the University of Calgary, University of Alberta and Casper College libraries, and the University of Alberta archives have my gratitude. Lorna Dabbs and Howard Bentall were helpful with theological references. Friends and colleagues, especially Donald V. Currie, Angela Connell, Albert Ludwig, Douglas Cass, David Coll, Don and Betty Peterson, Gus Christopher, Neil Richardson, Julia Jones, Ted Matthews, Debra Scott, Mike Byfield, John Shiry, Laurie Watson, George Koch and Gillian Steward kept me pointed in the right direction. A word to aspiring writers: don't try to do this alone.

Some 85 subjects participated in more than 100 interviews to help me complete my research. I thank them all. My reading list exceeded 150 political science, history and economics titles; Preston Manning is an intellectual, and if one wants to understand him, one had better be prepared to crack the books. The good news is that Canadian and American writers have done a fine job documenting democrats, populists, third parties and federalism. Before this book appeared, there was already a substantial bibliography directly on Preston Manning, his family and the Reform Party of Canada. Since the Second World War only two Canadian politicians have accumulated more titles, as far as I can discern: Pierre Trudeau and Brian Mulroney. A selected bibliography is included at the end of the book, but I must single out for special acknowledgement John Barr's *The Dynasty*, Ernest Watkin's *The Golden Province*, Tom Flanagan's *Catching the Wave*, *British Columbia Report's Act of Faith*, Preston Manning's *The New Canada*, Carl Sandburg's six-volume study of Abraham Lincoln titled *The Prairie Years and The War Years* and Saul Padover's *Jefferson*. Unattributed opinions expressed in the text are mine.

Finally, there are my readers. Without you, nothing.

I have fought the good fight, I have finished the race,
I have kept the faith.

— St. Paul, The Second Letter to Timothy

IN THE FIRST weeks of 1996, as the Canadian prairies lay in the grip of an exceptionally brutal winter, Ernest Charles Manning, the eighth premier of Alberta, retired Canadian senator and lifelong lay preacher, was dying of lung cancer. His son, Preston, cofounder and leader of the Reform Party of Canada, remained in Ottawa, where he was working twenty-hour days to preserve the battered fortunes of his party and its caucus. Preston Manning is not a demonstrative man—"not a hugger," as a close friend once described him. He usually keeps his emotions well masked. Now the haggard face, which most around him took as the result of political trials he endured midway through his first parliament, betrayed the intensity of his feelings for the man whose year-long final illness was drawing to its end.

When Ernest died, on February 19, Preston flew back to Calgary. His wife, Sandra, met his flight. A newsman photographed the couple out in the frigid afternoon, as their car pulled away from the curb. Sandra, her irrepressible effervescence for once subdued, was driving. Her sunglasses hid her grief. In the glare of the flash gun, Preston simply looked bleak—thinner than ever, battered, drawn.

Ernest Manning's funeral, on Friday, February 23, at the First Alliance Church in Calgary, where he had worshipped in his final years, drew an eclectic crowd of twelve hundred, in spite of the sullen late-winter weather. They scuttled in from the gusty, ice-encrusted expanse of the parking lot. Later, at the graveside, the men would be able to shed their coats as the afternoon warmed, but those crowding into the sanctuary shivered in the frosty damp. Inside, the vaulted ceiling lifted the faithful into the realm of prayer and worship. The scents of wood oil and fresh flowers, blended with the perfumes and shaving lotions of the congregation, wafted through the sanctuary, while the the organ played the old, familiar hymns.

The somber dress of the mourners reflected the wide diversity of Ernest Manning's friends and followers: the dark suits and tailored dresses of the affluent; the ill-fitting, thumb-stained shirt collars of older working men with work-gnarled hands, the trendier fashions of adolescents and twenty-somethings. Among the mourners were Ernest's widow, Muriel; his closest political associate, Orvis Kennedy; his grandchildren; Preston's wife, Sandra; a wide circle of the friends he had gathered round himself during his years as a lay preacher and religious broadcaster; aging Social Crediters; the younger faces of the Reform Party; journalists, politicians and the merely curious. Preston asked his political aide and personal friend Ron Wood to greet and usher the great and near-great, including journalists, Reform caucus members and the honorary pallbearers: Alberta premiers Peter Lougheed, Don Getty and Ralph Klein; Manitoba's former premier Duff Roblin; Alberta's ethics commissioner, Bob Clark, who had been in Manning's later caucuses; the Liberal Leader of the Senate, Joyce Fairbairn, who had covered Manning as a *Lethbridge Herald* reporter; and Reform House Leader, Ray Speaker.

There were prayers, and the congregation sang some hymns. Two preachers recalled Ernest's second career as a popular radio evangelist.

Preston's daughter Andrea reminisced warmly about "Grandpa," a wry, witty patriarch who expressed his love for his grandchildren as much in what he did for them as what he said to them.

Preston Manning is a man who chooses his words deliberately. When he stood at the pulpit to speak about his father, his notes were titled "Tribute," which is a spoken gift of respect, gratitude and affection. This was no orthodox eulogy, no formal paean. His words were clearly from a grieving heart, suitable for a father who had no political vanity, whose credo had been common sense, who had listed his home phone number and had taken calls from anyone and everyone wanting to speak to the premier. For Preston's entire life in politics and in business he had lived in the shadow of this man and shared his passion for business, farming, reform and religion. Now, when he asked the congregation to celebrate his father's life, not mourn his passing, the words echoed with a deep, loving sorrow that exposed Preston personally, in a way he would in other circumstances never permit.

"I have tried to find an appropriate phrase to express Ernest Manning's love for Alberta and Canada, a practical not a sentimental phrase, for he usually expressed his affections by doing things for, rather than talking about, the object of his affections. And the best phrase that I can think of is simply that he was a builder," he told the mourners.

"All the old populist movements of the West—the Progressives, the CCF, Social Credit—had their colourful and bombastic "wrecking crews," politicians who could attack and demolish the old political establishments and obsolete ideas and systems they were trying to displace. But to make the transition from mere protest movements to governing parties required builders; less colourful than the wrecking crews but constructive and even more essential in the long run," he said.

It was his father's sense of political balance that allowed him to offset his fiscal commitment to debt-free government with the real purpose of politics, which was, said Preston, "the betterment of the lives and living conditions of hundreds of thousands of people."

For a few moments, Preston reminisced about some of the projects his father, "the master builder," had devoted himself to as premier: rebuilding the government's credit and finances and the Alberta economy after the Depression, creating modern educational, health care and social services systems, establishing a regulatory and legislative framework for the oil industry, inoculating its wealth against political corruption, "turning the valves on" at half a dozen major oil and gas pipelines, and launching commercial oil-sands development. He pointed out his father's working relationship with five Canadian prime ministers, from Mackenzie King to Pierre Trudeau, and his attempt to change Alberta from the maverick complainer of Confederation to a nation-builder. "If Ernest Charles Manning the builder could have one last political word on this day, I think I know what it would be," Preston concluded. "He would say on behalf of himself and all the many others who have toiled so hard to build this country from sea to sea, through wars and depressions, through booms and through busts: 'Do not let internal discord do to Canada what wars and depressions and hard times were unable to do. Continue to build! Continue to build.' "

Speaking from the heart about his father, the son had defined his own task as the inheritor of a political estate. In the quiet rustle of the crowd, as Preston sat down, one could almost hear Ernest's response: "Go thou and do likewise."

CHAPTER ONE

Bloodlines

The people are, under God, the original of all just power.

—OLIVER CROMWELL, *A Resolution of the Rump Parliament*, 1649

IN THE LAST year of the nineteenth century, after the Victorian era had faded into the graceful Edwardian years and before Europe could guess at the shadow of war fifteen years ahead, one could scarcely find a more English place than the prosperous market town of Bury St. Edmunds, home of a young horticulturalist named George Henry Manning, on the Lark River in West Suffolk. Some of Britain's richest agricultural land spread eastward across the rolling countryside from the town to the North Sea, broken by pleasant stands of deciduous forest, lonely heath lands and moors, slow-flowing rivers and low escarpments oriented northeast across the plains.

For a millennium, migrating Northern Europeans and their descendants tamed and cultivated this land of cattle, fruit and corn. On the coast, the sea yielded its bounty to fishers with generations of skill. The women of Suffolk perfected the art of weaving flax into fabric, while their men built the landmarks of civilization—barn, church and manor hall—from local stands of timber and deposits of stone. Bury St. Edmunds was still part of that separate, earlier England.

Just 70 kilometres northwest of London and 40 kilometres east of the university town of Cambridge, the town knew little of the urbanity and ambition of the city, the sophistication and affectation of the academic world or, as yet, the disruptions of industrialization. Part of the genius of the English at their zenith was the rich tapestry of communities they wove across their homeland. Bury St. Edmunds was, if no longer bucolic, still the insular, agricultural, orderly world elsewhere found only on the pages of the Brontës, Trollope and Hardy.

Known by its ancient name of East Anglia, the region had a thousand-year history of a tenacious independence of mind and spirit. Its people fought Celtic and Northern European invaders and were a rebellious thorn in the side of the Roman world. Feudalism broke down early there, and freeholders and yeomanry prospered from their rich farmland and their sagacity as merchants and traders. Isolated by geography from the intrigues of London's royal court and economically self-sufficient, these taciturn folk gave and withheld their political allegiance deliberately and thoughtfully. They were not people to be trifled with. They resisted arbitrary power, were suspicious of authority and asserted their own freedom, property rights and rights of citizenship.

When the Calvinist Protestant Reformation swept across the English Channel in the sixteenth century, it rooted quickly and deeply on these farmsteads, desolate moors and heaths. Calvin's Puritanism replaced the authority of religious hierarchy with the right of individual judgement on spiritual matters, and licensed personal discipline and rational thought. It was a system compatible with the disposition and experience of the East Anglians.

In the civil conflict between the monarchy and Parliament for political supremacy during the seventeenth century, Puritan country squire and member of Parliament Oliver Cromwell recruited the nucleus of his zealous Ironsides soldiers from among the self-styled independents of East Anglia. These ardent fighters crushed the monarchist Cavaliers, defended the brief-lived republic, guarded Parliament and enforced the peaceful restoration of Charles II as a constitutional monarch. In the rivalry between Episcopalians, Presbyterians and Catholics for spiritual preeminence, the nonconforming Puritan influence of the East Anglians tipped the scale in favour of religious liberty.

God, prosperity, Parliament, the Queen—these were the pillars upon which the life of Bury St. Edmunds was grounded. In 1899, however, it held no future for George Manning. An orphan, the youngest of thirteen siblings raised by his oldest brother, George was quiet and reserved, a gifted horticulturist employed in an uncle's nursery garden and greenhouses. He enjoyed no advantages and had little education and no prospects that he could offer his boyhood sweetheart, Elizabeth Mara Dickson, who seemed destined for a life in domestic service in London's wealthy and titled society. Yet he had ambition and the gritty determination that had been bred into the bone of so many children in this region.

The British merchant navy, the commercial lifeline to the empire, offered promising careers to young men with no other opportunity. Manning made his way to London, planning to go to sea for a few years to make his packet and then return to marry Elizabeth, who in the meantime took employment as a lady's maid in Picadilly. He enlisted and was about to embark when it was discovered—because he had no talent for deception—that he was underage. He was abruptly put ashore.

But the crowded streets of London carried gossip of other opportunities. It was rumoured that the Canadian government and the Canadian Pacific Railway were recruiting homesteaders to the western plains. Canada offered free land and had a partiality for British subjects and a preference for young men like George who actually knew how to grow things.

In 1900, Manning boarded a steamer, sailed to Montreal and got on a train bound for Winnipeg. In Manitoba, through the aegis of the CPR, he obtained work as a farm hand for two seasons and learned the basics of planting and harvesting the hybrid Red Fife wheat, which had been developed to thrive in the North-West Territories' harsh climate, and accumulated enough cash to establish his own homestead and break his own land.

In 1902, he selected a homestead near a village called Carnduff on what, three years later when the territory was carved into provinces, became part of Saskatchewan. It took George a year to build livable accommodation and establish a basic farming operation. Then he wrote to England, and Elizabeth Dickson made the long journey to Carnduff, where the two were married in the Baptist church in 1903.

The rich, unbroken grasslands and cottonwood-lined river banks of Carnduff were half a world away from the pastures of West Suffolk. The searing heat and the violent thunder and hail of summer storms, the winter frost and the weaving of the northern lights across the sky were new and frightening experiences. The Mannings were very young and frail to be contending with the rigours of homestead life. George was small and scrawny; Elizabeth ashen and tubercular. Yet this rigorous place and its demanding climate were the making of them. Her lungs cleared, and she gained a new vivacity; he became wiry and tough, although he could not shake his reticence. His physical strength began to match the Suffolk stone of his character.

The first years of George and Elizabeth's marriage and life in Canada offered enough trials and setbacks to challenge the resolve of the toughest East Anglian. Their farm was idyllic, situated on a watercourse with the charming name of the Antler River, amid rich grasslands that promised abundant crops, especially at the hand of a trained and talented horticulturist such as George. Their first son, William, was born here in 1905, and the happiness of the house increased. But the violent summer storms that blew hail and tornadoes in across the North Dakota boundary, a mere 30 kilometres south, destroyed the Mannings' crops three years in a row.

Their second son, Ernest Charles, was born in the autumn of 1908. The following spring the family moved onto a quarter section at Rosetown, southwest of Saskatoon, near the Alberta border. George erected a sod hut in a shallow valley facing west and plough-broke the thick grasses that had sustained the buffalo for ten thousand years and nourished the prairie loam.

Ernest, his older brother, William, and a younger brother, Roy, who was born in 1910, worked hard on the land and toed a strict line, which their taciturn father enforced more with his belt than his words. Their mother, whose vivacious, gregarious side flourished with her new-found health, could scarcely endure the isolation and drudgery of the homestead. So she filled the house with what books and music the family budget could afford.

The Puritan passion of East Anglia was muted by distance and circumstance into a quiet, lukewarm faith. The Mannings, who had attended the Baptist church in Carnduff, now associated with the Methodists and, after the union with a branch of the Presbyterians, the United Church of Canada. Although the Bible was the chief volume in the family library, it gathered as much dust as honour. George and Elizabeth were, in their quiet way, praying people, but they did not speak easily of the deepest things of the heart and spirit, and God was honoured in deed, not word. Politics were never spoken of. Liberty and independence of mind were not ideas in this home; they were a way of life.

Ernest was as bashful as his father, and his taciturnity undoubtedly contributed to his indifferent performance as a student, for he was a demonstrably clever lad. He completed grade 8 in the one-room schoolhouse and did not go on to secondary school. None of the teachers who boarded in the Manning home apparently sparked his enthusiasm. For two years, the young man drifted along, helping his father, working on a threshing crew around the district during harvest, playing his violin at community events and tinkering with farm machinery. Since he was hopelessly shy, his social life was limited to activities with his brothers or the invitations he received to entertain with his violin.

George Manning's farm was prosperous, and he appreciated Ernest's contribution. As the boy outgrew his father's physical discipline, their relationship became friendlier, though it remained distant. Ernest settled into a comfortable, humdrum existence and seemed destined to drift into the quiet life of a hard-working, forgotten country bachelor.

Then, after the harvest of 1924, he took one hundred dollars from his earnings on the threshing crew and purchased a Montgomery Ward mail-order, battery-operated radio. It was his Christmas gift to the family and to himself. Life in the Manning home changed that Christmas when George, Bill and Ernest ran up the 30-metre antenna, while young Roy and Elizabeth waited by the cooling dinner. After the chores in the long winter evenings that followed, the family listened in the lamp-lit kitchen to radio signals from across the continent.

In November 1925, 300 kilometres away in Calgary, high school principal and self-trained Bible scholar William Aberhart made his first religious broadcast over CFCN, The Voice of the Prairies, from the stage of the Palace Theatre, in the name the Prophetic Bible Conference. Overnight this obscure, workaholic lay preacher became a phenomenon in the frontier communities within broadcast range. Ernest was an avid listener.

Through the seasons of 1926, from planting to harvesting, as he followed Aberhart's teaching, Ernest underwent a conversion, making a personal commitment that went beyond theology. This kind of commitment is an emotional and spiritual experience as well as an intellectual conviction and is lived out by those who make it. Some regard themselves as Christian by birth, others by persuasion. Ernest Manning was both. His explicit Christian commitment transformed him from a quiet, aimless youth to a focussed and energetic man. To his Puritan belief in religious freedom, the authority of Scripture and the right of individual judgement on spiritual matters, he added Aberhart's New Testament evangelism and Old Testament sense of prophetic mystery and awe.

As Manning intensified his study of the Bible, guided by the Prophetic Bible Conference's publications and broadcasts, Aberhart planned to expand his religious empire. He organized the funding and construction of a permanent home for the conference and established a Bible seminary, to be called the Prophetic Bible Institute and launched in the autumn of 1927.

In February of that year, Manning took advantage of the winter lull in work around the farm and travelled by train to Calgary to introduce himself to Aberhart and seek admission to the institute. He checked into the downtown YMCA and went uninvited to the Aberharts' home in his only, ill-fitting suit, to discover it was the wedding day of Aberhart's eldest daughter.

It was a comic moment—the ungainly farm kid pushed into a corner of the family parlour while the portly Aberhart blustered about, getting ready for the ceremony, and his elegant wife, Jessie, did her best to hold his famous temper in check. Aberhart did find a moment to pump Manning's hand, clap him on the back and direct him to the evening young people's meeting at his church, Westbourne Baptist, in the city's residential east end. Manning was not the least taken aback by the hurried meeting with his preoccupied hero. As soon as applications were available, he registered for fall classes at the Prophetic Bible Institute.

On a bone-chilling autumn day, November 1, 1927, when Aberhart arrived to open the stolid, new, brown-brick institute in downtown Calgary for the first day of classes, seventeen-year-old Ernest Manning was waiting in the street for him, in the same dark suit of the February visit, which failed to cover his work-thickened wrists, his white socks or his enthusiasm. He had come to study for the ministry; he believed God wanted him to be a preacher.

Aberhart had an empty place in his heart that winter as he approached his fiftieth birthday, corresponding to the emptiness in his home because of the recent departure of his two daughters, Ola and Khona. Ernest Manning, quiet, hard-working, committed, thirsty for everything Aberhart could teach him, filled the void that the absence of his children had left. Manning reminded the older man of himself as a youth on a farm near the town of Goderich in Huron County, Ontario. To his detractors—and there were many—"Mr. Aberhart," stern and disci-plined, was an unlikely friend. In the inner circle of his family, however, he was "Abie": gregarious, affectionate and vulnerable. Manning was admitted to that circle; it was Abie that he came to love.

Ernest Manning proved to be everything that Aberhart had hoped for when he built the Calgary Prophetic Bible Institute. An adult life of activist dissent had progressively edged Aberhart onto the fringe of Calgary's Protestant churches, which distrusted him and were reluctant to associate with his radical, apocalyptic interpretation of the Bible. His workaholic habits and his overachievements as a principal, Baptist lay-man, broadcaster and lecturer isolated him. He had associates who admired him, but no close friends. Manning was the first vindication of the risks Aberhart had taken in founding a Bible institute where young people could be trained "in the truth once delivered" without the errors and apostasies Aberhart decried in mainstream theological colleges. The lackadaisical attitude of Manning's boyhood disappeared; he became a highly motivated, exceedingly bright pupil, absorbing and excelling in his studies.

A striking depth of love, camaraderie and mutual respect quickly grew between the hefty teacher and his slender protégé. The relationship that matured between Manning and Aberhart was a meeting of the minds, based on a shared spiritual experience, a common view of the world and a mutual sense of mission. The result was an easy companionship, a reciprocal trust and a deepening affection. Manning was the son that nature had denied Aberhart. In turn, the older man soon displaced, in influence if not affection, Manning's hard-working, undemonstrative father.

Manning's aptitude as a student and his undisguised enthusiasm for everything his mentor did flattered the older man's considerable vanity. Aberhart needed Manning's undivided loyalty. Aberhart's impetuous style and his propensity to make all important decisions himself meant that he had a large turnover of associates. Manning had a gift for administration, valuable because Aberhart's unflagging twenty-hours-a-day schedule could no longer keep pace with his commitments and ambitions. Manning became the detail man. Aberhart established him as the institute's resident janitor and night watchman.

William and Jessie Aberhart hosted a Saturday evening roast beef dinner each week in the institute's social hall; Manning became the centrepiece and informal leader of the circle of young, single Christian students who gathered for this weekly hour.

After Manning completed his two-year course in 1929, he stayed on at the Prophetic Bible Institute as resident secretary and administrator. His aptitude for organization and problem solving allowed Aberhart to expand his enterprise far beyond what it could have been without Manning to rely upon.

In 1930, Manning began to participate in the Sunday radio broadcast, *Canada's National Back to the Bible Hour,* which now commanded five hours of air time, starting with a radio Sunday-school class and ending in the evening with an hour of hymns and music. Much of the planning and preparation for the broadcast was done with Aberhart at his home in his study.

The Aberhart house was built into the prairie bluff above the Elbow River. The ground floor opened onto the front lawn and driveway, and was split into a garage and a bedroom with half bath. The Aberharts invited Manning to take over the suite. Aberhart installed a second desk in his study, where he and Manning worked together, often through the night.

William and Jessie were generous, gregarious and outgoing. Domestic life in their home centred on the breakfast and dinner tables; when the girls were growing up, and later when Manning took up residence, those were the only times the family could be sure of being together. Frequently at mealtimes there were guests. As the girls grew older, there had often been a boarder. There was laughter and camaraderie at table and music in the parlour. Mother and daughters were able pianists and they shared William's love of music.

Jessie Aberhart did not entirely agree with her husband's religious views, and that created tension in the home. The family never prayed together or shared devotions. However, they loved to sing, and the common experience of faith was through family hymn sings. Jessie participated little in the Calgary Prophetic Bible Institute or Westbourne Baptist Church. She was deeply involved in the community, but in more conventional volunteer activities such as the Red Cross. Manning was captivated by her style and confidence. It is not surprising that in many ways she resembled the woman Manning would marry, another frequent guest in the Aberhart home: Muriel Preston.

CHAPTER TWO # A Very Political Household

From the day I was born to the day I left home to attend
university, I lived in an environment shaped by the
consequences of the political explosion on August 22, 1935.

—PRESTON MANNING, *The New Canada*

O NTARIO-BORN MURIEL was the product of a rare thing for the time: a broken home. Her mother, Mary Hutchison, was a dour Catholic Scot and schoolteacher. When Muriel was five years old, Mary's marriage to William Preston, a musician, crumbled, and the couple separated. Mother and daughter came West, where Mary obtained work in a series of rural schools. Muriel was sent to a convent school in Prince Albert, Saskatchewan. For the child, it was a lonely, unhappy start to life: without mothering, without a home.

After the First World War, Mary gained a position with the Calgary school board. Muriel was moved to the Sacred Heart Convent, in the city's Catholic enclave on the banks of the Bow River, which incorporated the convent, the Gray Nuns' Holy Cross Hospital, St. Mary's Cathedral and the home of the bishop of the Southern Alberta diocese and other residences for priests and nuns. The nuns who ran the Sacred Heart convent school were bright, demanding women, and Muriel Preston received an excellent, if lonely, classical education. They also taught her the piano, and she became an accomplished concert pianist, earning a degree from the Royal Academy of London.

In the meantime, Mary had become a follower of Aberhart's Prophetic Bible Conference, converted to evangelical Christianity in 1923 and joined Westbourne Baptist Church. Muriel went with her mother to services and joined the young people's group, and Aberhart was charmed and impressed with her ability at the piano. In 1925, when Muriel was fourteen, Aberhart's organist moved to Vancouver, and he told the young girl that she was to take over as his pianist at the movie-theatre Bible classes. When she refused he insisted, and the two began an enduring working relationship.

Muriel inherited her mother's grit and determination. She easily matched wits with Aberhart and overcame his domineering nature; for that, Aberhart respected her all the more. The Aberharts welcomed her into their closest circle. She and Jessie were made of the same cloth, shared many interests and had the same broad, intelligent view of the world.

Muriel was a stunningly beautiful young woman with dark hair, a perfectly sculpted face, flashing eyes and breathtaking smile. She dressed handsomely, and her looks were enlivened by an effervescent wit. She was intelligent, gifted and tough; Aberhart admired her unerring common sense and good judgement. She was, most important to Aberhart, a deeply spiritual woman.

After graduating from high school in 1928, Muriel Preston worked as a promising legal secretary in the Lancaster Block, a downtown office building that housed Calgary's brightest and best young lawyers, including future prime minister Richard Bennett. It was the best business address in the city, the hub of Alberta's pre-Depression prosperity: the gilded letters on the frosted glass of the office doors carried the names of top real estate, oil, insurance and agricultural enterprises and law firms. Muriel learned what made the wheels turn in the city's establishment and how to manage the egos and ambitions of powerful men.

As Ernest Manning expanded his role as Aberhart's lieutenant and administrator, Muriel worked with him because now she was the music director of the institute. Abie had the knack of identifying promising young comers and encouraging them in their careers, and these two were closest to him. It would have been surprising had their boss not wanted Ernest and Muriel together; he was incurably romantic. Yet for a long time, the two knew each other simply as part of the circle of promising young people Aberhart drew to the institute. Before romance came friendship, then respect.

The Depression intervened abruptly in the orderly affairs of the Calgary Prophetic Bible Institute, and interrupted love's progress between Ernest Manning and Muriel Preston. By the end of 1930, Manning and Aberhart were keenly aware of the plight of their followers, especially on the rural back roads of the West. They received regular correspondence from their radio listeners who wrote in, pouring out their troubles and pleading for help. Ernest read the letters during the broadcasts; Aberhart brooded. At night in the family study, the two men talked. Their faith was one to be lived; they could not separate their lives into the secular and the sacred, so they looked for the work of God in the politics of the Depression. They believed that just as God called them to preach, God also called them to the poverty and loss of those terrible days.

Deputation workers from the institute travelled regularly, in threes, to visit home Bible-study groups that subscribed to the Aberhart-written curriculum. The teams consisted of a speaker, a musician and a Bible teacher. Muriel was a frequent traveller: she drove the group, played the piano and counted the offerings. As the drought and Depression lengthened, she reported back to Ernest and Abie on the devastation of families who had had no cash income for several years, had exhausted their resources and were living on canned gopher and muskrat meat, making clothes from sacking and sandals from tires.

Aberhart organized and directed informal charitable relief from his affluent followers to help those who had fallen into the economic abyss. It was in his high school classes, however, that Aberhart was radicalized and pushed into politics. "Why spend your life preparing young people for the future when they have no future?" he asked Manning.

In 1932, a young man Aberhart had particularly admired committed suicide a few days after graduating from Crescent Heights High School. As principal and classroom teacher, Aberhart was a stern taskmaster, showing little affection for his students. However, the young man's death left him stricken. Aberhart travelled to Edmonton, as he did annually to supplement his income marking departmental exams. He roomed each year with another teacher, Charles Scarborough. That year, Scarborough lent Aberhart a book called *War and Unemployment* by British actor Maurice Colbourne, which popularized the economic theories of a pedantic aircraft plant manager, Major C. H. Douglas.

Had Aberhart been introduced to Social Credit, as Douglas's theory was named, through the writings of the Major, he might well have dismissed it as dull, unimportant, pretentious and spiritually empty. Colbourne's book, however, was written in an idiom that Aberhart understood: angry, rebellious, with a sweeping vision of history. It was apocalyptic and prophetic and prescriptive. The book resonated with Aberhart's dissenting spirit.

The frontispiece quotation, from Aberhart's favourite German poet, Goethe, inflamed his rebel blood: "If anyone advances anything new, which contradicts and perhaps threatens to overturn, the creed which we for years respected and have handed down to others, all passions are raised against him and every effort is made to crush him."

In the first chapter, Colbourne quoted another Aberhart favourite, John Ruskin: "Civilization is heaps of agonizing maggots struggling with one another for scraps of food." In his own words, Colbourne wrote, "Man although able to keep alive is unable to live fully, he exists but with bent back and brow weighted with anxiety and care."

Aberhart had been sucked under by the horrible reality of the Depression—his young students in work camps; naked children evicted with their parents from their farms; women struggling to feed their families with nettles and ground squirrels; suicide, starvation, illness and the despair that caused people to raised their angry fists against heaven. Impulsively and intuitively, he believed that God had given him the tool to fight back.

As the morning light streaked into his university dorm room, William Aberhart signed on to Social Credit. He endorsed the theory without much scrutiny because it offered the first hope he had encountered during those desperate times. In Colbourne's fluently written text, hope came in biblical cadences capable of igniting Aberhart's spirit. When he first expounded Social Credit later that summer in his radio broadcasts, the teacher was barely a lesson ahead of the class. In Aberhart's hands Social Credit was a weapon to goad an indifferent government to hear the voice of the people. He seized on Social Credit as a means to put money back into the hands of penniless victims of the Depression, kick start employment and restrain the banks from the heartless farm fore-closures that had ruined many families.

Previous to this, Aberhart's only knowledge of such matters was of Colonel Anthony Van Egmond, the secular saint of town-pump politics in his boyhood community of Egmondville, Ontario, near Lake Huron. Van Egmond was a retired soldier from the armies of Napoleon and a Reform Party politician in the early 1830s. In the Upper Canada Rebellion of 1837 he was rebel leader William Lyon Mackenzie's only experienced military officer. When the rebellion was broken, Van Egmond was arrested and imprisoned in the Toronto jail. Housed in a dank cell with a soaking blanket that froze stiff at night, Van Egmond, an elderly sixty-seven years, caught pneumonia and died. Aberhart walked to school, passing the Colonel's ruined estate every day. Fed on stories of Van Egmond's political martyrdom, Aberhart came to politics hostile to authority and believing in the righteousness of insurrection.

In the autumn of 1932, Aberhart and Manning began the crusade that took them away from the pulpit and into public life. Manning was detached, almost noncommittal about Social Credit theory. He did not share the passion of Aberhart's conversion, but he was ever the loyal lieutenant and he did prepare—and frequently give—a stump speech explaining its basic principles. For the next three years, Aberhart taught Social Credit instead of prophecy, though he did not distinguish between the two. He organized the movement into home study groups, often the same gatherings that the previous winter had been his Bible-study groups.

In the summers of 1933, 1934 and 1935, Aberhart took to the road, with Manning driving, on gruelling, two-man tours. It was a singular cam-paign against the ravages of economic and social injustice. In a radio broadcast in 1934 Aberhart said: "For the past fifteen years, I have preached to you about your eternal and your future welfare, and for the last two years I have pressed also for your temporal and material welfare here and now. I am glad to say you are nearer the solution in Alberta than any other place in the world." To those who challenged him he said, "If you have not yet suffered enough, it is your God-given right to suffer some more."

It was against Aberhart's better judgement, however, that the movement became a political party. For a time, he tried to persuade the United Farmers of Alberta (UFA) government of John Brownlee to convert to Social Credit. But like other Canadian politicians, Brownlee was paralyzed by the Depression. He was also trapped in a sex scandal engineered by the Liberal Party. The daughter of a leading Liberal mayor ensnared Brownlee in a furtive affair, which ended in a messy law suit. It was apparent that Aberhart's new secular gospel would be forced to challenge the incumbent government in the election of 1935.

Impatient and impetuous, relying on Manning for the organizational details, ignoring the criticism of the authors of the theory and its orthodox followers, Aberhart bulled ahead. What he craved was action. He believed in history as a series of dramatic, decisive moments. He believed in a God who controlled the destiny of the people of the earth and who was now poised to correct the injustices, the poverty, the hunger and the misery of the Depression. As Aberhart swept on, driven by idealism, egoism and passion, he led his protégés into an entirely unexpected life of politics and power. For Muriel as well as Ernest, this singular enterprise was now the family business.

In the Alberta election campaign during the oppressively hot summer of 1935, William Aberhart and Ernest Manning crisscrossed the sun-baked back roads of the province in their battered black Ford on the final progress to power. Aberhart was leading the newly formed Social Credit Party; Manning was nominated as a candidate in Calgary. The portly, balding man wearing the pince-nez and the rumpled suit filled the long, dusty hours between stops by poring over pamphlets and correspondence or writing and rewriting speeches and radio scripts. Often he'd turn to the neatly groomed young man at the wheel and utter a trademark question: "Well, Manning, what do you think of it now?" Then he'd launch into a characteristically exhaustive cross-examination on some problem the crusade faced. Or he'd commence a diatribe against one or another of his many opponents, his voice rising, his face flushing and his meaty palm slapping the dash.

Aberhart and Manning faced an array of powerful and bitter enemies who felt Social Credit threatened their own interests. Social Credit was thought of as, in the words of the urban Economic Safety League, "an omnium-gatherum of political odds and ends, business failures, social misfits and imitating parrots, reciting ready-made speeches which they do not understand . . . led by a political parson with no business experience, with no knowledge of the law and with ideas of political economy that were discredited and discarded, repeatedly, before he was born."

Communist Party leader Tim Buck unselfconsciously nicknamed them the Something for Nothing Gang. The insults were often venomous; Aberhart was described by one prominent newspaper columnist as "a mountainous, glistening heap of flesh."

As the UFA's campaign foundered, Aberhart gained momentum. To the platform of monetary reform, he added a call for the abolition of poverty and the introduction of state medicine. The party started a small weekly newspaper for the campaign. The presses of the Calgary Prophetic Bible Institute churned out translations of Social Credit pamphlets in French, German, Ukrainian, Greek, Italian and a half dozen other languages.

But Aberhart was ambivalent about the outcome of the election. He disliked the gritty side of politics and didn't run for office himself. In his mind, Social Credit would elect a minority conscience in the legislature, opposing the UFA. After the election, he could go back to Crescent Heights High School and the Prophetic Bible Institute, and the Social Credit opposition caucus would become a branch plant of his greater movement.

Aberhart's campaign closed with a triumphant procession by train across the province, ending on the evening of August 22, 1935, at the Calgary Prophetic Bible Institute. A large crowd waited in the muggy heat to hear the election's outcome. At 10:30 P.M., a messenger brought a telegram to the podium from the Canadian Press office at the railway station. Aberhart announced that Brownlee had conceded the election, and suddenly slumped against the pulpit, overwhelmed by the realization of what had happened.

Ernest Manning signalled Muriel at the piano, and the congregation began to sing: "O God our help in Ages past, our hope for years to come, our shelter from the stormy blast, and our eternal home." Social Credit had won 54 per cent of the popular vote and fifty-six of sixty-three constituencies. Every UFA candidate was defeated; opposition consisted of five Liberals and two Conservatives.

Aberhart may have been a reluctant premier. He was certainly astonished to have been elected to the post, but he rose to the challenge with characteristic energy. He and Jessie moved to Edmonton. They took up residence in the Macdonald Hotel, a grand railway establishment high on the north bank of the North Saskatchewan River, a five-minute drive from the Legislature. A few doors down the hall from the Aberharts' suite, Ernest Manning took a room. He was twenty-six years old, about to be appointed provincial secretary and the youngest cabinet minister in the British Commonwealth.

Politics had again broken in on his romance with Muriel. Although she was fully engaged with the Social Credit, the demands of the long campaign had kept them apart. Now, with Muriel in Calgary and Ernest in Edmonton, the marriage was put on hold.

They were, however, part of a network of young men and women with energy, intelligence and an intensity of commitment that formed bone marrow of the new party. The burden imposed on them by their domineering, demanding leader and their Biblical sense of responsibility for justice and economic recovery had made them serious beyond their years. Unlike Aberhart, however, they had companionship in the cause. They had embarked on careers before the Depression changed the direction of their lives. Edith Rogers was a schoolteacher. William A. C. Bennett and Orvis Kennedy were hardware proprietors. Manning, of course, was a professional clergyman and Muriel a stellar legal secretary. All of these young adults were in the thick of the election of 1935. The results of that battle took away their carefree years.

The autumn of 1935 provided a flicker of happiness for Aberhart, the only such moment in his eight years in office. Leaders of the Social Credit movement from around the world courted him. He picked his cabinet and travelled to Ottawa to meet Prime Minister R. B. Bennett. He successfully negotiated federal loans to relieve a debt crisis created by the Depression. He won a by-election in the safe seat of Okotoks-High River, south of Calgary. He drafted the reams of Social Credit legislation with which he intended to transform the province.

He barely noticed that Bennett had been thrown out of office in the federal election, replaced by William Lyon Mackenzie King. While Bennett had at least understood and was willing to work around the eccentricities of Aberhart's politics, King was hostile, unyielding and sworn to bring Alberta's new government to heel.

Manning's fortunes ascended. He was given a second cabinet

portfolio: minister of Industry and Commerce. As acting premier, while Aberhart took a lengthy Christmas break in Vancouver, he began to renegotiate the province's debt. Aberhart had no patience with the parliamentary process. He so disliked the Legislature that he did not make a speech in it until 1938. From the outset, he surrendered the management of legislation to Manning. The Executive Council, cabinet, was Aberhart's exclusive forum.

The political honeymoon was brief. On February 6, 1936, the legislative session began, and the government plunged quickly and deeply into trouble. The first budget alienated its strongest supporters because it contained no Social Credit measures. A Recall Act giving electors the right to fire their member of the Legislative Assembly was turned against Aberhart in his own riding, and he forced cabinet to rescind it. Alberta's relationship with Ottawa collapsed; King and Aberhart could barely speak to one another. Without federal help, Alberta defaulted on its debt in April.

When the legislative session ended that month, Ernest and Muriel were married in Calgary. The engagement had been made during the winter when Aberhart and Ernest were in the city on business. After Muriel accepted the overdue proposal, the two went straight to their mentor's room in the Palliser Hotel to inform him. "What took you so long?" he beamed. At the wedding, Aberhart gave away the bride. A wonderful reception was organized by Jessie Aberhart, complete with flowers, piano music, formal toasts led off by William and a fine dinner in the Palliser. The honeymoon was a family affair. The couple travelled by train to Vancouver with William and Jessie, who now vacationed there regularly in the spring with their daughters. From there Ernest and Muriel travelled on alone to California.

When they returned, they moved into a rented house on Edmonton's south side—the first of several temporary homes. Muriel had given up her career as a legal secretary, so they had only Ernest's modest income from his cabinet post. In addition Manning's puritan attitude and indifference to money, they were careful in their expenditures because Manning had very modest tastes and because his position as the British Commonwealth's youngest minister of the Crown seemed at first impermanent. The prospect of political defeat and a return to nonpolitical life was always a consideration in family affairs.

In the first autumn of their marriage, the political crisis deepened.

Social Credit legislation started to move through the Legislature, only to be struck down by the courts, the federal cabinet and the lieutenant governor as unconstitutional. Aberhart could not understand why the judges, the Crown and that hated man Mackenzie King would permit something as intangible and untidy as the Constitution to stand in the way of action that would put desperate men to work, bread in starving mouths, shoes on frozen feet and roofs over the heads of the homeless.

For the next eighteen months, Ernest Manning and William Aberhart were overwhelmed by the repudiation of Social Credit legislation and insurgency within the caucus. Manning's health was nearly destroyed. Overworked and under great stress to meet the demands the premier placed on him, Manning contracted tuberculosis, his mother's disease, from a pleurisy spot on his lung. He was given two years to live. There were no children in the family, so rather than being placed in a sanitarium, he was sent home. Muriel was given a crash course in nursing. For three months he endured complete bed rest; she did not even let him lift a newspaper. His recovery was remarkable. Friends credited his restoration and return to political life to Muriel's intense efforts; she said it was prayer and the will of God. In March 1937 Manning resumed light duties; in July, he went back to work full time.

He thus missed the insurrection that started after New Year's, 1937. It pitted the party orthodox against Aberhart for his failure to deliver Social Credit law. The premier brooked no challenge to his authority and crushed the uprising without compunction. The cure was nearly worse than the disease: Aberhart and the party were never at ease with each other again. Had Manning been at Aberhart's right hand during the crisis, his political career might have died with Aberhart in 1943. He was absent, however, and therefore untarnished.

In 1938 it began to rain again, and the people of Alberta regained hope. It also seemed that the worst years for Social Credit might be over. Aberhart tried unsuccessfully to extend the reach of the party in the Saskatchewan election. Back home, he produced a more conventional government, creating, for example, a regulatory framework for the fledging oil industry, transferred in 1931 to provincial jurisdiction.

Ernest and Muriel had settled into an ambitious regime. They were widely regarded, inside government and out, as the most promising couple in the province. He managed the Legislature and the most important issues of government, while Aberhart did high politics. Together, they positioned themselves for the expected 1939 election. Muriel was directing the music and acting as Aberhart's administrative proxy for the *National Back to the Bible Hour* and learning her way around the Social Credit women's auxiliary. Each Sunday, the young couple drove back to Calgary for the broadcast and services at the Prophetic Bible Institute. They began to plan for a family.

Of course, no one reckoned on the war. It delayed the election and put on hold the personal lives of families just recovering from the Depression. Now instead of going to work camps, fathers, sons and daughters were off to war.

In May 1939, a few weeks before the outbreak of hostilities, the Mannings had their first son. He was named William for the family patriarch but was called Keith, his middle name, by the family. Keith's delivery was extremely difficult: he had been deprived of oxygen for several minutes and suffered brain damage, which arrested his development and motor coordination and left him with epilepsy. Children with Keith's disabilities were routinely institutionalized, but Ernest and Muriel were not routine people and were determined to care for him themselves as long as possible.

After Keith was born they built a tiny white bungalow, little more than a cottage, on 112th Street across from the University of Alberta campus in Edmonton's Garneau neigbourhood. They acquired a dog, a large St. Bernard called Monty. Muriel developed an attractive garden.

In the election of March 21, 1940, the party's popular support slumped to 37 per cent. Social Credit won only thirty-five seats and faced a sizable twenty-two-member opposition. Chastened, it limped through three more brief legislative sessions under Aberhart. The premier was more and more subdued, isolated and exhausted. He did not know why he could not maintain his energy. A stiffening of his intemperate, autocratic ways and sometimes erratic behaviour marked the onset of serious illness.

In those somber days, a contrasting joy came to the Manning home: the birth of a second son on June 10, 1942. He was called Ernest for his father, and Preston—his mother's maiden name. He was the younger son; however, because of his brother's infirmities, he carried his parents' hopes for the future of the family.

CHAPTER THREE

The Younger Son

Oh for boyhood's time of June,
Crowding years in one brief moon,
When all the things I heard or saw,
Me, their master, waited for.

— JOHN GREENLEAF WHITTIER, "The Barefoot Boy"

A YEAR AFTER Preston's birth, the Manning household lost its patriarch. Aberhart's body had continued to fail and his mind became more eccentric. He dabbled on the fringes of the occult; studied numerology, palmistry and the unorthodox theology of the British Israelites, a Christian cult that believed the British were a lost tribe of Judah. He flirted with some of the leftist ideas of Social Gospel and the Canadian Commonwealth Federation.

He was dying. At the end of the spring session in 1943, he took his usual vacation rail trip to Vancouver. He took seriously ill on the train; when he arrived on the coast, he was hospitalized. In a matter of days he was dead of cirrhosis of the liver. Ernest and Muriel were stunned.

In the last years of his life, William had been so unhappy in Alberta and so vilified that Jessie decided to bury him in Vancouver.

Ernest was not only Aberhart's successor of choice, he was preferred by the party. His selection as the eighth premier of Alberta by the Social Credit caucus was uncontested, and he was sworn into office on May 31, 1943. The job didn't seem much of a catch: Ernest's prospects were daunting, discouraging. He grieved for his irreplaceable mentor. The province was in default on its debts, a national embarrassment and international pariah. The Social Credit Party was in possibly terminal political trouble. The bloody Second World War was dragging on, and many of Alberta's best young men were absent from home, dying in it. By contrast, the new premier's home offered refuge, and Muriel was determined that it would be an island of security for Ernest and their sons.

So Preston Manning was raised in a certain world, and the memory of his early childhood includes a sense of freedom and possibility. He was surrounded by the love of his parents, the unqualified affection of his brother and the mystery of a compassionate God. Although the family had limited financial means, the home was full of music, books, a respect for learning and knowledge, and the parental example of leadership, responsibility and engagement in the world beyond the front porch. His spirit was stimulated by his parents' faith in a loving, merciful, forgiving God with whom one conversed in companionable prayer and worshipped reverently but joyfully.

He was encouraged to excel in everything he did. His parents were people of initiative and action, and Preston followed their example. It was a family with routines that overcame the pressures and distractions of running the government and the *National Back to the Bible Hour* broadcasts. The five-hour broadcast from the Prophetic Bible Institute in Calgary had shrunk to an hour and was now broadcast live on Sunday from a movie-theatre stage in Edmonton. The Mannings did things together. Sunday was the family's day; during the week they often attended formal political and ceremonial occasions or socialized with people from church or the *Bible Hour*. His mother's first commandment for the home was: "Be not idle," and Preston was an obedient, compliant and therefore busy child.

After he was born, the Mannings moved six blocks up 112th Street from the tiny white bungalow to a larger, green-painted, two-storey clapboard home closer to the edge of the University of Alberta campus. Garneau was a prosperous enclave of two-storey homes and neighbourhood schools that had escaped the worst effects of the Depression. The cottonwood-shaded streets with their well-tended gardens facing the stone archways and clock towers of the campus could have been set down in any Canadian city's university quarter in the 1940s.

This university and the ambience of the Garneau neighbourhood were chiefly the work of one man, Henry Marshall Tory, a brilliant Canadian scientist and engineer who presided over the founding of two permanent universities: Alberta and Carleton; one temporary college: the Khaki University for Canadian troops awaiting demobilization in Britain in 1919; and two government research establishments: the Alberta and the National Research Councils. The neighbourhood of Preston Manning's nativity, and later his university alma mater, bore the brand of Tory's cultured, informed personality and his enterprising, creative spirit.

Garneau's north side had a commanding view of the North Saskatchewan and the deep, wooded river valley it cut through the city. On its east side Whyte Avenue, a wide European-style boulevard, offered fashionable red-brick store fronts and a marvellous, heavy-set fire-hall topped by a large Canadian Red Ensign. This was a neighbourhood populated by professors, lecturers and middle-income professionals. The man who lived next door to the Mannings' tidy home was John W. Fry, the mayor of Edmonton. Preston played with the sons of lawyers, university professors and the eminent doctors of the university's medical faculty.

In the spring of 1943, a few weeks before Preston's first birthday, Ernest signed an agreement to purchase a run-down, 355-acre dairy farm a half hour's drive from the city on the North Saskatchewan River. The cashless years of the Depression had left their mark on its wind-scarred, sagging outbuildings. There were a dozen wood barns, sheds and grain bins, and a tiny white cottage without indoor plumbing. Ernest had always wanted to farm his own bit of land. He and Muriel intended to build a home on it and make it into a financially self-sufficient sanctuary away from the pressures of government and the

Back to the Bible Hour broadcasts. It would be the perfect place to raise this newborn son and perhaps a place where they could keep Keith out of institutional life. In December, they closed the sale with $11,000 in financing, scraped together in spite of their modest income.

They named the farm Westerlea. For several years, it was a weekend project while the family improved it and saved sufficient money to build the house. It was at Westerlea on a sunny spring day shortly after Aberhart's death that Ernest picked his first cabinet, while shingling the barn roof with his best friend and confidante, Orvis Kennedy, the Social Credit Party's secretary and chief political operative. When the two men stopped for lunch, they wrote their decisions down on a brown-paper sandwich bag.

The war had only an echo on the streets of Garneau and the grass-lands of the farm, but that faint music was stirring as well as sobering. Members of neighbourhood families were fighting and some were dying overseas. Edmonton was a patriotic city, and civilians took the war effort seriously as a kind of community enterprise, but the actual battles were impersonal, far-away things and their hellish nature never penetrated Garneau. Preston, in any event, was far too young to have anything more than a sense of the great conflict.

As parents, the Mannings were rather formal; their love was considerate, gentle, harmonious and distant. Emotional expression in the home was restrained. Ernest was a quiet man like his father. He was busy and travelled a great deal on provincial business. When he was at home, he was a consistent but punctilious father who disappeared after dinner to work on his government files or his sermons for Sunday. Muriel was busy with radio broadcast business and Social Credit women's matters, so nannies and housekeepers often took care of the boys. And caring for Keith placed a large demand on the parental energy. As a child, Preston was hushed by the nannies and housekeepers, told to be good and not a bother to his parents. "They have a lot to deal with, with Keith, so you be good," they said.

Muriel's convent upbringing and childhood relationship with her dour, absent mother had deprived her of close parenting. When they were together, Mary had been strict and unaffectionate. Muriel had learned some parenting from William Aberhart, who had been gentle with her and frequently counselled her stern mother, "Don't hold so tight a rein." Aberhart had also taught Muriel to attack life with vigour, to be uncompromising, to give no quarter in pursuit of her goals. On her fifteenth birthday, he wrote in her diary: "The difference between one mind and another, between the weak and powerful, the great and the insignificant is *energy* invincible and determined—a purpose once formed, and then death or victory." Muriel demanded this of herself and expected as much from her husband and her sons. Even Keith was not permitted to do anything less than his best, regardless of his limitations.

The paradox of family love in the Manning home was that it was rock solid and unqualified, yet expressed in strict codes of formality and action. The bonds that knit the four together were rooted in the compassion of New Testament Christianity and Christ's first commandment: "Love one another as I have loved you." Among the measures of the parents' love was their determination to have Keith in the home and care for him; others placed such children in institutions.

Keith's brain impairment affected some of the joy that the family might otherwise have shared. His love for his younger brother was huge and unconditional, but he could not keep up with Preston, who was lithe and graceful in play, serious and bright in conversation. Keith also suffered from regular seizures, which often occurred when the family was out together. This embarrassed Preston and made him highly apprehensive on social occasions. Nor could Keith join in boyish games and rough-and-tumble, but he loved to be in the gang and wanted to sing, to read, to hike the river bank, and to hang around with his younger-older brother.

It took Preston some time to master the frustration, resentment and anger he felt in the situation. Over time he learned first patience, then tolerance, then compassion in living with Keith. The two became extremely close; their many separations while Keith was being treated were hard for Preston to understand or accept.

In the first years of Keith's life, Ernest and Muriel exhausted many avenues and a significant sum of money to have him diagnosed and treated. He needed medication to control his seizures, and his medical expenses strained the family's budget. Keith spent a great deal of time with Grandma Preston, who lived near the family. Although the experts had proclaimed Keith uneducable, the dour old teacher taught him to read and to write a little at about age seven. His parents took this breakthrough as a harbinger of a better life for Keith, and they sought all the harder for a solution to his situation.

Preston eavesdropped on those lessons and, relatively unnoticed, mastered reading and writing before he was old enough to attend school. He wrote his first book in block letters on a sheet of 8-by-11-inch paper, folded into quarters. It was called *How to Live*; its thesis was "be nice." He could write the words, but not his name yet, so at the bottom of the title, he scribbled his age: 5. The content of the story, as much as the achievement of writing, provide an insight into Preston's early relationship with his family. Burdened by Keith, his parents did not need problems from him, so he sought their approval by being obliging.

Dr. Walter Mackenzie, dean of the medical faculty at the university and a great admirer of the premier, devoted a great deal of time to Keith's treatment. He put Ernest and Muriel in touch with the legendary Montreal neurosurgeon Dr. Wilder Penfield, who told the Mannings to bring Keith to him after Keith turned twelve; the boy would be as developed as could be expected, and he could make a proper examination. So, after Keith's twelfth birthday, Ernest and Muriel took him to Montreal. Dr. Penfield spent several hours with him, then called the parents to his office. "Do not waste any more time, money or grief on this boy," Penfield told them. "He was a perfect baby until the moment of his birth. Now you must learn to accept his situation and spend your energy making the best of it."

Again with Dr. Mackenzie's help, the Mannings found a doctor in upstate New York who with his wife operated a residential school that proved suitable for Keith. There he was treated and educated further. However, this meant that he was away from home for most of the year. From the time Preston was ten years old, he was, for all intents and purposes, an only child.

Keith had a large place in Preston's boyhood. The younger son could see that his older brother had disadvantages that were no fault of his own. At the same time, he himself had a quick mind and strong body. The difference drove him to make the best use he could of his abilities. "Preston," his mother once said, "looked at Keith and resolved to make good use of his brain." As Keith grew to adulthood, his uncomplicated love of God and his faith, however childlike, helped Preston deal with his own inevitable periods of religious doubt. Most important, the two brothers loved one another: with Keith, it was uncompromising, huge, emotional; with Preston, it was discerning, thoughtful, tinged with regret.

With Keith gone, Preston played with a group of about seven or eight chums in the neighbourhood. They were all from families far more affluent than the Mannings, and from an early age, he learned that he could not expect to have the same possessions as his friends. However, Preston's friends regarded his father as the most important in the neighbourhood. Preston was a natural leader of the group, initiating the games, the hikes along the deep, wooded river valley, and the pranks.

In many respects, it was the midcentury Canadian equivalent of being a child of the manse: the Mannings were comparatively poor, but cultivated and genteel. The family's status didn't depend on their money, and Preston's indifference to wealth as an adult has been influenced by the fact that he didn't need it to make his way in one of Edmonton's privileged neighbourhoods as a child.

Ernest's war, as an important political leader in a combatant nation, was burdensome and stressful, chiefly because the province was bankrupt. He was only in his mid-thirties and was doing a job that in most Canadian provinces was the task of men old enough to be his father. He had to manage the province's affairs in a political milieu controlled by the federal government through the War Measures Act and its extraordinary crisis powers. He had to establish personal credibility with angry, suspicious creditors in New York and London, restore harmony to the relations with Ottawa that Aberhart had destroyed and rebuild the party's standing with voters.

For a time, it appeared that the CCF would gain power in war-end elections in Alberta and Saskatchewan. Financially, Manning had little to offer to the electors. His postwar plans were for budgets that would generate the surpluses needed to refinance the debt. The socialists talked of state programs that Alberta could not afford. Manning hated socialism because it was materialism writ large, and feared its blurry connection with Marxism. Like many politicians of his generation, he feared a postwar clash with communism in North America as well as Europe. This perspective was coloured as much by his interpretation of the Bible and Christian prophecy as it was by the information he received through his extraordinarily wide political contacts outside Alberta.

In any event, on August 8, 1944, two months after the Allies invaded Europe and a week after Tommy Douglas won a landslide election margin and became Saskatchewan's first CCF premier, Manning accomplished one of Alberta's political miracles. The Social Credit Party not only escaped the defeat that many feared Aberhart had ensured, it won 51 per cent of the popular vote and fifty-one of sixty-two seats in the Legislature. Ernest had emerged as a political power in his own right, and life in the Manning household now felt more financially secure.

The Edmonton of the mid-1940s and early 1950s was a frontier town in which a fur-trading, coal-mining, homesteading past blended—effortlessly it seemed—with the refinements of university, government and finance. It was an imaginative, storied city and couldn't fail to stimulate Preston's inquisitive sense of history, romance and adventure.

In spite of nearly two hundred years of development, Edmonton in the first years after the war remained a raw prairie town, parts of it still treeless and unpaved. Its business was as much the rough and ready northern Canadian enterprises of mining, timber, agriculture and transportation as it was the more sedate professions of government, banking and education.

There was no lack of ambition or vision, but the Depression had held the city back. Capital was in short supply, jobs were precious and the ravages of hard times in rural Alberta were evident on the streets, as homeless men and families drifted in from repossessed farms and bankrupt coal mines. The war brought an artificial recovery, based on the strategic need for Alberta's resources. It was hoped—but there were no guarantees—that peace would bring permanent prosperity.

Young Preston Manning saw the world through the lens of the end-of-war dreams, ambitions and potential of a city that always saw itself on the edge of something new. A contemporary landscape entitled *Skyline of the North*, painted by Ontario artist Charles Comfort on commission for the House of Seagram in the early 1950s, depicts the vista from Garneau with which Preston grew up. In the foreground, energetic automobile and rail traffic are crossing the river; an electric power station stands opposite on the north bank below the Legislature and the bright, new buildings of the city's centre; overarching the city is a powerful prairie sky with cumulonimbus clouds extending the reach of the urban towers and industrial smokestacks upward to a modern, four-engine airliner flying over the vista. This Edmonton was Canada's gateway to the North and the mineral riches of the Arctic archipelago, Mackenzie Valley, Beaufort Sea and mountains of the Yukon. Preston grew up aware of the bush pilots and prospectors moving in and out of his city.

He tackled postwar life on Garneau's movie-set streets with an almost unfailing cheerfulness and an insatiable inquisitiveness. He played hard; in spite of his slender, frail-looking cast, he had wiry strength and boyish endurance. His slender body was nurtured and hardened by Saturdays and holidays working at the farm, where he became a master horseman. He learned as much about dairy cattle, dogs, fishing poles and hunting rifles at the farm as he did about sports, politics and books in the city.

Like most small boys living in Edmonton he loved football and the Edmonton Eskimos, although he'd play any competitive sport. He and his pals were partisan fans, and their passions were fed in those years by the frequent contest for the Grey Cup between the Eskimos and the Montreal Alouettes.

When he began school, he walked a dozen blocks to Garneau Public School, a brown and red brick edifice with high-ceilinged classrooms and long, well-waxed halls. He had a particular aptitude for mathematics and science that extended beyond the classroom. In a family with different values, he might have been promoted as a prodigy.

The Mannings were very busy people after the war. In addition to running the government and leading the *Back to the Bible Hour*, Ernest had the farm to care for: the family needed the income it provided. Fortunately, he had his best friend, Orvis Kennedy, to run the Social Credit Party.

As a young father, Ernest was the carefully dressed presence at the breakfast table who disappeared for the day, returning for a family dinner, after which he retired to work on his sermons. On Saturday he'd dress down for the farm, but on quiet Sunday he again became the rather formally dressed man now preaching at the podium into the radio microphone and to the audience in the borrowed cinema-cum-broadcast studio.

Muriel had parallel responsibilities to those of Ernest. In the 1950s, political wives, like wives of the manse, were expected to share the careers of their husbands, picking up the slack on chores that no one else covered and cultivating the family's public persona. Muriel, married to a premier and a preacher, drew double duty.

She was expected at formal government occasions, and her participation in the affairs of the Social Credit Party went far beyond her nominal role as a political wife. She was a back-room operative of supreme importance in the party's women's institute; at elections, in the privacy of the voting booth, women of all political persuasions set aside their partialities and cast for Muriel Manning's husband. Ernest often joked that the day after an election, he could never find anyone who admitted to voting Social Credit; one of the reasons is that Alberta women of a certain background were reluctant to tell their husbands their vote had been part of Manning's large plurality.

As the musical director of the *Back to the Bible Hour*, which now had a North American following, Muriel organized every aspect of the hymns, the musicians, the instrumentation and the live performers, the soloist, trios, quartets and choirs that became a trademark of evangelical worship in the second half of the twentieth century, largely because of the influence of religious radio broadcasting.

Muriel made a point of protecting the privacy of the family. It was a time when there was no public expectation that a politician's personal life be exposed to scrutiny, but the Mannings erected a stouter wall than many of their contemporaries between their personal and public lives and were certainly very aware that the family circle was sacrosanct. Preston was not encouraged to invite his friends home for dinner.

Although the premier had a listed telephone number and took calls from petitioners at home, there were seldom visitors for a meal, and then only when the guest was well known to the family and trusted because of some political or religious connection. They had little time for entertaining and few close friends that they didn't see regularly in public social settings. And they struggled with the evangelical dialectic of being, to use the New Testament phrase, "in the world but not of it."

They practised a Christianity that included a full agenda of social responsibilities undertaken for their own sake and not as part of a religious campaign. But Ernest and Muriel steered away from the blandishments and perks of politics that conflicted with their puritan mores and strong ethical stands. Preston was forbidden the movies and, when he was older, dancing and other "worldly" entertainment.

The family turned out, however, on suitable occasions. Once a year, they invited the members of the Legislative Assembly and their families to a reception, and there were other government events, such as the lieutenant-governor's social occasions and various ribbon cuttings and community activities to which the Mannings were invited. Many of these were recreational, and combined family holidays with the premier's political obligation to show the flag. Preston went to the 1955 Grey Cup football game in Vancouver with his father and sat in the premier's official car during the parade. Each July, they travelled south for the Calgary Exhibition and Stampede and watched the Stampede Parade from one of several suites on the lower front floors of the Palliser Hotel equipped with French windows and an ornate balustrade for the viewing of public events.

Church and *Back to the Bible Hour* social events also created occasions that were always family affairs and were especially appealing to children. Many of Preston's acquaintances and colleagues later in life first met him at picnics at which Ernest, always dressed impeccably and never loosening his tie, served the ice cream and soda.

One of the advantages of having a father who was a premier and a religious leader was constant exposure to bright, engaging adult company. Preston thrived on this exposure; he loved the company of adults, held his end of the conversation well. If, on first meeting, the men and women he met indulged his presence and his chatter because of his father's position, that soon gave way to a recognition this was a bright, well-read chap with a fresh, serious way of looking at the world. If he was at times naive, unformed and immature, he was also interesting, entertaining and amusing. He was the kind of boy men respected and wanted to mentor. Women praised him and encouraged him. Everyone said that he'd never break his parents' hearts the way so many careless and reckless young men do, and that he'd make his mark in life: boys like that always do.

Preston was relaxed and at ease at these events. He loved to watch his father work the room and to be photographed with his mother. In his grey flannels, blue blazer and dark-rimmed glasses, he was a serious study. Only the sun-bleached brush cut and the squeaky voice reminded those who observed him that he was still just a boy.

CHAPTER FOUR

Westerlea

O prairie mother, I am one of your boys . . .
Here I know I will hanker after nothing so much as one more
sunrise or a sky moon of fire doubled to a river moon of water.

—CARL SANDBURG, "Cornhuskers"

Ι N THE SPRING of 1954, when Preston was twelve, the
ranch house at Westerlea that Ernest and Muriel had
designed for themselves was completed. In the eleven
summers they had worked the place, the farm had prospered and had
become self-sufficient. It was now ready as a retreat from the world of
politics and the home in which their younger son could grow to man-
hood. The Mannings sold their house in Garneau and moved to the
farm permanently.

The farmyard bore scant resemblance to the ramshackle, wind-
blown property acquired in 1943. The scraggly caragana hedges had
been replaced with neat shelter belts of young firs and hardwoods.
There was something of a lawn now, not the sorry, sun-scorched,

brown-patch thing that had barely survived the Depression. The battered old buildings had been torn down one by one, and new, well-constructed, neatly painted barns, equipment sheds and grain bins had taken their place. The new house dwarfed the old cottage, which had been fixed up a bit for the help to live in.

Esther Galloway, the housekeeper at Garneau, was married to an experienced cattle farmer and skilled herdsman, Ron, who needed work to supplement the earnings from his own land, so the Galloways were engaged to manage the dairy operation and moved into the cottage. Now when the parents travelled, Preston—and Keith when he was around—were cared for by the Galloways, who became part of the boys' extended family.

This was good, rich land laid flat by ancient seas and then carved up by the glacial knives of the ice ages. Winters were harsh and summers brief and intense. The thick prairie grass that built up the soil had been displaced by hay and grain, the buffalo had been eradicated and herds of cattle now dotted the land. Homesteaders from Ukraine and other parts of Eurasia loved it deeply because it reminded them in topography, climate and flora of the steppes of their homelands. The North Saskatchewan River was invisible with only a green line of cottonwoods on the horizon to indicate where it cut deeply into the plain. When one reached the lip of its escarpment, it was spread out below in a deep valley, its swift waters were muddy with the rich western soil it had gathered on its journey from the foothills.

His parents intended that Preston would live an outdoor life and learn to ride horses, to fish and to farm as his grandfather George Manning had once learned horticulture. Ernest loved to farm; more than a hobby, it was the life from which it had once been imperative that he escape but to which he could now safely return. Muriel, who was never comfortable with the protocol and formality of being the premier's wife, had her refuge in teaching Preston the value of hard work and bringing Keith home from time to time for good food and fresh air, to be with his family and to have a taste of the boyhood that circumstances now denied him. They wanted the boys to grow up with horses and dogs, the expanse of the prairie as a playground and nothing between them and the sky. The transition from the mature, stately streets of Garneau to the rawness of Westerlea with its wind-blown shelter belt of struggling saplings was a family milestone, as important as the parents' wedding day eighteen years before and the birth of the boys.

As a result of the move, almost by accident, Ernest Manning, who never talked about politics at home and never encouraged Preston's interest in public life, nudged his son across the line into the adult world of the premier's office. His parents did not want to pull the boy from Garneau School before the year ended. Conveniently, the Legislature building on the north bank of the North Saskatchewan River was a ten-minute walk—faster by bicycle—from the school on the south bank, across the High Level Bridge. So father and son commuted from the farm each morning. Ernest dropped Preston at the front door of the school at 9:00 A.M., and at the end of the classes Preston raced across the bridge to the marble floors and wood-panel silence of the Legislature building.

On some afternoons, Preston wandered the somnolent halls, which were soaked in the scents of lemon oil and history. Up the great stairs, in the alcoves and on the landings and balconies hung dark oils of the great and forgotten makers of Alberta's past. A fountain trickled in the rotunda under the dome. Behind the thick oak doors of the ministers' offices, one could hear the muted clatter of a typewriter. In the empty Legislative Assembly, the ranked desks of the members stood in the cool currents of spring air that blew in through open windows and doors, bearing the scents of grass and river. The caucus, cabinet and committee rooms, with their vast, polished tables, oozed with the mysteries of power.

Down in the clatter of the basement cafeteria, Preston sat at tea with the friendly people who worked in the building. According to Conservative MLA Ernest Watkins, many in the cabinet were "Aberhart's extinguished volcanoes," and they spun old yarns of the hard days of the Depression and the glorious summer of 1935, of barnyard politics and back-country meetings in musty community halls, at which the politician was expected to pour coffee from large, chipped-enamelled pots and pass the cookies, if he hoped to be reelected.

On most days Preston went to his father's large, sunny room, past the outer office with its two indomitable secretaries. Ernest's desk commanded the chamber from a 23-centimetre-high riser built across the east end of the room. The balance of the space was taken up with a maze of couches and chairs for visitors. On one wall there were two doors: one led into a walk-in safe and the other opened into an anteroom with a desk at which Preston was permitted to do his homework. As he worked, he could listen in on his father's meetings with an endless procession of delegations and interest groups. He could overhear conversations with cabinet ministers or the office staff. From this vantage point, he could see, first-hand, his father testing his ideas against the common sense of the common people.

When he asked, his father said that the first test of public policy was "Does it pass the judgement of the people of Alberta?" Ernest, however, was not a naive politician, and he also tuned Preston's ear to hear the subtle sound of axes grinding when people and organizations petitioned the premier. Behind the curtain, Preston observed the value of his father's legendary patience; he saw that good policy required hard work on detail as well as insight.

Preston soaked up this aural primer of political lore, absorbing impressions, experiencing for the first time the character and quality of ambition, vanity and, occasionally, selfless public service. He began as well to read the statutes that the Legislature was enacting, and his father taught him to see the human story behind each dry, dull bill. His father had previously invited him to visit his office, but for these precious weeks, this was an everyday thing, an immersion. Afterwards, through high school and university, Preston seized the opportunity to visit the Legislature as often as he could. Midway through high school, he purchased his own copies of the *Revised Statutes of Alberta* and *Revised Statutes of Canada*, precocious for a kid, and he soon became better versed in the law than most of his father's caucus members.

Although Ernest never played the role of a political journeyman with a young apprentice, Preston's taste for public life began in those sojourns across the bridge after school. The boy's interest concerned the premier, for whom political life was a poor second choice to a career as a preacher and an interference with his preference for farming. Ernest should not have been astonished: Preston's curiosity about politics was seeded and nourished by his parents' sense of responsibility and their engagement in important public affairs.

Preston learned, to his frustration, that his father did not readily answer the questions he asked on rides home to the farm. He never responded in ten words if five would do. What Ernest passed on to Preston was dragged out of him by his son. His father would disappear for a week, and Preston would follow what he was doing—a first ministers' conference, for example—in the newspapers. When Ernest came home, however, he said not a word; it was as if nothing had happened. It was only when Preston interrogated him that the story of the past week would be told. Calving and branding or breaking a horse were easier. Preston honed his interviewing techniques sharper and sharper.

Too soon in that spring of 1954, school and the afternoons under the Legislature dome ended. The open days of summer beckoned. The river flowed full of fish; the heat of the prairies rose up to the towering cumulonimbus of the afternoon storms. The thickets along the river bank, where the porcupines and owls loved to torment the dogs, were lush with saskatoons, raspberries and chokecherries. The night sky, after the long white dusk of the northern solstice, was thick with stars and falling asteroids.

Muriel organized an endless list of chores to be done. Ron Galloway was delighted to have the boy around, to teach him about horses and dairy cows, because he already had a strong back and a keenness for hard work. Even for a boy as serious as Preston, politics could take second place to the hours in the hot sun. His muscles thickened; his bones strengthened; his skin browned. He learned to wrinkle his eyes against the sun and spit out the dust.

Preston started school at Horse Hills, a nearby settlement that long since has been absorbed by Edmonton's expanding sprawl. This was a world away from the university quarter of Garneau. Here people worked with their hands as well as their minds; they were practical, sensible, close to the earth. Muriel saw the difference at the PTA meetings. In Garneau, parents would talk of the latest educational theory and how it might be applied to their children. In Horse Hills, parents organized a hockey rink for the winter: "I'll get the lumber, you get the hose, he'll string the lights, they'll flood and scrape the ice."

Even with the postwar prosperity, with land holdings that represented a great deal of wealth, and with the oil exploration companies paying cash on surface rights for their seismic lines, drilling rigs and pipelines, these families seldom had cash to spare. At Christmas the first year, the children in Preston's class drew names and were instructed to buy a present, spending no more than twenty-five cents, for the student whose name they held. One lad did not have the quarter, but he raised rabbits, so he selected the best new bunny as his gift. Preston was deeply impressed and envious of the child who'd been given the pet.

Preston became part of a circle of boys who called themselves the Fearless Five and after school lived a *Boys' Life* existence of dogs, horses, fishing and rodeos. They played hockey in winter and baseball in summer. They understood the river, arrowheads and teepee rings. They went down to the gravel pits in the evenings to sneak up on the parked cars and scare the romancing couples. Preston joined 4-H, raised cattle and exhibited them in competitions. When he finished primary school, he went on to Horse Hills High School, where he excelled in sports as well as academics.

The farm was a busy place, with more than seventy cows milking. Ron had to hire and supervise help, and Preston had his own demanding list of chores that his parents expected him to complete. Some of the best days came when Keith was home from the New York residential school and could be shown the ways of the farm. When that school could do no more for him, he was sent to the Red Deer School Hospital in central Alberta and later moved to Edmonton, where he was employed in a sheltered workshop and lived in a group home.

The fact that his father was the premier and his Sunday broadcasts were popular around Horse Hills was taken in stride by Preston's pals. Ernest was referred to as the father who owned the dairy farm and worked in the city for the government. The Mannings gained an easy acceptance, though their life was different from that of the neighbours. They holidayed at places such as California and Lake Louise Lodge, which were impossibly exotic by the standards of their cash-strapped neighbours. Preston was seldom asked to invite his friends over. Only one boy, named Ed Wilkins, cracked the invisible barrier at the Mannings' front door and won frequent invitations into the home, or to stay for a meal.

In spite of his unpretentiousness and the fact that he took the initiative to organize outdoor activities with his friends, Preston was indelibly marked by his parents' public prominence and sense of civic obligation. It set him apart from his fellows because he had a rather singular sense of purpose and commitment for one so young. The social isolation his mother created inevitably established a gap between him and the boys he could never invite home. The gap widened because of his self-sufficient character, intelligence, seriousness of mind and maturity and the positions his family held in politics and the evangelical Christian church. As he grew older, he became progressively more isolated from the usual world of adolescent boys.

During Preston's high school years, his father had become exceptionally powerful even for a provincial premier in Canada. His clean desk, his impeccable files, his orderly routines and his efficient staff produced machine politics without requiring a large apparatus. He kept government simple, uncomplicated and direct. He never overestimated his own importance. He did not bother to scheme, second-guess, intrigue or practice duplicity, thereby eliminating the need for many aides and advisors. Thus, it could be said that the government of Alberta existed in a single head and in a single pair of hands—Ernest Manning's.

Throughout his career he always held one or more of the important portfolios in addition to his duties as premier. The other cabinet members were on standby, department managers from whom he expected little except political prudence and personal rectitude. Over the years only a select handful, such as Nathan Tanner in natural resources and Dr. James Donovan Ross on the health care file, had his confidence. Caucus, with its connectedness and sensitivity to the people—more than cabinet, with its ambition and compromise—was the forum Manning relied on to inform his policies and temper his politics.

He usually travelled alone on government business. He did not surround himself with an entourage of self-important file pushers, bath drawers and media buffers. In exceptional circumstances—and they were rare—a deputy or two might tag along to provide specialized support. Ernest flagged his own cabs and booked his own dinner reservations. If he had time to spare he called on his network of Christian friends, built up through years of directing and preaching on the *National Back to the Bible Hour* broadcast.

Ernest Manning was the most emotionally self-sufficient man to grace Alberta's political history. He simply did not need other people, and this was disconcerting to those around him, including his neighbours at Horse Hills. He once had a man in cabinet who was also a close friend. David Ure had been his agriculture minister, but David was killed in a highway crash. His executive secretaries, Peter Elliot and Russ Shephard, had a sparing amount of access. Orvis Kennedy was the exception: a powerful confidant, proxy in party affairs and friend with whom he shared Christian as well as political fellowship.

When Ernest came home, he left his job behind in the city. Government and political people were never entertained at Westerlea, nor were people from the *National Back to the Bible Hour*. He rarely brought home files; on one exceptional occasion, Preston watched him at the kitchen table with an adding machine working on the provincial budget. Normally in the evening, Ernest worked on his radio scripts and sermons. His family was as isolated as possible from his political life.

When Ernest first succeeded William Aberhart, Muriel was extremely apprehensive that she would not be able to match Jessie Aberhart's gracious social conduct. Fortunately, much less was expected from a politician's wife after the war, as social attitudes to women changed. She need not have worried because she was, in her own right, a capable hostess and a social success, but she was just as glad to be at the farm away from politics. She preferred to be away from scrutiny, and would have been quite happy if she'd not been expected at the few social occasions Ernest hosted, such as an annual reception at the Legislature for the caucus members and their spouses.

Like all their friends, Muriel and Ernest lived disciplined, dedicated lives focussed on faith, family and politics, They followed a demanding regime that began early in their years together. Late in his life Manning confided in one of his former MLAs, Albert Ludwig, that he had always wished to learn to sail or to fly a plane. But, he asked, "where was there a lake to sail near enough Westerlea? And when was there time to learn to fly?" When Preston spent time with his father at home it was because the two of them were working on farm chores.

The Mannings found their closest friends in the political and religious circle around Social Credit and the *National Back to the Bible Hour*. These serious men and women saw the world as a broken place in need of Christian love and enlightened government. The Kennedy family were among their closest private friends. A year older than Ernest, Orvis served his Social Credit apprenticeship in federal politics, sitting from 1938 to 1940 as a member of Parliament. Then he became the party's national political organizer and took a seat on the board of the Alberta Social Credit League, the party's powerful command centre. Orvis delivered Ernest a functioning political machine that held power in two provinces, Alberta and British Columbia, and provided a third force in the Canadian Parliament through the 1950s and early 1960s. His son, Ed, and Preston were friends and collaborators on church projects in their university years.

Another close and remarkable friend was the American J. Howard Pew, the Sun Oil heir and chief executive who, along with Ernest and petroleum engineer Sidney Blair of Canadian Bechtel, was trying to commercialize the oil sands. Pew was a well-connected evangelical Christian who counted among his protégés the young Billy Graham. Pew and Ernest spent a great deal of personal time together including at least one week a year at Lake Louise, where they talked about faith and families and fishing.

Muriel had a remarkably contemporary view of the place of women and the gifts to occupy her own position. She played an integral role in the music for the *National Back to the Bible Hour.* She was also intensely partisan, more so than the characteristically detached Ernest. She was active in Social Credit Party affairs, viewed by many of its members as the hidden influence behind Ernest, almost the assistant premier. In a 1968 speech recalling her husband's career, Muriel said that it was good government provided by Social Credit as much as the oil boom that after the war made Alberta prosperous. That was the kind of partisan claim Ernest would never make.

The Sunday broadcast gave Ernest and Muriel a common interest large enough for their very keen minds and high energies. It was the activity that kept "Abie" alive for them and constantly reminded them of the romance that brought them together, But it also set them on a pedestal, and Preston was pulled up onto that perch with them.

Keith was away most of the time. Ernest commuted to the city during the week. Muriel was often away on *Back to the Bible* broadcasts or Social Credit women's business. Preston kept the fort with the Galloways, who were now his extended family. They may have been, respectfully, at the beck and call of his parents but Preston's relationship with them was more open, easy going and intimate. However, they were adults, and through them Preston was again being drawn out of the world of ordinary adolescent concerns.

In the end, when all the rules and rituals of the family were taken into account, Preston's was an increasingly lonely life, with Ed Wilkins his only important and lasting friendship outside the farm gate. He was forbidden by the strictures of his parents' evangelical life style from entertainment such as dancing and the movies. And he endorsed their standards because he accepted their faith. It simply never occurred to him to chase after booze, cars and necking in the gravel pits. Girls were *terra incognita*. In terms of moral strictures, his was not that unusual an upbringing for rural Alberta teenagers in the late 1950s, and it never occurred to him to resent it or to rebel. He loved his life, he loved his parents and he wanted to please them, the Galloways, his teachers, Orvis Kennedy and any other adult who crossed his path.

So while there was loneliness, he found an outlet in his studies, and not just in his school work but also in his other interests. He had the knack for turning everything he did into a serious piece of curriculum. He persuaded his parents to purchase a chemistry lab for him. He installed it in the Galloway's basement and added some fairly sophisticated instruments to it over the years and did some quite advanced experiments. Mendeleev's periodic table of elements fascinated him: it showed the order of the physical world and the creative imagination of a good scientist. He memorized it and regaled his pals by reciting from it.

His father was given Will and Ariel Durant's ten-volume *Story of Civilization*. Preston read it cover to cover. It gave him a sense of the unbreakable connection between history and politics: each was part of an indivisible continuum, and whether or not an event was one or the other depended on when you were born. He began to put the lore of politics that he'd absorbed from his father into a framework, an intellectual construct. He saw that there were patterns and common human values and needs that didn't change even if cultures and systems that contained them rose, ran and faded. He could see in his father's approach to government an appreciation of the common sense of the common people, his deference to the judgement of ordinary Albertans who looked the premier's phone number up in the telephone book and called him at home.

At the same time, he sorted out his faith through intensive personal study, reading widely and beyond his years to determine what he himself would believe. The Society of Friends speaks of the distinction between "Quaker by birth and Quaker by conviction." Preston was Christian by birth; he now achieved the conviction and personal commitment for an authentic and lasting faith able to endure the transition from adolescence to adulthood.

He observed that the Christian passion for justice and compassionate social relationships had a bearing on contemporary life. The history and politics of the Bible and the history and politics of the twentieth century were not removed from one another but bound together by the human longing for reconciliation as the remedy for broken relationships, and for peace as the remedy for civic strife. This wholistic sense of spiritual and secular values was not a matter of bringing a hidden agenda or a secret list of Christian objectives to politics; rather, it was a matter of political style, of, in the language of the Old Testament, "reasoning together" rather than making laws through adversarial processes.

Long before Preston was out of high school, he had set the course of his intellectual inquries for the next half decade and discovered the themes that would preoccupy his politics for the next forty years.

CHAPTER FIVE Rites of Passage

. . . take no thought of the harvest,
But only of proper sowing.

—T. S. ELIOT, Choruses from "The Rock"

PRESTON MANNING GRADUATED from Horse Hills High School in the spring of 1960 and the following fall registered at the University of Alberta as an honours science undergraduate, majoring in physics. His choice of faculty was a rather arbitrary one; he had excelled in math and science in his final years of secondary school, but he had done well in all his other courses too. He had no career plan. There was little counselling in his school, and his parents were not the type to influence his choice of profession: that was in other hands. The Mannings that believed there was a divine plan for every life and that in time God would reveal his calling for their son.

Preston worked at the farm over the summer and read voraciously. He looked deceptively frail, geeky, behind his dark-rimmed glasses; his clothes tended to hang loosely on his frame. When he was in a suit jacket, his big hands stuck out of the sleeves awkwardly. He had the stoop and gait that rural Alberta boys seem to develop at an early age from hours on horseback. His body, however, had been hardened by physical labour into a lean, wiry frame. His hockey-playing friends knew that those hips could deliver a painful bodycheck, those wrists were capable of a hard, fast shot. On horseback, he was graceful, almost balletic. People said he was the most natural rider they'd ever seen; he belonged in a saddle.

When he started classes that autumn, he attended as a day student, driving back to the farm each evening. His courses were demanding, and he had little time for extracurricular interests beyond a bit of hockey and some church activities. Edmonton's winters are unbroken by the chinooks of the southern part of the province, and the campus buildings vent great gouts of steam into the air around the clock in the subzero temperatures, creating an almost surreal Arctic cocoon that hides the serious student away from the rest of the world. Daylight from the beginning of November to the end of February is confined to a few hours between 9:00 A.M. and 3:00 P.M., and the long drives to and from Westerlea were dark, windblown and lonely. Nights he spent at his desk. The weekends were divided between chores, studies and the family's Sunday mornings at the Fundamental Baptist Church in Edmonton. Through the winter, as he maintained a disciplined study schedule, Preston remained suspended between adolescence and adulthood.

He felt obliged to keep in touch with the Social Credit Club but was not active in campus politics. He established contact with the student group that was to have a much greater influence on him than the Socreds: the InterVarsity Christian Fellowship. IVCF was a North American nondenominational, evangelical organization engaged in an impressive initiative to provide intellectually satisfying, emotionally mature leadership to young Christians wrestling for the first time with the demands, doubts and pressures of an adult world. Its publishing house was turning out the best books and magazines in the evangelical church; its triennial missions conclave at the University of Illinois in Champagne-Urbana, was *the* career hothouse for North American Christians. Preston was impressed by its senior staff member in Alberta, Cathie Nicholl, a former nurse with intellect, sensibility, commitment, uncompromising faith and an empathetic ear for undergraduates. She was easily his intellectual equal, and as yet he'd met few evangelicals besides his parents who were. In his first year of studies, however, Preston had little time, even for a group as attractive to him as this one.

Occasionally, he commuted to the city with his father, and as often as he could he visited Ernest in the Legislature building. However, the university's academic requirements were demanding even for a bright student and left little time for other interests. Preston didn't know what life he was preparing for, but he wasn't taking any chances scholastically with his future. That summer, he again worked for Ron Galloway at Westerlea and made new living arrangements for the fall term. He had found that commuting, especially in bad weather, was too time-consuming, and he was ready to try life away from his parents. His best friend, Ed Wilkins, would be attending the University of Alberta as well, and the two rented an apartment together in his old boyhood neighbourhood of Garneau.

Eight years had subtly changed those familiar streets. Old houses on the eastern edge of the community were being sold and torn down to make way for walk-up apartments filled with students and poor young academics at the beginning of their teaching and research careers. Fraternities were buying some of the largest homes and turning them into residences. Other, more modest houses were being converted to collectives by late beatniks and the early neoradicals who opposed the war in Viet Nam and the political and economic establishment and were into folk and rock music, psychedelic drugs and sexual freedom.

Preston Manning was no child of the sixties, and the University of Alberta in the first half of the decade was removed from the counterculture that had begun to form on other campuses in North America. The campus was smothered by the province's small-town ambience, which was antithetical to more cosmopolitan influences. The high proportion of day students still living in the parental home hindered experimentation, and the deans still considered themselves to be *in loco parentis*. Nevertheless, a diluted, muted version of the coming ethos was on the threshold, with its antiestablishment insurrection, experimentation with sex and drugs, and flamboyant, insubordinate rhetoric so quickly abandoned after graduation by most of its devotees. Preston Manning had no inclination for any of it, however diluted. He was tuned in to his parents' generation: abstemious, chaste and temperate. Many of his friends thought he was one of those guys who'd been born old and had missed childhood. One could easily miss his wit, his prankish humour, his flaring brilliance and see only the sheepish grin, cowboy gait, careful manner of dress and slow, drawling thoughtfulness.

He and Ed lived a monkish, bookish undergraduate life compared with their most extravagant peers. They were farm boys in the big city, with sense enough not to do anything stupid. Preston, away from the home in which he had been compliant, cheerful and ready to please, found that the real freedom of the city lay in the opportunity to think independently about the assumptions and commitments of adolescence. If his upbringing had been precocious, it had also been untested. Now he could get some perspective on himself.

That year he had more time for IVCF and young-adult church functions. He began to find his own spiritual voice. Because of his father's position and his own abilities, he was expected to assume leadership in his church. He knew that. But he wanted to sort out what he believed for himself from the doctrines his parents espoused. Like most Christian young men of his generation, he could also see that social change was placing great stress on the evangelical and fundamentalist sectors of the Protestant church. The venerable doctrines of the mainstream denominations were crumbling under cultural pressure and social criticism and began retuning their theology to a socially acceptable expression of faith to stop the erosion of membership, funds and church attendance. IVCF was part of a movement that didn't want to rewrite theology. Rather, it sought to express the old faith in the new idiom of its generation, and to face the new realities of late-twentieth-century life. IVCF was a fresh voice for scriptural Christianity that was as tough, cool and engaged as Preston, and he found it appealing and worth pursuing.

Living close to campus gave Preston and Ed access to ice time for pick-up hockey, and they attended football and basketball games. Preston sat as a Social Credit backbencher in the model parliament. He read a few things that piqued his curiosity outside his course lists. He and Ed kept the apartment, prepared meals, enjoyed long conversations with pals. There were visiting lecturers and films. He visited his father more frequently. He began to think about his future. He came to the attention of some of the men who had built the Alberta economy, through what was called the golden decade, which had been really fifteen uninterrupted years of development from the benchmark discovery of the Leduc oil field in 1947.

One of these men was Sid Blair, who had been a University of Alberta petroleum engineering graduate student in the 1920s and who'd done his master's thesis on the commercialization of the oil sands. He then spent twenty years out of Canada in the refining business, including a wartime secondment as comptroller of aviation fuel for the Royal Air Force, before returning to head Canadian Bechtel. Blair, Ernest Manning and J. Howard Pew had worked together since 1949 to get an oil-sands industry started and were engaged in the advanced planning of the first plant. Blair, who knew most of Preston's teachers and had heard that the young man was a real comer as a research scientist, was leaving the premier's office one afternoon during the term when he bumped into Preston at the door and inquired about his summer plans.

Although Blair was a weekend farmer himself, who raised prize sheep on a farm outside Toronto, he thought Preston's time could be better spent. He recruited the young man to go to San Francisco, the world headquarters of the privately owned construction giant. In May 1962, Preston found himself living in a tiny apartment on San Francisco's cable car line and working in Bechtel's research facilities. He worked on mathematical calculations for a radiation shield at a plant to process spent fuel rods from a nuclear reactor and was commissioned to write a report on the commercialization of laser (electron beam) and maser (electromagnetic wave) technology. He was introduced to researchers at Berkeley, Stanford and the Lawrence radiation labs. He was given an introduction to the project management of the biggest domestic research, engineering and construction undertakings in the United States, a world of high finance, high politics and advanced applied science.

One of the "what-ifs" of Preston Manning's life concerns his career with the Bechtel family. The Bechtels recruited the brightest and best engineers and scientists in the United States for a sprawling, multibillion-dollar corporate powerhouse. They incubated the careers of scores of smart young California Republicans. The family had started in the early part of the century building dams, roads, bridges and rail lines in California and the southwest. Bechtel flourished in the Second World

War building ships, refineries and pipelines, and the company had come to Canada to develop the Norman Wells oil field and build the Canol pipeline from the Mackenzie Valley over the Mackenzie Mountains to Whitehorse, Yukon. After the war, Bechtel was the prime contractor to North America's petroleum and electric power industries. Canadian Bechtel had a hand in every major Canadian pipeline, refinery and oil sands development from 1943 to 1965, plus ports, the Churchill Falls and Baie James hydroelectric projects and the Chalk River nuclear power laboratory.

Preston was favourably evaluated by Bechtel's human-resources talent scouts during his summer with the company. Had he been interested, they would have written his ticket to any graduate school in North America and put him on the fast track in their research program and in the United States' most successful corporate meritocracy.

But these were wise men with superb antennae for human nature, and by the end of the summer they told Sid Blair that this young man did not want to spend his life locked up in a laboratory. Preston had been more taken by the consultants and project developers than by the researchers. Although they might have groomed him as Sid Blair's successor in the Canadian arm of Bechtel, he would first have had to complete a long apprenticeship as a scientist. Every success there—and his success was considered almost a sure bet—would have made them reluctant to waste him in executive management. What Preston found missing in the labs, the Bechtel executives realized, was people.

Back in Edmonton, as Thanksgiving passed and Christmas approached, Preston wrestled with his first career change: he wanted to switch his major and he had to do it by the end of 1962 to complete the requisite courses and earn an honours degree. Dr. Walter Mackenzie, the family friend who had helped the Mannings make the best of Keith's future, counselled Preston to go into medicine. He would have a promising future in biophysical research, on the leading edge of new medical technology. But Preston wanted something closer to the politics that he saw in his father's office and the project management that he'd seen at Bechtel. He began to ponder what kind of consulting he could do that would place him in that arena.

In his dilemma, Preston's new confidence in the Christian faith kicked in, and he began to pray about his future and to study the

Scriptures for guidance. As part of his decision process, he was reading widely in other disciplines. He included on his eclectic reading list the journals of John Wesley, an eighteenth-century English religious dissident. Educated at Oxford, Wesley was ordained as an Episcopalian priest. Then, in 1738, he was converted to evangelical Christianity, and with his brother founded the Methodist religious society that got them banned from the Church of England. Wesley spent the rest of his life preaching for the moral and spiritual reformation of England. He campaigned for public education, the care of the poor and social justice. He welded piety with politics in a gritty, practical combination that had a lasting influence on both England and America. Preston found this impressive, and while he didn't want a career in the Christian ministry, he did want to emulate Wesley's public mission. To do this, he decided to complete his education in a field that touched on public affairs.

In the spring of 1963, Preston did the paperwork to switch to the faculty of arts and science for an honours economics degree. He went to the farm for the summer of 1963, and in the fall he started classes, cramming into a single year the full load of economics courses he needed to graduate. During the winter, he also found time to read the impressive academic literature on Canadian reform and populist movements dating back to the eighteenth century. He observed that political parties, business, the church and government all needed at one time or another to be reformed. If breakdown and failure were inevitable, he reasoned, then the art of mending things, of reconciliation, should be a constant too. Rapprochement was the stage on which people and their social institutions met, and managing that stage was a business opportunity. The outline of a career was taking shape.

By the New Year, 1964, Preston knew he was going to succeed in getting his degree that spring and he considered graduate school. But not for long. He craved action, engagement. And he began to see business and government consulting as a link between the problems that corporations and institutions faced and the experts who could solve them. The two sides—the problem and the solution—didn't know how to find each other and often couldn't even talk the same language. Preston could broker the relationship and make the linkage work. He had seen Bechtel do this, and he was sure he could do it himself. He guessed that such consulting would inevitably lead into politics.

During Preston Manning's undergraduate period, the University of Alberta had been a singular environment for the development of political talent. Many of its undergraduates from the mid-1950s to the mid-1960s were the "A" team of Alberta political life for the next thirty years. The team's leading lights included Peter Lougheed, later the province's premier; Grant Notley, who led the New Democratic opposition to the Lougheed government; Joe Clark, a future prime minister, and James Coutts, the future principal secretary to Prime Ministers Lester Pearson and Pierre Trudeau. Ray Speaker, who founded the short-lived Representative Party before joining the Reform Party of Canada, and Preston Manning were the populists of the team.

These young men reached adulthood in Alberta during a flourish of prosperity and confidence. They had seen government in Alberta succeed in burying the damage of the Depression and rise above war. There had been good fortune and a treasury of resources to build on, but there had also been brains and a fresh, unfettered culture in which merit, not inheritance, mattered most.

They had a surfeit of role models in business and the professions. They had also seen in the rise and run of John Diefenbaker's career that a Western Canadian could take federal politics by storm and command the nation. With the certainty of all young men, they were sure they could avoid his mistakes and do better than he, both tactically and in lasting results. But they considered him great for his vision of Canadian development in the West and the North, and were sure that the men of Bay Street and Parliament Hill who had so hated the Chief simply didn't realize the wealth in resources, people and new ideas that was out there in the Canadian hinterland.

So they all went to graduate school in places such as Harvard and Oxford, or to work as lawyers, accountants, consultants, and teachers, knowing that sooner or later they would be in politics and that Canada would need them. Preston Manning had the additional advantage of an insider's view of the zenith of his father's premiership. In the period from 1955, the province's Jubilee, to the 1963 election, Ernest Manning stood astride an awesome political machine, forged from the alloy of a grassroots consensus on the purposes of government and complete public confidence in the premier's integrity.

Through those years, Manning commanded 55 per cent of the popular vote, personal approval ratings 20 points higher and 60 of 64 seats in the Legislative Assembly. To celebrate the Jubilee, the province built auditoria for the performing arts in Edmonton and Calgary that bore on their portals these words, approved of by Premier Manning, from the Roman Suetonius: "I found a city built of bricks, left it built of marble."

That was the mission of government, and Ernest Manning had expressed it not just in public works but also in medical care, new elementary schools, the creation of a second university, homes for the elderly and a relatively enlightened system of welfare for the poor. The combination of the liquidation of the Depression-era default, payment of the debt, balanced budgets and oil prosperity gave Manning the opportunity to be the highest per-capita spender on health, education and social services of all the premiers in Canada.

In his final year at the University of Alberta, Preston was closer to his father than he had ever been. He frequently sat in his father's office between classes in the autumn of 1963 and was there when American President John F. Kennedy was assassinated. As a courtesy, the U.S. State Department called within minutes of the President's death to let Ernest know bombers had scrambled over Alberta. Such moments indicated the father's acceptance that Preston's long-standing fascination with politics was going to be part of his son's entire life.

He saw that Preston's boyhood interest in politics came from his effort to know his father and define their relationship. Preston was curious and inquisitive: he wanted to know what Ernest did when he was away from home. He wanted to break through Ernest's taciturnity. It was frustrating most of the time to pry responses from his father, but it produced results.

His father told him stories, and from those stories Preston learned the three-dimensional lore of lawmaking. To the bare facts he added a young boy's sense of excitement and drama. A bill passed in the Legislature was more than a sheaf of paper drafted at an obscure desk in the complex of government office blocks north of the Legislature grounds. It was the product of phone calls at night between well-known people, of the delegations sitting in his father's office, of the wisdom and insight of public servants for whom his father had a keen appreciation, of farmers gathered in their yards and of men in somber suits arriving at Ernest's office in long black cars. Budget making was watching his father sit at the kitchen table after dinner, amid papers, file folders and binders, banging away at the keys of a manual adding machine.

Ernest introduced him to other, more loquacious men, who told him more stories of politics and politicians present and past. Preston learned the stories of the forgotten ghosts imprisoned in the oil paintings hanging in the Legislature building. He read books about the political founders of Western Canada, he read the papers, he read the statutes that emerged from each legislative session. He had an insatiable thirst for the whole of it. Politics was the family business, and he was the son of promise who watched as his father practised public duty.

From Ernest he absorbed the democratic values that were the Manning government's trademark—hard as Alberta's limestone mountains and just as immovable. The core was a belief in the rights and responsibilities of individual judgement, common sense, the limits of government, the dangers of arbitrary authority and the preeminence of citizen lawmakers gathered in an elected parliament. In the most common cliché used to describe it, it was government of the common people. Ernest applied those values in a stark critique of fascism, collectivism and socialism, which he regarded as threatening intrusions on prairie political life, and a culture emerged in Alberta that was skeptical to liberalism and hostile to social democracy.

Preston had tested what he'd learned in the crucible of university life. Ernest was pleased with his exposure to Bechtel, proud of the reviews that had come back to him and impressed with the process that his son had used to evaluate his career and switch from physics to economics. Preston was still his son, but he was no longer a boy. It was time for the father to take his son off the sidelines and put him into the game. He'd earned it.

When he started university, the points on Preston's compass had been family, faith and political vision. Now, as he graduated and began his adult life, he would set his own direction, but he would do so with the same magnetic needle.

He had defined his own political identity, crafted his own adult faith and set the terms of engagement on which he would build his place in the world. He was looking not for a conventional career but for the opportunities to experiment with his ideas and hone his talent. Like any other fresh-faced university graduate of his generation, he needed a little experience before the rest of the world would take him seriously.

CHAPTER SIX

Experiment and Experience

"You are the truest person I have ever known."

— WILLIAM NICHOLSON, *Shadowlands*

ALTHOUGH HE HAD dismissed the idea of graduate studies, Preston's plan to establish a consulting business after he received his B.A. Hons. (Economics) in 1964 was vague. What he most wanted was to work with his father. There was plenty to do. The Social Credit Party was winding down like an old watch with a worn-out mainspring. It needed repair and rejuvenation. The premier, who had been musing openly about his retirement since 1962, showed surprisingly little overt interest in the long-term future of the party. He didn't initiate it, but when his son and a handful of other young men offered ideas and proposed projects, the patriarch was receptive and gave this new blood some rein.

Preston, of course, enjoyed the freedom that came at the end of four years of hard academic work. He had more time to slip out to the farm to ride and fish. Keith was living in a group home in Edmonton, and Preston spent a great deal of time with him, taking him for meals, to movies or to church. His older brother had grown into a big, friendly bear of a man—demonstrative, a hugger, a singer. His medications were reliable, and Preston could relax and enjoy his visits without worrying about seizures. Although he was much more reserved, being with Keith drew out a degree of warmth in him and a tenderness that was otherwise well contained. Preston continued to play pick-up hockey and to call on his father's legislative office. Ernest was as sparing with his words as ever but now seemed more willing, as one adult to another, to answer Preston's questions about the important events of government.

Ernest had renewal on his mind—but not the political kind. Canadian evangelicals had as keen a sense as any national network in the 1960s of the depth and extent of social change being wrought by this turbulent decade. Critics inside and outside the church were flaying the faith for its irrelevance. Canadian journalist Pierre Berton's *The Comfortable Pew*, Toronto clergyman Ernest Harrison's *Church without God*, and Harvard theologian Harvey Cox's *Secular City* were manifestations of this storm of reproach. Theologians and churchmen in the major Protestant denominations reexamined their faith, repealed great chunks of theology and reformatted their delivery in an attempt to break through the alienation and indifference of their congregations. It seemed to be a losing battle against Sunday golf and brunch. Marriage-counselling institutes, day-care centres, political action and guitar music in the sanctuary displaced Wednesday prayer meetings and strawberry socials.

Ernest Manning and his like-minded colleagues responded differently. The problem wasn't with the old, unshakable truth; it was with the old, rebellious human nature. Their answer to Christianity's crisis of credibility was "spiritual awakening," a sixties way of expressing the old concept of "revival." This theme was being established by evangelical leaders such as Billy Graham.

On the *National Back to the Bible Hour*, Ernest devoted a great deal of energy to proclaiming an ambition to restore Biblical faith and focus to people's lives. Many his age were alert to the desire of young Christians to actively move their faith into every nook and cranny of life but were also afraid of the risks. The sophistication of urban life was more likely to dilute the faith than was the faith likely to mitigate the despair that seemed to come with change. Ernest was quietly glad that Preston showed no inclination to take risks with his faith.

Preston Manning's first major research project after his convocation was to assemble a body of literature on the Protestant Reformation and the history of English evangelical "awakenings" and American revival movements. He studied this material intensively for several weeks, created his own synthesis, then wrote a paper and developed some speeches about spiritual awakening in the 1960s. This exercise foreshadowed twenty years of reducing problems to sheaves of paper in a briefcase—an analytical model of going into retreat to study, read and write, then emerging with a new prescription and launching a campaign. Of course he received no income from this work: earlier, his father had insisted that this kind of work be unpaid.

Preston gave his talks first on the *National Back to the Bible Hour.* Orvis Kennedy's son, Ed, shared Preston's enthusiasm for the subject, and the two young men organized a cross-Canada speaking tour that autumn and winter, with the help of Ernest's and Orvis's networks of contacts. They got themselves invited to preach on Sunday, spent weekends at retreats and dropped in to weeknight dinners in church basements.

Many of Ernest's friends and listeners speculated that the young man would do what his father had wanted to at the same age, before politics intervened—become a professional minister. The compliant son, always eager to please the father, might now win ultimate parental approval by following in his father's footsteps. Preston's friends, those his own age, worried a bit that he was drifting, reacting to his father rather than getting on with his own life.

There was, however, a distinctive thread to Preston's themes: he was not a Bible preacher in the conventional sense. He did not prepare and deliver homilies. He was a layman. He stood up to the pulpit or microphone and talked conversationally, shrewdly, intellectually about connections between faith and the society in which he and his listeners lived: business, politics, science, relationships. He wanted to show how the greatest accomplishments of science and intellect revealed God in new ways, how the broken could be mended, relationships healed and conflict reconciled.

His study of the church's European and American history allowed him to see the deep mark that the Reformation and four subsequent centuries of Protestant dissent and nonconformity had placed on North American democratic political thinking. His father may have unconsciously absorbed George Manning's puritan East Anglian outlook by living with it. Preston picked it up from hard study. The hallmark of this outlook was a skeptical attitude towards authority and a preference for a political culture in which every citizen was obligated to exercise individual judgement in political matters.

Preston was now walking on a religious high wire. There is a dialectic in the evangelical church expressed in the dictum to the Christian to be "in the world but not of it." If a young man wandered too far over the invisible line between the two, he could count on being yanked back or losing the approval of his elders. And the line was drawn in a completely subjective fashion. The controversies over the distinction between legitimate and illegitimate participation in the affairs of the world were a primary cause of generational conflict, rebellion and rejection of the faith.

In reconciling faith and politics, Preston had to resolve a second, more intellectual tension. The New Testament kingdom of God is proclaimed as being at hand, but how close was it? Politically active Canadian Christians in the first half of the century had answered the question with the Social Gospel, a prescription for social justice based on the communal love of the New Testament church. The Social Gospel emerged quite gracefully from the Protestant tradition. It did not challenge the authority of the church, but drew on the authority of Scripture and the example of Christ's life of service to challenge civil governments indifferent to the poor and oppressed. But the best work of the Social Gospel was social democracy—the CCF. In Ernest Manning's mind this was the failure of the Social Gospel: collectivism was three quarters of the way to totalitarianism and communism.

Aberhart had avoided the pitfall of collectivism by blending political dissent with the Old Testament apocalyptic view of history, in which God was the active agent in human affairs and each individual was responsible for establishing a redemptive relationship with God and his or her neighbours. Aberhart wanted to improve capitalism, to give it a sense of spiritual purpose, not purge it. Preston Manning faced the problem of how to conduct politics in a Christian way, with practical remedies for the problems governments are mandated to solve, but without forcing his faith on others or interdicting the work of the state.

Canadians were accustomed to prime ministers and premiers of strong private faith. Men like Ernest Manning did not separate the sacred and secular parts of their private lives, but in public life kept church and state apart. Canadians found it difficult to understand the obstacle that John F. Kennedy, a Catholic, overcame in 1961, becoming the U.S. president only after persuading the country he would not be a proxy for the Pope. But the evangelicals of Preston's generation had a faith that cut much closer to the bone. It was harder for them to say "everything that is, is holy" and not to follow through by seeking to redeem everything unholy in public life. On one end of the spectrum, ending the war in Viet Nam and banning the A-bomb were considered Christian acts; on the other end of the spectrum, so were banning abortion and the teaching of evolution. The issues and the stakes were escalating, and it was Preston's generation that had to find a way through the dilemma, not Ernest and his peers.

Meanwhile, there was secular politics. The Social Credit Party had not been rejuvenated since 1946, when thirty-eight-year-old Ernest Manning dragged it out of the shadow of Depression-era, eccentric monetary reform and into the second half of the twentieth century. At the end of the war, Manning brilliantly settled Alberta's defaulted loans. In 1946 he took one last shot at modernizing Social Credit theory. He tabled an Alberta Bill of Rights to guarantee citizens free education, medical benefits, an annual income of six hundred dollars and access to a provincial banking system. The law was struck down by the Alberta Supreme Court. In March 1947, the premier repudiated the party's last vestiges of anti-Semitism in a showdown with the fossils on the party's board who stubbornly continued to espouse the unacceptable notion of a so-called "international monetary conspiracy of Jewry" and who were effectively purged. This freed him to bring in a new era of staid, contemporary government whose hallmarks would be conventional conservative economics and enlightened attitudes towards education, health care and social services—the primary human services provided by provincial governments. His timing was perfect: the oil boom and the golden decade that started in 1947 paid the bills

for Alberta's smooth transition to an urban, industrial era and its atten-
dant government machinery.

In 1965, however, the party's arteries were hardening again. The
cabinet was aging and lacked ideas. After another election sweep in
1963, when he'd won fifty-nine of sixty-three seats and 55 per cent of
the popular vote, Ernest Manning was thinking of retiring from public
life. He was still relatively young. He could lead the party in one more
election and then leave after his sixtieth birthday to work in the corporate world—which was now showing an unguarded interest in his
executive talents. He was reflecting on the legacy he would leave, and
he began to think about a kinder, more humane touch for a party and
government that was faceless and coldly institutional. Oddly, however,
he prepared no succession plan and groomed no one to fill his shoes in
Alberta.

Nor, although he controlled the federal wing of the party, which
had a small caucus of MPs from the West and Quebec, did he express a
vision for its future. As a prairie force in the House of Commons from
1938 to 1962, Social Credit never had the stature or influence of the
Progressives or the CCF. The operations and finances of the national
organization were controlled by Orvis Kennedy and Ernest Manning,
who, at best, ran it as an Alberta branch plant and, at worst, as an after-
thought. Premier W. A. C. Bennett's success in creating a loosely
affiliated Socred dynasty in British Columbia provided a strategic
alliance that gave a vague raison d'être for the national party and
allowed it to survive John Diefenbaker's sweep to power in 1957 and
1958. In truth, the only common denominator between Manning,
Bennett and Kennedy was that they had all been young men in Alberta
in the summer of 1935, caught up in Aberhart's tidal force. They all had
more in common with Diefenbaker's prairie populism and his affinity
for outsiders, the poor and the disadvantaged.

In the 1958 Diefenbaker sweep, the Socred relic of nineteen MPs in
Parliament was wiped out. In 1962, Diefenbaker faltered, and Social
Credit regained a caucus of thirty members; in 1963, however, when the
Liberals swept Diefenbaker aside, Social Credit began its final fade. Only
four western Social Credit MPs held seats; the main force was its twenty-
member Quebec wing, the *ralliement des créditistes*, under the mercurial
car salesman Réal Couette. In 1964, at the party's convention in Red

Deer, Alberta, a Manning-inspired resolution proposed a "philosophical realignment" with the Conservatives as an ideological alternative to the Liberal hegemony. The idea died on the convention floor.

In 1965, twenty three-year-old Preston plunged into active politics for the first time in his life, as the Social Credit candidate for the federal riding of Edmonton East in the November general election. It was a curious undertaking: the national campaign had no focus, no message and nothing to link the western and Quebec candidates. On one hand, Preston was nothing more than an accommodating piece of cannon fodder, running against a safely ensconced Progressive Conservative, Bill Skoreyko, and an entrenched Tory machine controlled by the ruthless ethnic and labour bosses of the city's blue-collar neighbourhoods. On the other hand, he was presented, in the rhetoric of the day, as the "voice of youth." Campaign material ran his obviously youthful visage (did he need to shave yet?) with pictures of other candidates as proof that the Social Credit party embraced a demographic spectrum, vaguely defined in the text.

He was being patronized and exploited for his name: his organizers sent a letter from his father to every home in the riding, expecting that the endorsement of the premier would deliver the riding. Preston tromped around to the ethnocultural church offices, cultural festivals and meeting halls of the east end's minority power brokers. Ukrainians, Latvians, Germans, Poles, Francophones, Greeks, Estonians; exiles, refugees, the grandchildren of homesteaders; Lutherans, Russian and Eastern Orthodox, Anabaptists: Alberta had more than one hundred identifiable minorities. Edmonton East had at least a few families from most of those groups, and Social Credit, since 1935, had been routinely translating campaign pamphlets into five or six of the major languages. Preston met a lot of people and made no impact. The political chieftains in this part of town controlled the mayor's office, voted Liberal provincially and Conservative federally. They liked Preston, but not that much. Skoreyko was a Diefenbaker Conservative. He was first elected to the House of Commons in 1958, and after he clobbered Preston by 13,596 votes to 6,762, he remained the MP until he retired in 1980.

On November 8, Liberal Prime Minister Lester B. Pearson was reelected to a second minority. Social Credit retained only fourteen seats and was the fourth party in Parliament, behind the Conservatives and the NDP. It was an inauspicious entry into elective politics—an apparently quixotic venture. For federal politics, Preston was too early and in the wrong town. When John Diefenbaker was expelled from the leadership of his party two years later, the resulting western anger and disillusionment gave Ernest Manning the lever for a second attempt to merge Social Credit with the Tories and thus realign Canadian politics along a two-party ideological "left" and "right" divide. When that stratagem fizzled, the slow-gestating seed of the Reform Party of Canada was planted in politically fertile prairie soil. But Edmonton has never proved to be an easy town for Preston Manning to win.

He had paid his dues, however. He had earned his way, by more than his father's name, into a circle of young men who now turned their efforts to salvaging a future for the provincial Social Credit party. There were storm warnings that the party was losing touch and that younger voters, especially in the cities, were ripe for an alternative. It was becoming very clear to the young Socreds that if they didn't create the alternative, the older men and women of the leadership would let the party fade away.

Preston's demonstrated skill at research, analysis, synthesis and writing put him in great demand. He had an incredible capacity for hard work—partly inherited from a father who routinely worked sixteen-hour days with no ill effects and partly from the strength he gained from a physical life of farm work and sports. And Preston got a paying job. As a candidate, he'd worked with a senior fund raiser and strategist for the campaign, David Wilson, who was director of the newly formed National Public Affairs Research Foundation (NPARF).

The NPARF was financed by wealthy Albertans led by Home Oil's chief executive officer, Bobby Brown. Brown was a second-generation oil man with a prodigious capacity for Scotch whisky, a brilliant ability to create wealth and an inherited sense of civic responsibility. He and the cosponsors of the foundation wanted a source of good ideas for the provincial Social Credit and federal Progressive Conservatives in the leadership transitions that both parties faced. Beyond partisan boundaries, they slowly evolved a Western Canadian vision for the future development and growth of Canada, founded on market capitalism and grassroots democracy. Wilson was one of their bright, young resources who'd proved himself an able political administrator. Wilson hired Preston as a policy researcher.

Preston's initial assignments at the foundation sprang from his father's interest in reconnecting Social Credit to the reforming passion upon which it had been founded and rewriting that ardour in an idiom suited to the last quarter of the century. If Ernest Manning could steer his party, caucus and cabinet back to the sense of mission to care for the welfare of the people, which had made the winning difference in 1935, he would be remembered for more than cold, prudent administration. And he would lay the groundwork for the political transition in Alberta following his retirement and equip his successors with new ideas. Father and son were working as a team, with Preston's patrons footing the bill. It was heady, perfect stuff.

Then, romance intruded on the smooth course of politics. In the spring of 1966, Preston, now twenty-four years old and two years out of university, went on his first date. He had behaved for his six years away from home as if girls didn't interest him very much. His social contact with them was mostly at the Fundamental Baptist Church, where interested young women quickly discovered he had no idea that girls were on the map. One of those young women was Sandra Lillian Beavis, a twenty-two-year-old nursing student. Now Preston was, finally and rather suddenly, swept off his feet. No one was more surprised than Sandra, who broke her way into his heart and life without realizing it, until he called to ask her out. They had known each other casually for several years. Their parents were close friends. Her father, Gordon, was a popular church tenor who sang for Muriel Manning on the *National Back to the Bible Hour*. Preston and Sandra attended the same church and its Career and College group, although Sandra had been away at college for three years.

She was a talented musician and extroverted social instigator—drop-dead gorgeous, life of the party, leader of any group of young women larger than two and constantly surrounded by young men. She had grown up the eldest of four daughters in a noisy, voluble household where everyone was expected to have an opinion and to express it. Her parents met while both were serving in the air force in the Second World War and based in Ottawa. He father was a brilliant businessman with a strong reputation for integrity. Her mother, Mary, was a determined, handsome woman who prayed hard, worked hard and expected her daughters to excel first and ask questions later.

Sandra gave her parents fits as she grew up. She was pretty, articulate, popular, flirtatious and romantic. She dated until they were distracted. To the dismay of many young men, however, Sandra was solidly grounded and reserved her greatest passion for the love of God. Her romantic sensibilities travelled in tandem with a profoundly spiritual nature. She knew what she wanted: a career as a medical missionary. She worked summers through high school at the Oliver Mental Hospital, near Westerlea, and planned to study medicine at the University of Alberta.

Sandra graduated from high school with a major scholarship, but she put that on hold to attend the Prairie Bible Institute in Three Hills, Alberta. Prairie Bible Institute had very rigid ideas about appropriate social conduct, and her friends thought she'd never cut it. But she had discipline and she paid the price, graduating with a bachelor's degree in religious education, with a major in music.

When Sandra returned to Edmonton, she registered at the University of Alberta school of nursing for the winter term of 1965–1966. Preston was campaigning that fall, and Sandra was getting oriented to the nursing program, so it wasn't until the New Year that they began to chat a bit at the church College and Career group. Sandra was a bit in awe of Preston, the son of a religious and political giant, who was launched on a public career and was so apparently self-contained and sure. He didn't seem to know much about women, but that was immaterial to Sandra. They certainly had some things in common, and she appreciated the evident spiritual maturity he articulated.

Still, they were barely acquainted, and Sandra was startled when Preston phoned one evening in the spring of 1966 to ask her out for dinner on a double date with his pal Ed Wilkins and another young woman. Sandra stuttered. She stunned herself by saying, "I don't know—I guess I'll have to ask my Dad." She was of full majority, had been away from home for nearly four years and knew more than most women her age about managing young men. And she was telling this guy she hardly knew that she needed to ask her dad before she went out.

Her father chuckled but also told her quite seriously that he'd been thinking about the two of them and had even prayed that they'd take an interest in each other. Not fair, thought Sandra. But she accepted the date, and through the summer the two spent a great deal of time together. By the autumn, the solid companionship they enjoyed, the common interests—horseback riding, professional football, books, family—the shared evangelical faith had ripened into love. On October 23, they agreed to marry the following June, after Sandra's second year of nursing ended.

New Year's Eve, 1966, was cold and snow-bound in Edmonton, one of those nights of ice crystals and frosty air with diamond-chip stars that freshens the blood and sharpens scents and tastes. Preston and Sandra watched on the park grounds of the Alberta Legislature as Ernest ignited a natural gas flame in the centre of a marble, altarlike monument built for Canada's centenary. It was an evening of extraordinary optimism and promise across the country. The television klieg lights backlit the gathering. The crisp new red and white Canadian flags snapped in the wind. South, across the North Saskatchewan River Valley, the lights of the university campus, the sodium street lamps and the apartments and houses in Garneau wavered in the heat rising from the furnace chimneys. There was a sense of history and of limitless possibility, as the VIPs at the podium spoke the *bon mots*, of this centennial occasion.

It was possible that night for a young couple certain of one another's love and certain of a guiding hand directing their future to believe that there was nothing they could not do with their lives. Later, after the handshakes and the cheery best wishes had faded and the stars turned across midnight, Preston and Sandra talked long and late about their commitments and moved the wedding day up to March 23.

The Mannings had a flawlessly organized wedding at the Fundamental Baptist Church, with baskets of gladiolas, white carnations on the groom's lapel and the same for his father and father-in-law. This was a bonding of prosperous, professional families. "Mr. and Mrs. Perfect," a friend said, perhaps a little sharply, at the cut-and-dried competence of the event. The mothers, Muriel and Mary, wore chic suit dresses cut an inch below the knee. Sandra wore an elegant, understated white wedding dress and a single strand of pearls. The tone of the day was confidence and poise. Preston and Sandra flew to Vancouver for a four-day honeymoon and moved into an eighty-five-dollars-a-month basement suite near the nursing school. Sandra went back to classes and Preston to the National Public Affairs Research Foundation. They planned to balance home life, careers and church, and they felt the limitless energy and high motivation to do it. Everything seemed possible.

CHAPTER SEVEN # The Whiz Kids

The end of an age
And the end of an afternoon
Are one and the same to grinding fortune.

—Douglas Lepan, "Tuscan Villa"

IN 1966, THE year he courted Sandra Beavis, Preston Manning worked at the National Public Affairs Research Foundation on an agenda for the social and political issues facing Alberta, which was enjoying a second lengthy cycle of post-war economic growth that matched the first expansion following the 1947 oil discovery at Leduc. Ernest Manning was uneasy. The cruel years of the Depression that had propelled Social Credit into power still informed his political values. Yet his government seemed disconnected from the fire of its birth. It had grown fat and forgetful, insensitive to the lives of its electorate and the disparities between its communities. Now the electors were annoyed, if not angry, and had an alternative.

In 1965, the leaderless Conservative Party, which had garnered only

19 per cent of the popular vote and no seats in the 1963 election, found a new leader. Peter Lougheed was an intense, thirty-six-year-old Calgary lawyer and construction executive with impeccable family and business connections. His grandfather, Sir James Lougheed, had been a senator and a pioneer in law, politics, oil and cattle-ranching in the North-West Territories. Lougheed was a protégé of the powerful and secretive Mannix family, who owned the province's most serious fortune. With his energy, enthusiasm and fresh ideas, Lougheed was a contrast to the arthritic, listless cabinet. He was attracting a young, vigorous following—and plenty of news coverage.

The Social Credit Party and the government needed a response, and a ginger group of young men provided it. Some were in the caucus, most notably Robert Clark, a teacher from central Alberta and an amateur athlete and coach, and Ray Speaker, a rancher from the south. Some were in the civil service, notably deputy minister Les Usher. Some were the new breed of professional political technocrat, including ex–United Church Minister Don Hamilton and *Edmonton Journal* editorial writer John Barr. Some were at the university, including Preston, Owen Anderson (president of the campus Social Credit Party organization) and Erik Schmidt, a Baptist theology drop-out doing a graduate degree in sociology. Preston held the passkey to the premier's office. Their political opponents in the Conservative Party labelled them the Whiz Kids; the *Edmonton Journal* called them the Young Turks.

In 1966, Ernest Manning created the Ministry of Youth, put Clark in the cabinet to run it and gave him Les Usher as his deputy. Clark created the Alberta Service Corps, through which university students would volunteer for community service. Don Hamilton was hired to run that. Erik Schmidt was hired as an executive assistant to the cabinet. Preston—funded by the National Public Affairs Research Foundation— wrote a White Paper on Human Resources, a study on poverty, regional disparities in the province and the government's social services. Schmidt, who had become a close friend of Preston's during their final years together at the university, worked closely with him on the document.

The White Paper, a year in the making, was a technocratic response to a messy package of political dilemmas. Preston wanted to humanize a government that he believed had become "fixated" on economics, the exploitation of Alberta's vast pool of natural resources and the development of industrial infrastructure by giving it a new mandate for social welfare and regional development. He wanted an alternative to the liberal welfare state—either U.S. president Lyndon Johnson's Great Society or the democratic socialism that Prime Minister Lester Pearson's minority governments were stealing from the New Democratic Party.

Preston's systems-analysis diagnoses and prescriptions were enthusiastic but naive. They lacked the salt of political realism because they assumed that good ideas could win out over the vagaries of political ambition and compromise. His prescriptions depended on the rightness of an idea overcoming the quirks of human nature that would impede it. He used case studies to analyze social problems and created inventories of resources to address them. He broke down significant areas of social and political responsibility into small, manageable tasks and recommended high-sounding bureaucratic machines—the Human Resources Research Council, the Human Resources Development Authority—to undertake the solutions. His prescriptions depended on neat, tidy divisions of responsibility between the public and private sectors and sharply defined functions—prevention, rehabilitation, maintenance—within the system. Few of his calculations took into account the capriciousness of elected political officals, conflicting pressures on the public service and the impetuous demands of the people to whom new, high levels of physical and mental health would be delivered.

Nevertheless, the White Paper he produced revealed a great deal about his adult political style and helped to cast some of his fundamental ideas in stone. As Sandra was learning and told others, Preston took his time with ideas and had endurance for research and analysis. But once his mind was made up, it stayed that way and once his ideas were formed, they didn't often change. It was a way of doing politics that tended to isolate him because it required long periods of study and reflection followed by advocating ideas that were subtle, complex and, therefore, not well understood by others.

Preston called on an academic passion he'd developed in his study of economics: systems analysis—the study of the inputs, components, constraints and outputs of an organization to solve its operational problems and improve its productivity. Preston believed this was a dynamic tool for balancing conservative economics with social priorities. It would allow the services government provided to people to be organized and delivered rationally. Using systems analysis, the government would make human resources its priority. The world would be divided into areas of private and public responsibilities for the "free and creative development" of the people of Alberta. Systems analysis was also a potential proving ground for "prairie populism" that would show the commonality of "right" and "left" populist movements and the ultimate folly of pigeonholing people on a political spectrum.

The 1960s was an idealistic decade in which a young man with no experience of the venial side of human affairs beyond books and no exposure to practical politics beyond conversations with his father could conceive such things, unselfconsciously, and get a serious hearing from his elders. In its outcome, the text of the White Paper was an odd mixture of youthful idealism and pedantic droning. It reduced resources development to a schematic in which manpower, physical resources, materials and finance were the human resources inputs and "free and creative individuals" and "the materials and finances required for distinctive creative activity" were the outputs.

"In developing new and positive approaches to the future requirements of the people of Alberta, pertinent data must be accumulated, comprehensive research must be undertaken, and a structural and financial capability sufficient to provide effective administration must be developed," he wrote. He dismissed most government and political activity as "piecemeal" and "uncoordinated." The starting point for systematic reform would be for "public men" to recognize the fundamental principles and values that "exist relative to the management of public affairs. Basic principles and values ought always to occupy a prominent place in the thinking of public men and to find concrete expression in public policy. It is imperative that the continuing effort be made by those in positions of governmental authority to arrive at a clearer understanding of fundamental political principles."

He enunciated five basic values (as important for his own long-term political career as for his father's fading government). "Human resources will be treated as 'intrinsically' more important than physical resources. Prior consideration will be given to human beings individually (persons), rather than to human beings collectively (society). A free enterprise economy, in which all individuals have maximum opportunity to participate, will be regarded as more desirable than a state regimented economy. A supporting function, rather than a domineering function, will be ascribed to the state relative to resource development. Changes and adjustments to changes will be proposed, but these will always be related to fundamental principles."

He seemed to say, "See how easy this is if people will just be reasonable and rational?" For most readers, however, it was eye-glazing stuff. The partisans in the Conservative opposition caucus scorned it as "pedestrian." Power, they thought, was about more practical matters. There was a certain zealous intensity to Preston Manning's writing that could be off-putting if the reader had a more easy-going nature or a more mature approach to politics.

It was, after all, a bit disconcerting to have a twenty-five-year-old, fresh-faced systems analyst hectoring the reader. "These principles and values are held with conviction. [They] are subject to modification or replacement as more wisdom and experience is gained, but they should be modified or replaced only when it can be clearly shown that fundamental error has been made, or that inconsistencies exist, or that there are other principles and values even more fundamental and demonstrably valid."

The Whiz Kids developing policy ideas for Ernest Manning thought at the time that it was refreshing to manage human problems systematically and analytically. Many elected MLAs in the Socred caucus, however, though it oddly cold and calculating. It did not take into account the compromises and concessions of politics and the subtle and hidden currents swirling around every legislative and administrative decision. It didn't seem to mesh with the world of working politics—the streets and barnyards of the province where the only output that counted was votes. The document, which many practical politicians found difficult to understand, was dead on arrival in the Legislature. Aside from some studies recommended to investigate economic disparity in the province, nothing recommended was undertaken.

All new ideas in politics need powerful champions and time to work their way into the system through the osmosis of governance. It wasn't enough for the White Paper that Preston was the boss's son; the premier's endorsement was reserved and his power diminishing. And the sand was running out of the Social Credit hourglass.

Premier Manning tabled the White Paper in March 1967 and went to the voters in June, riding on the euphoria of Canadian centennial parties. There he received a seismic foreshock, a signal from the voters that they weren't buying his new look. Peter Lougheed took 26 per cent of the popular vote and six seats. Three Liberals also were elected, and Manning's support dropped below 50 per cent (to 44.6 per cent) for the first time in twelve years.

Meanwhile, Preston was on to his second initiative at the foundation: an exploration of the basis for merging the federal Social Credit and Progressive Conservative Parties. The impetus for this merger came from the sponsors of the foundation, who saw an opportunity to reconcile the interests of an electorate that voted for Ernest Manning in provincial elections and for John Diefenbaker in federal elections. They looked at the Social Credit rump in the House of Commons, which itself was subdivided into the anglophone Socred wing and the francophone *ralliement des créditistes*, and thought the two parties should get together. For the Manning family, participating in the merger might provide a political monument for a premier who'd fought his last election.

There were desultory merger talks that had the guarded endorsement of both Peter Lougheed and Ernest Manning, but these had no support whatsoever either in the government or official opposition caucuses or in the respective parties' rank and file. Preston Manning and Erik Schmidt attended the talks on behalf of Social Credit. Joseph Clark, a law school drop-out and Lougheed executive assistant, and Merv Leitch, a brilliant, understated corporate lawyer and Conservative MLA, represented the Tory camp. The confidential meetings coined a name: the Social Conservative Party, and a Basis of Union statement was created, which included a process for merging the memberships before the next provincial election, expected in 1971. But Ernest Manning was a spent political force; his blood was in the water. Within his own party, ambitious men waited to succeed him. On the other side, Lougheed, Leitch and Clark tasted Manning's defeat in the wind; with it would come Conservative victory and power. Meanwhile, larger currents were flowing in the national Conservative Party, which was preparing for the September 1967 convention, which deposed Diefenbaker and elected Nova Scotia premier Robert Stanfield leader. The proposed merger had only three enthusiasts: the two Mannings and Schmidt.

So Preston worked with his father on the alternative: a book called

Political Realignment: A Challenge to Thoughtful Canadians, which would be published in Ernest's name and would propose the reform of federal politics by the creation of a rationalized two-party political system. This would occur when conservatives of all partisan persuasions, including blue Liberal, united in a single party. This party would combine free-market capitalism and enlightened social conscience, "hard heads, soft hearts," as Preston would come to call it, in a political movement that exhibited the sensitivity of populism and the pragmatic practicality needed for electoral success. The "left" would respond by forming into a single force on its side of centre, and voters would be given a simpler, clearer choice.

Political Realignment, a slim paperback published by the Toronto house McClelland & Stewart, followed the familiar template of the White Paper. It started with a strong statement of "social conservative" principles, followed by a detailed diagnosis of the current political parties and a proposal that a Social Conservative Party be formed to instigate the reform of the federal political terrain and, ultimately, to end the seventy-year hegemony of the Liberal Party of Canada and push its centralized, statist neosocial democratic agenda off the stage. *Political Realignment* went on to provide a comprehensive plan for the organization of the new party, almost arcane in its detail and cribbed from the meetings between Schmidt, Preston Manning, Clark and Leitch.

It was a work out of its time. While it might be too much to call the book the founding document of the Reform Party of Canada, it was certainly the bridge between the prairie movements of the first half of the century and the tides of reform in the century's last two decades. It was also the first time a prairie voice—Ernest Manning's, with Preston writing the lines—presented a federalist vision with national solutions to national problems that was not driven by the regional grievances and alienation that characterized Aberhart's anti-Canadianism and the western separatism yet to come in the 1980s. Its best ideas had to wait for the unfolding of history because it was written before the remarkable and unexpected rise and run of Trudeau liberalism, and without the later influence on conservatives of American republicanism in the White House from 1980 to 1992. In retrospect, the book revealed Preston for what he wanted to be if he ever pursued elective politics: a national politician and a reform federalist.

The book presaged the neoconservatism that twenty years later underpinned Preston's road to political power. It stated four

social conservative ideals . . . worthy of vigorous and continuous pursuit by Canadians and their governments:

1. The attainment and conservation of Liberty for each and every individual in Canada.
2. The attainment and conservation of a national Community of Diversity embracing all Canadians.
3. The attainment and conservation of Prosperity for each and every individual Canadian.
4. The attainment and conservation of Liberty, Community, and Prosperity, not only for Canadians but for all men everywhere.

Twenty social conservative principles, taken together, articulated a political culture based on the supreme value of the individual (an implicit rejection of collectivism); a free, eclectic and open society with political, religious, cultural and intellectual liberty; responsible (democratic) government; the protection of diversity and of the family and home as the fundamental social unit; and fiscal responsibility. The private sector, supported by government, was primarily responsible for economic activity, and the creation of free and creative individuals was to be the purpose of economic development.

The principles were distinctively Preston Manning's: a systems approach to policy making that recognized all problems, issues, policies and programs as interdependent; the use of the wisdom of the long history of Canadian conservatism to shape the future of the movement; the freedom to worship and acknowledge the sovereignty of God because the greatness of a nation is related to the spiritual strength of its people; and a recognition that social conservative principles are applicable "to all men and nations."

When *Political Realignment* was published in September 1967, it was panned as mischievous because 30,000 copies were purchased by federal Conservatives and distributed before the Toronto leadership convention. This was seen as a clumsy attempt at rainmaking by Ernest Manning, trying to seed the clouds for a movement to draft him to succeed Diefenbaker. Back home, sales of the volume were brisk, especially on the campuses of the universities of Alberta and Calgary, and the *Edmonton Journal*, with its former editorial writer and now Whiz Kids member John Barr playing a facilitating role, published the text of the book over two days.

Political Realignment was the subject of much cocktail conversation in Alberta through the winter, but it did nothing to preserve Ernest Manning's career in elective politics. In January he finally warned his most trusted cabinet colleagues that he would retire that year and they should reach a consensus on a successor among themselves.

By the time *Political Realignment* was published, Preston Manning was in Redondo Beach California, working for TRW Systems (later TRW Space and Electronics), a unit of TRW Inc., one of the world's largest technological corporations. His White Paper on Human Resources had received scanty acknowledgement in Canada, but had been read by Dr. Simon Ramo, the "R" in TRW. Ramo was a genius-level scientist, engineer, business executive, author and university lecturer who'd been the Chief Scientist in the development of the U.S. Intercontinental Ballistic Missile and held the Presidential Medal of Freedom and the National Medal of Science, among other honours. He and his partners were building a global enterprise, providing products and services with high-technology or engineering content to advanced manufacturing sectors such as the auto, aircraft, space and defense industries, and information markets including health care, education and municipal government. TRW had consulted on hospital development in Alberta. Ramo invited Preston, Ernest and Preston's titular boss, David Wilson, to dinner in California. During the meal, he read and commented on passages from the White Paper. Then he offered Preston a job.

Manning took a leave from the foundation; Sandra dropped out of nursing school, and the two lived for several months in Redondo Beach. Manning worked on a human-resources development model, studied requests for proposals as an alternative to traditional government contracting and developed a matrix to help TRW identify business opportunities that would develop because of continuous change in business and government. Once again, as with Bechtel, the door on a well-paid career opened a crack. Had he wanted it, he could have stayed with TRW, which needed thousands of bright young researchers.

Once again, he didn't make his move; the one thing that companies like Bechtel and TRW wanted was a lifetime commitment, and Preston Manning had obligations elsewhere.

He and Sandra were fascinated by American politics, especially the rage over the Viet Nam War. Manning was curiously neutral on the war; he listened to both sides of the issue that was violently dividing the United States, then decided to go see for himself what southeast Asia was all about. When he completed his TRW contract in 1968, they took the money he'd made and travelled to Cambodia, Japan and Hong Kong to see for themselves the changes that embroiled the Americans in a bloody war and unleashed the economic power of the rapidly modernizing Pacific Rim on unsuspecting industrial democracies. They also visited Protestant churches and missions in the region.

When Preston and Sandra arrived back in Edmonton, she was pregnant and the leadership campaign to replace Ernest Manning was under way. The Whiz Kids wanted Preston to join the race. He was articulate, intelligent and presentable; he had the cachet of the family name, as well as some seasoning at Bechtel, TRW and the National Public Affairs Research Foundation, and, more to the point, he had energy, enthusiasm and ideas—all of which made him a match for Peter Lougheed. Manning was ten years younger, and even that could be seen as an advantage because youth was one of Lougheed's high cards.

The group went to see the premier, who opposed the idea. Preston, he believed, was too young and inexperienced and would be chewed up by older, harder men. The senior Manning also disliked nepotism; as always, Ernest put probity and propriety ahead of other considerations. Internally, the Social Credit Party had polarized—the old-line political fundamentalists on one side and the brash reformers on the other—and the premier did not think the party could survive the conflict that a young man with new ideas would create in the old guard, which he considered the bedrock of the party. Preston had been away for nearly a year; tactically, he'd lost his focus on Alberta affairs and would not have time to recoup. The premier had failed to groom a successor and to encourage a fresh new candidate. Now he argued that change would have to come more slowly than the young men might want.

He threw his mantle over fifty-five-year-old Harry E. Strom, a quiet, religious rancher and nondescript cabinet minister. Strom was not his first choice, but education minister Anders Aalborg did not want to run because he'd had a serious heart attack. Ernest Manning's political judgement had failed him at a crucial moment: he had missed the chance for dynamic change in the government's style, which might have kept Social Credit in office.

Had the young Manning persisted in his candidacy (backed by men such as Barr, Anderson and Hamilton), he would have been an attractive candidate and, as leader, might have been able to hold the middle ground against the Lougheed insurgence for one more election. It was unthinkable, however, for Preston to oppose his father's advice; had he, it likely would have sundered the party as badly as it would have torn the family. In any event he already had half an eye on federal politics. So Preston followed his father's lead and worked for Strom, and the Young Turks fell in line. Sandra joined the Strom campaign when she could; their first daughter, Andrea, was born that year. But the young couple was often together at political events, and Sandra added verve and vitality to Preston's wry and shy persona.

The old-line Social Credit adherents were uncomfortable with the prospect of the first-ever Social Credit leadership convention—open to the media, televised, with balloons, pretty cheerleaders, buttons and assorted hoopla. They looked anxiously for reassurance and found it when the party establishment—Orvis Kennedy, Manning and his son—signalled their endorsement of Strom. That was good enough for a solid core of the 1,672 delegates who crammed into Edmonton's Jubilee Auditorium to vote on Friday, December 6, 1968, after a day and a half of tedious party business.

The day, however, was a disaster for the party; there were five candidates and Strom failed by 23 votes on the first ballot to win the 837 endorsements needed for a majority. He was more than 500 votes ahead of the man in second place, Gordon Taylor, an old cabinet war horse. But in the wheeling and dealing between the ballots, faint fractures in the brittle old party cracked, and when Strom won on a second ballot, with 915 votes, his 54 per cent support was less important than the 46 per cent who voted against him.

Ernest stepped out of the limelight. He and Preston incorporated M & M Systems Consulting ten days after the leadership vote and began to look for consulting contracts with private business. For a long time, government was out of bounds as a prospective client, and what Preston did for Premier Strom in the next thirty-two months was unpaid.

Lougheed's opposition caucus of six grew to ten through by-elections and the recruitment of one independent MLA. One of those seats came directly at the Mannings' expense. On February 11, 1969, a rangy, personable lawyer named William Johnson, the Social Credit candidate running in the retired premier's constituency of Edmonton Strathcona, lost a stunning by-election upset to a peppy research engineer named William Yurko, whose margin of victory was a squeaky 470 votes.

Preston had run the campaign; his father and the entire Strom cabinet had door-knocked through the riding. Preston was mortified and sad that he'd let Johnson down. Of all the cabinet, only Ray Speaker showed up at the campaign office to take the medicine with the candidate and the campaign manager. The whole affair had the stink of defeat, and proud old Socreds didn't want to catch the smell. The fractures in the party split a little wider that night. The men who stayed away consoled themselves with the closeness of the vote count. It was an aberration; they'd get the seat back in 1971. It showed that those young guys—even the former premier's son—weren't all that smart; in fact, wasn't it a good thing that the pups had been smacked?

The Tories, in a boozy celebration at the Edmonton Inn, next to the municipal airport, saw beneath the numbers. "Social Credit was dying and we know it, if they don't. This is the big one," Conservative President Roy Watson told reporters.

The Whiz Kids hung on, working overtime to breath some life into Strom's administration. Barr, Anderson and Hamilton worked as ministerial assistants; Bob Clark and Ray Speaker were in the cabinet. Preston eased himself out of the Social Credit orbit but, feeling personally responsible for the transition out of the Manning era, took calls from the other Whiz Kids and put scores of unpaid hours into the cause.

They put together a task force to reform urban policy and asked Strom for other, similar policy reviews. They opened a new university at Lethbridge and created an intergovernmental affairs department. They advocated cabinet reform. It didn't work. John Barr later sadly said, "There is only one thing worse than to refuse to reform, and that is to promise to initiate reform and then not carry through." Change had no champion at the levels that really counted—cabinet, caucus, the premier. Preston Manning and his friends could write all the white papers and task force reports in the world, but they had no power base to implement their bold ideas.

In 1970, Ernest accepted an appointment to the Senate of Canada, giving Preston the opportunity to move to the fringe of national politics, reading widely and seeking consulting assigments that would broaden his contacts and looking for opportunities for political realignment. His own family drew him further from politics: in 1969, he and Sandra bought their first house in a modest northeast Edmonton neighbour-hood. In 1971, Avryll, their second daughter, was born.

The new team to replace the old team belonged to Peter Lougheed. On August 30, 1971, thiry-six years and eight days after William Aberhart's stunning victory changed the face of Alberta politics, Social Credit was crushed. The Progressive Conservatives emerged from the hot, dusty, dry summer campaign with 46 per cent of the popular vote and forty-nine of seventy-five seats. Preston Manning was out in the political cold.

CHAPTER EIGHT

The
Contented
Exile

*I remember no other time in my life of such untroubled affection.
We were famously snug together.*

—C. S. Lewis, *Surprised by Joy*

LESS THAN FOUR years after the election of the Conservative government, what was left of Ernest
Manning's dynasty was obliterated. On February 24,
1975, Lougheed won reelection with 69 per cent of the vote and sixty-
nine seats, and Social Credit was reduced to a fragment of four seats
and 18 per cent support. The Socreds clung to the dream of a restoration, even in the diaspora. As successive annual conventions argued
over a political identity and sought a credible leader, Preston Manning's
sense of responsibility for the family party faded. The remnant of the
tribe felt betrayed when Ernest accepted his Senate appointment and
started joining the boards of the business establishment he'd fought as a
young premier. The old guard decreed that the former premier had

gone over to the enemy and his son was not to be trusted. And the word of the old guard was holy writ because it was now the power in the party. Everyone else had lost interest.

There was no place for Preston Manning in Peter Lougheed's politics. Even after time passed and other young, urban Social Credit supporters drifted into the Conservative orbit, Preston held to his loyalties. Lougheed would have happily recruited him, but he would have been nothing more than a prize of war. He had little taste for Lougheed's style or the purposes of his government. He was not certain that Lougheed was a small "c" conservative; no one was, not even other Conservatives. Within eighteen months of the 1971 upset, the Organization of Petroleum Exporting Countries started spiking up oil prices, and Alberta became a national oil power and pariah. Lougheed was locked in a bitter jurisdictional battle over resource management, and while Manning thought the federal government wrong constitutionally, he had grave concerns about the way Lougheed was using the flood of oil dollars. This new breed of politician holding power in Alberta was pragmatic, not principled, and the economist in Manning cautioned him that commodity cycles go both ways: the Conservatives were being profligate, and there might come a time when the well of dollars dried up. What would Alberta do then to finance its newly acquired taste for public spending? In the meantime, the Tory party rode on the glitz and glamour of smooth public relations and advertising, a well-oiled constituency machine and a ruthless sense of its strength. None of this fit Manning's mold.

Nor was there a federal platform upon which he could stand. The Social Credit caucus in the House of Commons had disappeared. He would never join the Conservatives, because they had rebuffed political realignment and laughed off social conservatism. Manning's politics were about set ideas; everyone else was brokering power. He was not of a mind to compromise or concede his intellectual foundation. He acknowledged to himself that grassroots political parties seemed to have a natural life span. After a long hegemony, Social Credit had quit the field with an honourable record. None of the existing parties interested him, so he waited on his moment and honed his ideas.

He was now primarily a business consultant with a home to care for and children to feed. He turned his attention to earning a living, the pleasures of his growing family, and to reflecting on and writing about faith, politics and his community. This was a political exile from the world of power, influence and government, but it was on very happy terms.

Once the 1971 election was out of the way, business thrived. His former University of Alberta fellow undergraduate, James Coutts, who was principal secretary to Prime Ministers Pearson and Trudeau and the *éminence gris* (or prince of darkness, depending on the perspective) of the Liberal Party, described one of his own self-imposed periods of absence from Ottawa and politics as an attempt to keep the addict away from the drug. Manning was on mandatory withdrawal.

His father's role in Manning Consultants Limited, as the company came to be called, was the door opener; he knew who to call. Preston closed most of the deals. Ernest was busy with other things, so he'd look at work at the beginning of a project and at the end; Preston hired the team and managed the contracts. Although they had a steady stream of marketing, strategic planning and human resources commissions, a great deal of their work came from the petroleum industry, helping companies manage a changing social and political milieu in which the corporation was becoming accountable to new special interests. In addition to shareholders, directors and customers, the oil companies found themselves being called to account by the communities in which they operated, by environmentalists and by new, more invasive regulatory bodies.

The Mannings' business strategy was to identify business needs and make proposals to companies rather than wait for potential clients to call. This was a playing field on which Preston excelled. His systems approach produced clear, understandable briefs. He wrote in excellent, unambiguous prose. He could catch a client's inarticulate vision and put it into words, or he could take a client's nuts-and-bolts ideas and rewrite them into strong, strategic statements and plans.

Slowly, the business base expanded to a national list of senior corporations and organizations. Much of the work was in the energy industry, though Hockey Canada hired him to conduct long-range planning. A group of wealthy Albertans commissioned him to develop an awards program for innovators and sent him to Europe to study the Nobel Prize process; then they revealed that the decorations they intended to establish would be named the E. C. Manning Awards to honour his father.

Preston Manning taught himself a working knowledge of corporate finance, administration and strategic planning. He developed expertise in utility regulation and wrote landmark studies on rate-setting and regulatory processes. The Mannings' client list grew to include a who's who of pipelines and electric utilities. He advised on a host of government relations problems and developed something of a name for himself as an analyst of the business and property-rights effects of constitutional change.

He had a decent enough income, but Manning Consultants didn't make a great deal of money, because he had the habit of reinvesting time and cash in unpaid community and political projects that interested him. He sometimes acknowledged that the business was more a means to develop political ideas and have the work paid for than a means to become wealthy. Money was not high on his list of priorities. His father had cared nothing for wealth, had not sought it and did not have any financial security until he left politics and started to collect director's fees and the Senate paycheque. Ernest and Muriel had sold Westerlea in two parcels for a total of $575,000—it was valuable because of a gravel deposit and nearly a dozen surface leases for oil wells and pipelines—and the proceeds formed a substantial part of their estate. Fortunately, his parents did not rely on a dividend from their equity in Manning Consultants.

His in-laws, who were affluent, wondered if Manning had any idea what was involved in developing financially security, and they worried about Sandra and the children. But when they goaded Manning, he simply laughed them off. Sandra, fortunately, was a superb family financial manager.

In fact, she was the linchpin of the family, which grew steadily. A third daughter, Mary Joy, was born in 1974; a first son, David, was born in 1977, and the fifth child, another son, Nate, was born in 1980. Preston was travelling on business about half the time; Sandra kept the finances, managed the house and chauffeured the children, who were as engaged in life as their grandparents and parents, to a growing list of after-school activities. As the girls grew older, they all became involved in competitive synchronized swimming. Andrea eventually earned a place on Canada's national team; Avryll and Mary Joy competed nationally and internationally on the leading Edmonton Auroras and Calgary Aquabelles YWCA synchronized swim clubs. Sandra became immersed, so to speak, as a volunteer in the Canadian Amateur Synchronized Swimming Association.

In 1977, the family moved to St. Alberta, a suburban community on the northwest edge of Edmonton. They bought a modest acreage in the Sturgeon River Valley, and the children roamed in the ravine, had a dog and generally ran wild as their father had done at Westerlea when he was their age. The Beavis family had gravitated to a single St. Alberta neighbourhood, where Sandra's parents, sisters and brothers-in-law all lived within a mile of each other. Once a week, sixteen children and eight adults congregated for those voluble, boisterous dinners that were the trademark of Sandra's parents. They gathered to watch the Edmonton Eskimos and Edmonton Oilers play football and hockey, or to sing. They prayed together, supported the Fundamental Baptist Church and worked in the yard and garden, and Manning organized touch football and fishing. Keith joined them as often as Manning could arrange it.

If he was never more than half a step away from leadership in politics, Manning was just as close to a significant movement in the evangelical church. He collected a group of bright young men from his Inter Varsity Christian Fellowship days and, over several years, got them to read and comment on papers he was writing on conducting contemporary politics in a Christian way. These review sessions dealt with the difficulties and ambiguities of being a practising Christian in politics in a society hostile to religion and a political culture polarized between left and right, with both Protestant and Catholic churches usually on the right hand of the spectrum on public issues.

One of his reviewers was an ordained Church of the Nazarene minister, Don Posterski, who had run the Inter Varsity Christian Fellowship in Ontario's universities before heading up World Vision Canada. Another was University of Saskatchewan history lecturer Don Page, who became a senior policy advisor in the federal external affairs department, leader in Parliament Hill's Public Service Christian Fellowship and later vice-president, academic, at Trinity Western University, a scholarly evangelical school in Vancouver.

In his memoranda, Manning argued that one's faith should have an effect on one's public service, that the love of Christ, which changed one's personal life, ought also to affect the way one made decisions and treated people. This was not a matter of policy. He was not talking about the Moral Majority or the Christian Coalition right-wing politics emerging in the United States. His populism ran against the grain of promoting or forcing a religious-based agenda item, such as abortion law, on the rest of the country. That was for the entire electorate to decide. And he feared and resented the caricature of religious politics that was drawn in the media.

The difference in conducting politics "Christianly," as he termed it, came in style and values. A Christian practised servant leadership; Christ had set this example by washing the feet of his followers in the classic New Testament account of the Last Supper. The purpose of Christ's life had been to express in practical terms the reconciliation of God with humanity. If one lived by the imperative to give up the world to gain spiritual liberty and guarded against losing the soul in grasping for the treasures of this world, then ambition and the acquisition of power took on a whole new meaning, opposed to filling a personal emptiness with power.

Two fundamental themes came forward in Manning's thinking about the relationship between his faith and his politics: sacrifice, as the opposite of personal aggrandizement, and making law through reconciliation, rather than doing it in adversarial debate. Followed through to its logical application—and Manning is nothing if not rational—this value system changed his perspective on parliamentary debate: his heart could never be in the cut and thrust of the House, and if he developed a taste for the blood of his opponent, it would be at great spiritual cost.

But Manning and other Christians with whom he discussed these matters did not regard their faith as soft. It required the constant disciplines of prayer and practical compassion. It had its own lines in the sand that could not be crossed. Reconciliation did not mean surrendering ground on the commitment to compassionate treatment of the poor or the mentally ill. Nor did it allow one to be fiscally irresponsible. One thing that Ernest Manning had impressed on his son is that the higher purpose of politics is to create decent conditions of life in a tolerant society, to care for the natural world in a scientifically enlightened way and to ensure individual liberty. The evangelical Protestantism that Preston Manning was digging out of Scripture and experience was a complex, demanding creed that allowed no easy way out to the politician willing to sign on to what theologian James Parker called "the long obedience in a single direction."

It will come as no surprise to those knowledgeable about Russian literature that as Manning went down this road, he grew fond of writings such as Leo Tolstoy's, particularly *Resurrection*, and Feodor Dostoevski's *Crime and Punishment* and *The Brothers Karamazov*. Both authors were great Russian Orthodox Christians who, in a different time and a different religious and political culture, wrestled with precisely the same issues of power and political conflict and rarely found unambiguous, much less easy, answers. The elusiveness, the ambiguity of practising his faith in daily life that Manning encountered contrasted sharply with Ernest Manning's and William Aberhart's formulaic, matter-of-fact certainty as they balanced political power and religious leadership. The only common ground across the generations was that the Christian's responsibility is to live the faith; believing it is never enough.

Malcolm Muggeridge, a British writer whose thinking appealed to Preston Manning and influenced his attempt to mesh his politics with his faith, thought Tolstoy was a particularly important example of how a Christian ought to go about the task of relating every aspect of contemporary life, including politics, to the eternal. Muggeridge thought every human life and every human event, "makes one pattern, tells one story, is comprehended in one prayer—'Thy will be done.'" Muggeridge was fascinated that Tolstoy, who described evil as the counterfeit of life and died with the words, "to seek, always to seek," was tormented by the paradox that the Kingdom of God, which was always at hand, was also unattainable in earthly terms. To search out the Kingdom is the imperative that directs the Christian to make the world a more brotherly place, Tolstoy believed, and, as a landowner, he used that as the basis for dealing with issues such as serfdom and emancipation in Russian politics. Manning was often more comfortable with Tolstoy than with high-profile twentieth-century Christian politicians such as Jerry Falwell and Pat Robertson.

As Preston Manning read these great authors, the difficulties of the Christian way of politics in the 1970s and 1980s seemed complex, compared with the well-illuminated, well-ordered path that his father and mother had walked. Ernest believed in the Protestant separation of church and state, and was trusted by Albertans to keep the two areas of his life apart, bringing to politics only his principles and integrity, and confining his preaching to the *National Back to the Bible Hour*. The time had come and gone, however, when a leading politician could take

Sunday off to preach on the radio. Preston understood that he would have to be more circumspect about his faith than his father was. He also knew that the landscape of his life and language of his faith were far different than those of his parents. He did not proselytize the way his father had, and he expressed his ideas in contemporary idioms, not biblical prescriptions.

On a practical level, the spiritual companionship he and Sandra shared compensated for his frequent absences and the financial strains imposed by his business style. She shared the theological road upon which he travelled. She had strong, practical opinions and advice, but she also knew the secret way to his well-hidden heart and she used that access to nourish him with a vivacity that leavened his dry, intellectual analysis.

Sandra also set the pace for the family's life with a dynamic, warm and off-the-wall home in which the children were permitted to be noisy, affectionate, rebellious and opinionated. The domestic arrangements followed the Beavises' model of freewheeling dinners, open doors, outspoken children and guests. "There was never us against the world; it was go find the world and drag it home," she said. As a single woman, Sandra had been the one to buy the hot dogs for the picnics of friends, invite acquaintances to the lake, instigate the weekend trips. This was most unlike Preston's quiet, socially isolated upbringing but he adapted.

One cold, dark evening after work when he went to his car, he saw a woman with two children sitting on a steamer trunk in the parkade. "You can't stay here," he challenged. "Nowhere to go," she replied. She said she had been abandoned with no funds by her common-law mate. "Well, you'd better come home with me," Manning said. The family stayed for two weeks, until Manning tracked down the man and helped the couple and their children reestablish themselves. He met one of his closest friends, Sam Okaro, on a plane ride from Toronto to Edmonton. During a stopover in Winnipeg, he observed Sam, a rather bewildered Biafran refugee, standing in the aircraft's aisle. "Where are you headed?" Manning asked. "Edmonton," replied Sam Okaro. "Better not get off here, then," Manning warned him. Manning helped him get a place to live and a job and helped pay for his wedding a few years later. Lucia Robalo, a teenager, lived with the Mannings for two years after Sandra extracted her from an abusive home. When she graduated from high school, they paid her college tuition and got her her first a job as a translator.

During the fifteen years he was on the sidelines of active politics, Manning helped some of Canada's largest corporations, including its biggest Crown-owned utilities, forecast and develop complex, far-reaching initiatives, but he lived in a household that usually didn't have a five-minute plan. Or if it did, the plan would change with the next knock on the door. The spontaneity caused friction. Privacy was a rare commodity, and the children competed fiercely for their parents' time and attention. Money was always tight, and Sandra occasionally had to defend her husband from her family's skepticism about his business. His frequent absences imposed on Sandra—sometimes felt she had all the responsibility for the children. She became accustomed to being in charge and was thin-skinned about criticism over that from her mother-in-law. Preston and Sandra annoyed and offended each other with the charming regularity of most couples—but her short fuse met its match in his quiet-spoken refusal to speak his anger too harshly. At times, to keep the peace, he caved in too easily, but they worked out boundaries and usually kept to them.

Although he was a politician without a party, Manning frequently managed to segue from community service to political experiment in his volunteer hours. Following the military coup in Chile and the assassination of President Salvador Allende in 1973, Alberta hosted hundreds of Chilean refugees. In Edmonton, they joined a large inner-city population of young families struggling to get by. Many had one thing in common: they were latchkey kids, children with both parents working long hours.

A small group at the Fundamental Baptist Church decided to organize an after-school program for these children. It was called Duck Inn and operated out of the church's building. Sandra's sister, Marian, had just graduated from the University of Alberta and took the job as director of the project. Preston and Sandra joined the board, and Preston got involved in dealings with the Alberta government. The board turned the bureaucracy inside out to find who regulated such a service. They found there were no guidelines, no funding and almost no interest. It seemed, however, to be a social service for which there was a pressing need and a sound justification. The volunteers persisted, and Duck Inn became the pilot project for new public policy covering after-school care.

The longest-running management consulting project that Manning ever did started almost the day he and his father opened the business and lasted twenty years. Characteristically, the company received virtually no compensation. One of the constructive outcomes of Manning's White Paper on Human Resources was a group of seven case studies on economically underdeveloped regions of the province. Lesser Slave Lake, in the northeast corner of Alberta, was one of the poorest areas studied—a mostly aboriginal community subsisting on fishing and hunting. The province, the federal government and oil companies exploring in the area all created development initiatives to deal with the crisis.

In 1969, four businessmen from the community, including the mayor, and one from Edmonton approached Manning Consultants for help in starting a community-development company. They incorporated Slave Lake Developments Limited, a vehicle for business start ups that would weave together social and economic objectives.

This was a novel approach for Alberta at the time. Manning joined the board and, until he moved the headquarters of the Reform Party, and his family, to Calgary after the 1988 federal election, he went to Lesser Slave Lake once a month for meetings. The first successful business was a housing project of two apartment blocks and forty-six town-houses. Manning and his associates not only arranged Central Mortgage and Housing and oil-company financing, they also helped with the sweat-equity investment. When Manning went to Slave Lake to spend a holiday finishing townhouse units, Sandra packed the kids and went along. The family camped out on the living-room floor of one of the units.

When it became apparent that Slave Lake Developments was going to continue its investment activities, and Preston his trips north, Sandra trekked north and found a lake-front property. She bought a mobile home and had it moved to the lot. She conscripted her family to help winterize it, build a porch and do the other renovations necessary to make the place livable. They named it Norwesterlea, after Preston's boy-hood home. Slave Lake Developments had only one business failure during Manning's tenure on the board—a failed attempt to provide res-cue financing for a local car dealership that collapsed in the oil-industry recession induced by the National Energy Program.

The success of Slave Lake Developments Limited opened more lucrative doors to Manning Consultants. Syncrude Canada President Frank Spragins engaged Preston to help create the Economic Development Discussion Group, which created a working group of major companies, the Alberta government and aboriginal businessmen to cat-alyze economic development for aboriginal peoples in the northeast's rich oil sands and oil fields.

Through these largely happy, productive years, there was always a cloud. Manning craved politics. He would say to Sandra, "I'll forget how. I haven't given a speech in three years." He continued to look for a way to bring the blueprint in *Political Realignment* to life, although he was ambivalent; he kept waiting for someone else to start the action. He had his own window into Ottawa through his father's Senate office; it cemented his oriention to federal politics.

In 1972, Joe Clark ran as a Conservative in Rocky Mountain, a rid-ing running north and south along Alberta's western border. He urged Manning to run for the party too, in Pembina, a rural constituency outside Edmonton. Manning sat up all night weighing the decision and filling a yellow legal pad with his reasons, the pros and the cons. Then he declined: he had little confidence in the national Tories, needed the kind of education in government that he could get consulting and had a "vague" impression that a "secession" crisis in Quebec might open the door at any time to the new party he and his father had proposed in their book.

Between 1974 and 1979, the constitutional issue of resource control created a fissure between the federal government and the western petroleum-producing provinces. The federal government imposed a domestic price on oil below the world price and an export tax to skim off the difference when the oil left the country. In Calgary, a fledgling separatist movement began to raise funds and brood about strategic options.

In 1978, Manning spearheaded the Movement for National Political Change. The name was a conceit—it was really just Manning circulat-ing a new series of papers he'd written on his core ideas of political reform and social-conservative policy and holding small discussion groups. He was well connected through his business, and the movement put some influential people on notice that Manning had some ambition and a number of good ideas that were grounded in values that could sell well in the West.

Before the 1979 federal election, Clark, now the Tory leader, sent his recruiters to Manning because he had been meeting with western Tory MPs who didn't like the drift of Liberal constitutional thinking. There was a high level of certainty that the Conservatives would win the election, but Manning again declined the offer of a constituency. Clark was a Red Tory and might as well be a Liberal as far as Manning was concerned. After the failed Conservative-Socred negotiations of 1968 in which Clark had represented Peter Lougheed, Manning put no stock in the blurry promise that westerners in a Clark government could accomplish something like the Manning realignment plan.

When Joe Clark was elected prime minister on May 22, 1979, it looked as if events had passed Manning by again. But Clark had a vulnerable minority with 136 of 278 seats and no natural allies in the opposition parties, except possibly the six remaining *ralliement des créditistes* members, and no one knew how to predict their behaviour. Manning watched, waited and thought. The fulcrum of Canadian politics was unstable and opportunity was afoot. He wondered if he ought to take on politics when his family had little financial security and the children were reaching an age when they would need him to help them through the crises of adolescence.

He asked Sandra. She told him that if he didn't take the initiative on his ideas, no one else would. She said, "Don't turn down the opportunity and then sit around wondering if you should have done it. Maybe it will go nowhere, but I won't be able to stand the heartache of listening to you when you're sixty-five saying, 'I wonder if I should have given it a shot after all.' "

CHAPTER NINE # The Fire in the Western Sky

Each one of us within his soul must make a decision.
No one wants the country split. The West wants to be
Canadian. But do we want to be Canadian at any price?

—TED BYFIELD, *Alberta Report*, February, 1980

THEN HISTORY INTERVENED. Events began to build the platform on which Preston Manning could reenter active politics. The Taoist master warrior Sun Tzu said that "military victory is determined by the opponent," and finally it seemed Manning's opponents were cooperating.

The political tremors that shook the West for the next decade began in the House of Commons on the night of Thursday, December 13, 1979. Prime Minister Joe Clark, having failed either to see the signs or to heed the warnings that his minority government was exposed, suffered a 139- to 133-vote defeat on his first budget. On one level, it was a simple bungle; someone on the Tory side forgot to count noses ahead of time. On a deeper level, it was a humiliation. In the West, the Liberals were seen has having once again mortified a westerner. Arthur Meighen, R.B. Bennett, John Diefenbaker and now Joe—everybody's kid from next door—all lost in the Ottawa quagmire.

The ground moved again just before midnight on February 18, 1980, when Pierre Eliott Trudeau returned, like a resurrected phantom, from what he clearly regarded as the ignominy of the opposition party benches to the glided ballroom of the Chateau Laurier Hotel, to celebrate a newly elected Liberal majority government. He seemed not to notice the tear in the fabric of the electoral map: the Liberals held not a single seat west or north of Winnipeg and had garnered only a quarter of the vote in that vast hinterland. A darkness was gathering over federal politics.

In the next four years federalism reached a historic nadir in the West. Prescient opinion makers warned, from the get-go, that Trudeau was poised to remake Canada in a fashion completely unacceptable to the region—and did not need to take into account the region's opinions because he did not need its votes. The West Fed Association of Alberta, a visceral, urban organization with a clear sense of rage and an inchoate sense of direction, held "Free West" meetings through the summer and autumn of 1980 to explore secession. Out of these frighteningly large gatherings of Free Westers came the explicitly separatist Western Canada Concept Party, which began to gain support in rural communities and British Columbia.

At the poker tables in the basement of the Calgary Petroleum Club there was dangerous talk of insurrection. The boozy oilmen talked about funding private investigations into Trudeau's personal life to discredit him. They ruminated about recruiting support in Saskatchewan, where politician Dick Culver was advocating that the West join the U.S. They considered the mechanics of Alberta and British Columbia joining the northwestern states in an economic union called Cascadia. At first it was the brandy speaking. Then in the summer and autumn of 1980 the Prime Minister overplayed his hand. With the confidence of a strong majority government and keenly aware that his political career was in its final years, Trudeau wanted to achieve his most important political dream—a made-in-Canada constitution. At the same time, he moved to deal with the economic and political consequences of the spiralling world price of oil. His constitutional and energy remedies brought him into direct conflict with the West and gave Preston Manning a doorway back into politics.

The British North America Act (BNA) of 1867, the basic document that sets out the Canadian Constitution, is an act of the British Parliament. On June 25, 1980, Trudeau had lunch in London with British Prime Minister Margaret Thatcher and advised her that if the Canadian premiers could not reach an accord that year on bringing the Constitution home to Canada, the Trudeau government would unilaterally ask the British Parliament to change the BNA to give Canadians the right to amend it in future, thereby making it a Canadian law.

Back in Canada, the barrier to an agreement was a two-decade-old debate on a constitutional amending formula that would preserve the interests of all regions of the country. What Quebec wanted to protect its unique linguistic and legal rights, granted in 1791, did not have the approval of the provinces. Nor could the West get provisions that would secure provincial control over natural resources and Senate reform. In meetings that went on through the summer and early autumn, the premiers could not agree. Trudeau was poised to act unilaterally and threatened to hold a national referendum to get popular approval for his decision. The premiers of Alberta, British Columbia, Prince Edward Island and Newfoundland, lead by Manitoba Conservative Sterling Lyon, met on October 14, 1980, to plot a way to stop Trudeau.

On October 20 in the Alberta Legislature, Premier Peter Lougheed articulated the position of the smaller provinces: "The unilateral patriation of the Constitution would make Alberta a second-class province. Ontario and Quebec will not only have vetoes [over constitutional amendments, offered by Trudeau] but they would carry the day in any referendum by virtue of their large populations."

To counter the federal referendum, Lougheed announced legislation for an Alberta referendum on the Constitution. Lougheed knew that unless western federalists could construct a credible strategy for dealing with Trudeau, western separatism was set to make very dangerous gains. That evening, at a $125-a-plate Social Credit fund raiser in Calgary, Ernest Manning gave his first political speech in the province in nine years. To a packed, hushed hall, he addressed the "people who wish to tear the Western provinces out of Confederation." He said, "I know the feeling of frustration in the West, but it is not as simple as it sounds to set up a new nation or to tear an old one apart." Listening to the present and former premiers, Preston knew that it was time to find other western federalists who wanted to find a new way to deal with old problems.

Meanwhile, throughout the summer rumours circulated through the oil patch of a new energy policy, one that would centralize at least some control over the resource in Ottawa. Misinformation circulated that this new regime would play Canadian independents off against the foreign-controlled multinationals, that the sugar on the pill would be competitive advantages to level the playing field, even tilt it in favour of Canadian companies. On Tuesday, October 28, 1980, Energy Minister Marc Lalonde stood in the House of Commons to table the National Energy Program. The needles on the seismic recorders of politics went off the Richter scale.

Wrapped in rhetorical cotton candy that promised national self-sufficiency and appealed to Canadians' sense of fairness and the virtues of westerners learning to share their growing petroleum wealth, the NEP, as it was called, was an audacious seizure of wealth, tax revenue and constitutional power. The tip of the blade at the western throat that night was the Petroleum and Gas Revenue Tax. It imposed a legally dubious tariff on oil and gas *production* as distinguished from *income*. In simple terms, oil and gas producers would pay, in addition to provincial royalties and federal and provincial corporate income taxes, a tax on revenues to be calculated at the wellhead and collected before the producers paid any of their operating or business costs.

Immediately, the tax impounded about 27 per cent of oil revenues for the federal treasury. Since equity values of resource companies had been calculated on future revenues, and since other costs of doing business, including interest rates, were exceptionally high and being driven higher by inflation, this wiped out up to 60 per cent of the asset value of public and private companies. The large amount of cash diverted to the federal government would prevent payment of other bills.

The political response was immediate. "This is nothing more nor less than a takeover of Alberta's oil and gas," Alberta treasurer Lou Hyndman told the province's legislature. "It will force Alberta to sell oil at less than half its value," Energy Minister Merv Leitch added. Oil company employee layoffs started in time for Christmas. Service and supplies companies found that their invoices went unpaid. Bank-loan payments fell behind. Companies started to go broke.

Then the long-term impact kicked in. Oil companies in 1980 had been reinvesting on average 110 per cent of their cash flow. Of course, they had to pay their bills, so they survived by raising new equity or borrowing against future revenues. To drill new wells and develop new fields, oil exploration and production companies were raising between $13 and $15 billion each year from investors or borrowing it at the banks. With equity values devastated and outstanding loans in trouble, investment capital dried up.

Commodity sectors are cyclical, and in the oil-exploration business, the cycles turn on a dime. Within a year, nine thousand jobs and one-third of the work force disappeared. Fifteen billion dollars of oil-sands development was shelved. The number of drilling rigs under contract, the most sensitive indicator of business activity, dropped by two-thirds. Through 1981, paper fortunes disappeared, and there were more layoffs, more business failures, more personal bankruptcies. The effects rippled out from the glass towers of Calgary and Edmonton to every little community that had oil-field workers and every cash-strapped farm that depended on those field jobs for a second income. Manning had a ringside seat as these events unfolded: these were his clients, and his consulting business was taking a hit, along with everyone else.

On February 17, 1982, the Western Canada Concept Party won the by-election to fill the vacancy left by the retirement of Robert Clark, a member of the now almost forgotten Social Credit Whiz Kids. Gordon Kessler, a young cattle rancher and rodeo rider, became the first western separatist to hold elective office. The men he beat were a young Conservative lawyer, Steve Stiles, and a Social Credit cattleman, Lloyd Quantz, but they were just unfortunate proxies for the real targets of voter anger—Pierre Trudeau and Marc Lalonde. Trudeau dismissed the outcome as a racist reaction to federal language policy, but that was a straw-man defence. The reality: the Olds-Didsbury riding, which Kessler won, was in the most intensively developed oil and gas district in the province. Since the early 1950s the local economy had been as dependent on oil and gas as on cattle and grain. These voters were using a provincial by-election to make a statement about the West's future in confederation: that the future was up for grabs.

Three Alberta federalists got the message. Premier Peter Lougheed worked overtime to develop a campaign for his November 2, 1982, provincial election and won back the seat. He went for many long, lonely walks that year, wrestling with the unity demon that would dog him for the rest of his career as premier and into his political after-life as a corporate lawyer and federalist spokesman. Already he carried the baggage of a tough political career. He had to live with the compromises he'd made to negotiate with the federal Liberals and seek amelioration of energy and constitutional policy. The price was high. For all the strength of his political machine provincially, he was voiceless in the federalist debate in the province. His positioning created a vacuum into which Manning could now move.

Ray Speaker, another former Socred Whiz Kid, formed a new populist provincial party. The Representative Party had a tougher, less compromising line on federalism than Peter Lougheed had and a social-conservative policy that contrasted sharply with Lougheed's Red Tory liberalism. In due course, Speaker's party came to naught, but it was a source of recruits for Manning when he finally made his move. One of the first of these was Ray Speaker himself.

The third federalist, Preston Manning, sat down with the leadership of the Western Canada Concept to assess whether the by-election signalled that Alberta was ripe for a new western populist federal party. It wasn't yet, but he could see that unless there was such a new party, the alternative would be a full-blown separatist movement. He continued to write papers and presentations on the political and economic issues that were fomenting a new political movement. He intensified his search for kindred minds and spirits who would join him when the time came. Liberal federalists, at least in the cabinet, did not get the message and remained in denial about the political realities the NEP created until they were thrown out of office in 1984.

The lasting anger that the National Energy Program induced in the West, and the reason that anger spread outside Alberta, had less to do with the economic impact than with the constitutional implications. The NEP was, in the western mind, a take-back of provincial jurisdiction over natural resources. This proved as inflammatory in the West as a federal intrusion on language and culture policy in Quebec. When Alberta and Saskatchewan were incorporated as provinces in 1905, control over natural resources was withheld, in spite of a long, hard fight between Frederick Haultain, the premier of the North-West Territories, and Prime Minister Wilfrid Laurier. This meant that the two new provinces were not equal to the older members of Confederation, which controlled their minerals and forests. The injustice was not rectified in law until 1930, and it took another six years and a supplemental agreement before Alberta could enforce that control and create its own regulatory and administrative systems.

The significance of that constitutional battle was not lost on thoughtful, politically active people in Manitoba and British Columbia, who had their own historical reasons to be wary of federal constitutional infringement. In Manitoba, the legacy was the hanging of Riel, followed by language and school disputes. In British Columbia, it was federal duplicity and double-dealing during the settling of U.S. border disputes and the building of the transcontinental railway, and British Columbia has the distinction of being the only legislature in the country to debate a secession bill. In 1980, old memories were dredged up and old suspicions renewed.

The NEP was widely interpreted not only as an intrusion on provincial control over resources but also as the use of unconstitutional tax law to prevent the nation's financial and economic centre from shifting to Alberta and British Columbia. Evidence of that came when oil company share prices collapsed on Canadian stock markets and stayed at historically low levels for months, and when the major banks began to write off billions in loan defaults. Meanwhile, to show the West's economic muscle as best he could, Alberta Premier Lougheed imposed regulatory limits on the removal of oil from the province, cutting pipeline shipments by 15 per cent in three, ninety-day periods.

The damage, however, was done. "The Ottawa government has, without negotiation, without agreement, walked into our house and occupied the living room," Lougheed said in a late-1980 special television address to the people of Alberta.

Through 1981, Prime Minister Pierre Trudeau's hard-line unilateralism on repatriation of the Constitution was taken as a continuing threat to the equality of the western provinces. Although the West and Canada's Atlantic provinces had tried to persuade him to relent, he refused.

When Trudeau overrode Quebec and brought the Constitution

home without the agreement of Premier René Lévesque, there was a surprising level of popular sympathy in the West for the Péquistes. Perception and symbols can be paramount in shaping political opinion. Westerners who were wounded by the NEP and fearful of this new, aggressive federalism shivered with trepidation in April 1982 at the sight of Queen Elizabeth II seated with Pierre Trudeau signing royal assent to repatriation.

Manning had no trade with the separatists, other than to endeavour to moderate their views and recruit them. He was a federalist. He was also an optimist who preferred positive people and positive ideas. He had an internal sense of balance and values and an external sense of confidence that made it difficult for him to feel alienated or angry; perhaps it was ten years of being a consultant, but he preferred to propose solutions to problems rather than wallow in them. His political style was based on his study of theories of mediation, reconciliation and sacrifice, drawn in part from the New Testament and in part from business common sense. Manning had confirmed the value of this approach in business—his worth to his clients consisted, he believed, of reconciling the conflicting interests that impaired their business success.

Manning believed that applied to Canadian politics, this style, as expressed in his new populist party, could mediate Canada's constitutional and economic conflicts, reconciling secessionists in the West and Quebec through a prescription of real equality in the federation for all citizens and provinces; social justice, the "soft heart" of politics, would be delivered with the "hard head" of fiscal responsibility.

The party's reconciling style would be at odds with the adversarial style of the House of Commons and the ruthless rough-and-tumble of partisan electoral politics; therefore, Manning predicted, its role might also require it to sacrifice its own interests to effect its program. For example, it might gain a platform by winning some seats in the House of Commons, present its ideas and have them picked up and used by the governing party. His party would get no credit for having brought the ideas to the table and might lose its seats in the next election because it was of no more use to the electorate. Manning's political creation would not seek power for power's sake but for what it could do when it had its hands on the levers, and this might shorten its life expectancy. This, he thought, was realistic. All populist and democratic parties in North American political history had had natural life cycles. The new party might even write a sunset clause into its constitution asking members to periodically evaluate whether they had still had a purpose in Canadian political life.

By 1984, the ardour of the secessionist movement in the West was cooling. Several sponsoring organizations had fallen under the control of extremists whose political eccentricity, advocacy of violence or thinly veiled anti-Semitism repelled many potential followers. The region's provincial premiers were leading several parallel processes with the federal government to counterbalance Trudeau's centralisim, and these seemed promising. And the Progressive Conservative Party, led by Quebec-Irish lawyer Brian Mulroney, was on the rise. He was recruiting bright young western candidates for the coming federal election. Typical freshmen in the class of 1984 were Manitoba teacher Jake Epp, Vancouver journalist Pat Carney, Lloydminster car dealer Don Mazankowski and University of Calgary chemistry professor Harvie Andre. There were reliable old hands such as former prime minister Joe Clark, and Mulroney was endorsed by powerful prairie Conservative bosses: Sterling Lyon in Winnipeg, Grant Devine in Regina, Peter Lougheed in Edmonton.

Mulroney talked a good line in the West. He would retract the aggressive hand of Trudeau federalism, roll back the National Energy Program (the Liberals had made only token adjustments) and deregulate oil and gas markets; he would shake up the bureaucracy and unwind the Grits' free-spending budgets and do something about Ottawa's horrific deficit and debt. He would let the West alone to prosper. This was already taking place: the resilient resource and agriculture industries were on the way back from a long commodity recession, and there was a budding economic relationship with the Pacific Rim. Even with Trudeau retired and the hapless John Turner, the interregnum prime minister, running in Vancouver as an ersatz westerner, Mulroney swept up fifty-eight seats in the region in the autumn election. The new prime minister, with his penchant for promising an Irish moon, had created high expectations west of Lake of the Woods that he would be the guy to fix the damage Trudeau had done.

Manning curbed his impatience. He and his father worked on a number of public-policy position papers. He and Sandra spent long hours at their Sturgeon Valley home with the children. They took summer courses at Regent College in Vancouver. He talked about starting some small political study groups, like those of Social Credit in 1933 to 1935, but Ernest and Sandra were more cautious.

Ernest and Preston had one propitious experience in 1984, a seminar sponsored by a private group called the Marigold Foundation, at which they made a day-long presentation on current public issues and made the pitch for a new, populist party rising out of the political turmoil in the West. The foundation was funded by independent oil man Jack MacKenzie and his wife, Sheila, and the event sealed their recruitment to Manning's gestating movement. Others were lining up, too. There were some pretty hard-headed old conservatives who had grave reservations about Mulroney and thought Manning's time would come pretty quickly: R. Campbell Todd, Jack Pirie and Bob Muir in the oil patch, wealthy Edmonton businessmen Dr. Francis G. Winspear (once a math pupil of William Aberhart), Dr. Charles Allard and Manning's Whiz Kids pal, Ray Speaker.

Some of the key figures at the Canada West Foundation, a Calgary-based economic and policy think tank and frequent client of Manning Consultants, were coming on-side: Stan Roberts, a Manitoba Liberal, academic and president of the Canadian Chamber of Commerce; David Elton, a political economist; Dr. Winspear; Jo Anne Hillier, a public affairs consultant, formerly with Atomic Energy of Canada; Fred Mannix Jr., of the Calgary billionaire family, and Cliff Breitkreuz, an Alberta municipal politician.

There is a time-worn cliché of prairie politics: "Send a farmer to Ottawa and get back a politician." By 1985, the powerful western caucus and the strong contingent of prairie and British Columbia cabinet ministers had been institutionalized and were falling into the trap of selling the government's decisions to the West instead of the West's agenda to the government. Mulroney had set the bar far too high and could not move fast enough to meet the expectations he'd created.

It took the Mulroney government more than a year to make substantive progress on energy deregulation. In 1985, University of Calgary economist Robert Mansell released a calculation that the NEP had resulted in a $100 billion transfer of taxes and price subsidies from the West to central and eastern Canada. The government still had not moved to repeal the program and would not for another year. Mulroney's attack on the deficit and reform of the political process was slow. He did not come west to visit. His lavish style offended prairie frugality. By 1986, the Mulroney Conservatives were badly tarnished.

Manning started making appointments for lunches and dinners, often accompanied by Sandra, to sound out his business and political contacts on the possibility of a new federalist political party based in the West. They'd see people individually or in couples. He'd ask, "Is this what you want? The discredited Mulroney Conservatives? Or discredited western secession?" He was firmer than he'd ever been. He gently twisted arms and brooked little recalcitrance from people he knew were ready to break with the Conservatives.

In June, his gathering momentum was interrupted when his brother, Keith, now forty-seven years old, suffered a fatal heart attack. He had been living in the McGugan nursing home in Edmonton, a specialty care facility, for five years and had been married for three to Marilyn Brownell, another resident of the home. These had been the happiest years of Keith's life, and his serenity, joy and abiding Christian faith had become an emotional anchor for Preston. Besides Sandra and his children, Preston had loved no one as deeply and completely as Keith.

He was devastated, but politics is a relentless master and he was soon back on the job of coalescing the Reform movement. Perhaps his biggest initial success was to win the support of *Alberta Report* publisher Ted Byfield. Byfield had been quick to size up Mulroney's shortcomings and was already thinking about a political alternative—perhaps the Christian Heritage Party. On August 25, Byfield wrote column headlined "The West needs its own party." In it, Byfield proposed a moderate, western-based party of economic and constitutional reform. Meanwhile, in British Columbia, Francis Winspear had created a $50,000 fund to explore federal political options with Stan Roberts and other prominent westerners.

In September, Manning wrote and circulated a memo called "A Western Reform Movement: The Responsible Alternative to Western Separatism." In it he said, "Many of the policies, plans, ideas and ingredients required to construct the platform of a responsible Western Reform Movement exist . . . the ingredients missing are: (1) the will to turn ideas, discussions, hopes and fears into political actions; (2) strong and respected leadership; and (3) the funds necessary to do the job." The encouraging response prompted him to draft a more specific sixteen-page draft called "Proposal for the Creation of a Western-Based Political Party to Run Candidates in the 1988 Federal Election."

This document argued that Mulroney hadn't fixed what Trudeau broke. It traced the roots of western Canadian "reform tradition," beginning with the two Riel rebellions and continuing through the Progressives, Social Credit and the CCF. It concluded with a deliberately incomplete sentence: "The next Reform movement?" The onus was on the readers to provide the reply. A friend of Manning's from evangelical circles, British Columbia journalist Lloyd Mackey, was working at *Alberta Report*. Manning invited him to lunch at the Mayfair Hotel on Edmonton's east side, popular for its noon-hour buffets, dinner theatres and, ironically, a favourite Liberal venue for membership conventions. After the meal, Mackey took Manning's "Proposal" back to Byfield.

A few days later, Byfield invited Manning to dinner with his editors and political reporters. Then he weighed in on the pages of the magazine with an endorsement for Reform. Byfield had developed two major Reform policy ideas through his columns. He was years ahead of Alberta's politicians in his concern over government debt and deficits: budgets had to be balanced and the overhanging debt load paid off. *Alberta Report* expended a large amount of its slender resources overcoming bureaucratic accounting trickery to compile an accurate account of how much the federal and provincial governments owed in unpaid borrowings and what portion of annual budgets were consumed by interest payments. And he provided the principle platform for Triple-E Senate reform: an elected Senate with effective lawmaking powers, in which the provinces were represented by an equal number of seats.

In September, Preston convened pivotal meetings with Winspear on Vancouver Island and in Calgary. Before the Calgary session, he sent copies of "A Western Reform Movement: The Responsible Alternative to Western Separatism" to Calgary oil man and Conservative supporter James Gray, David Elton of the Canada West Foundation and Ted Byfield. In a covering letter, he said that action, not further analysis, was needed. He asked the three for a meeting to discuss what should be done to turn six years of anger and talk into political action.

Still, he needed a flash point, something that would carry the idea of a new party out of the élite circle of western opinion makers and connect it with the grassroots. In October, Brian Mulroney gave him the spark. The federal government was tendering a large and lucrative maintenance contract for the Canadian Armed Forces fleet of 136 CF-18 fighter jets. There were two competitors for the deal—Bristol Aerospace in Winnipeg and Canadair Montreal. The $100.5-million Bristol Aerospace bid was lower by $3.5 million and outscored Canadair in a technical evaluation by a large team of civic servants.

News leaked from western cabinet ministers that the work was going to Winnipeg, proof that their government was good for the West. Then the Quebec Tory caucus intervened, and Mulroney threw the contract to Montreal.

The angry response from the West was instant and intense. The prime minister claimed that Canadair would be better at transferring the technology involved into other fields. This watery explanation aggravated the injury to western pride. "CF-18" entered the regional political code book on the same page as "NEP." Here was another Quebec politician using the power of the prime minister's office to stick it to the West. Preston Manning and the nascent Reform movement had their *cause célèbre*.

CHAPTER TEN # Roots
# of Reform

*I am satisfied that the mass of the people are sound—moderate in
their demands and attached to British [parliamentary] institutions;
but they have been oppressed by a miserable little oligarchy on one
hand and excited by a few factious demagogues on the other. I can
make a middle reforming party, I am sure, that will put down both.*

— GOVERNOR-GENERAL LORD SYDENHAM
Letter to Lord John Russell, 1840

THE PRESTON MANNING who stepped into the
arena in 1986 to form a western-based Reform
movement as an alternative to prairie separatism and
the Liberal-Progressive Conservative mainstream was a different politician from the naive, twenty-something Social Credit candidate and
whiz kid technocrat of the 1960s. He was no longer his father's eager-
to-please proxy or custodian of a family interest in Alberta politics.
Now in his mid-forties, he knew his own mind. He had the wisdom
gained from establishing a business career and a family. He had tested
his values in the adult experience of life. He had seasoned his political
experiences with a careful study of history.

Reading extensively to complete the politically related assignments that comprised about 20 per cent of his consulting practice, he had found a connection to the lineage of political reform in Canada and development of citizens' democracy in the United States. He had tested his ideas with others—such as his father, Simon Ramon, Ted Byfield, Francis Winspear, the directors of the Canada West Foundation—whose greater experience he respected. He was clear about where he had come from and where he wanted to go.

He was a social conservative: he believed in government with a hard head and compassionate heart. He advocated fiscally responsible government, free-market economics and prudent social policy that produced good public education, decent health care and social assistance for the disadvantaged within the limits of public financial means.

The heart and soul of his politics, however, was a carefully thought-out notion of the preeminence of the citizen-democrat in a political system in which representative government was paramount. He was a populist first and a conservative second. He had concluded that federal politics, when not attentive to and driven by the will of the people, produced National Energy Programs, CF-18 decisions and secessionist movements in Quebec and the West. Old politics and old parties had interests separate from those of the people.

Manning used the terms "populist" loosely to describe his movement. In fact, the Reform movement of the mid-1980s had less to do with the late-nineteenth-century American Populist movement for which the term "populist" was coined than with other political traditions. William Byron Jennings's organizational methods, agrarian orientation and monetary policy had a faint resemblance to those of Social Credit, but the parallel ended there. The Populists were demagogues and rhetoricians who were quickly and accurately judged by the people for what they were: a passing wind. When Preston Manning used the label "populist" in 1986, it was shorthand for what he called "the common sense of the common people."

He found Canadian and American antecedents for his movement. In American history, he learned from the U.S. Continental Congress and the birth of the Republican Party. In the Canadian West, he looked to the ideas behind the Riel rebellions, the struggle to gain provincial status for Alberta and Saskatchewan and the prairie populism of the Progressives, Socreds and CCFers. From the rest of Canada, he drew on the reform movements of the 1830s in Upper and Lower Canada and Nova Scotia, and on the great Reform coalition that dominated the Assembly of the united provinces of Canada from 1842 to 1851.

The essence of Manning's political reform, as it emerged after the NEP and CF-18s, was to change the processes of government so that public policy would "carry the judgement of the public" before it reached the legislative process, which would then pass laws accurately reflecting the will of the people. The essence of responsible government was much more than the election of representative parliaments and assemblies: it was to continuously reconcile the power of the legislature and the opinion of the people.

Preston Manning first observed this plain political thinking in his father's office, where it was a touchstone of everything Premier Ernest Manning did. Ernest thought the people had the right not only to be consulted but also to have their views brought to bear on public policy. He thought government relied entirely on the trust of people, and if a leader wanted the people's trust, the leader had first to demonstrate trust in the people by asking their opinions and giving those opinions influence over the public decisions affecting their lives.

Ernest had huge majorities in the Legislature and could have done anything he wanted. Nevertheless, when a minister or deputy minister came to him with a new scheme, he never asked, "Can we get it through the House?" Of course they could; they had the votes. He always asked, "Will it carry the judgement of the people?" The question wasn't asked for form's sake; he expected an informed, persuasive response. He also asked what will it cost and what good is it supposed to do. He believed, however, in the final analysis, the new idea wouldn't succeed in practice if it didn't have popular support. Ernest's knack for correctly evaluating and accommodating popular opinion explained his untrammelled success in nine elections and, perhaps, his reluctance to anoint his successor.

William Aberhart did not have this ability. His passion to destroy the economic system he blamed for the Depression and defeat a government indifferent to the people's suffering caught a tide of opinion and carried him into power. Aberhart never expected to negotiate or reconcile. In office, he was a reluctant politician; he did not know how to make the transition from protest movement to government, or how to make opinion into a body of law.

Preston Manning thought that Aberhart might have destroyed the Social Credit Party had he lived to fight the 1944 election. One of the reasons prairie movements had died out so easily in the past, Manning reflected, was that they'd flared up so quickly and intensely. It was easy to be a bombastic wrecking crew, tearing down the past. It was something else to be the colourless but constructive legislator creating an enduring future.

Manning preferred a cooler approach. His personal hagiology of democrats included American presidents Abraham Lincoln and Thomas Jefferson and Canadian reformers Frederick Haultain and Robert Baldwin. These men had lived his kind of politics, and their words gave expression to the political verities he himself was discovering. They were all politicians who came from outside the political establishment and were never accepted by insiders. Their critics and supporters both observed that these men all retained higher values than the gritty practice of power normally allowed for and succeeded in advancing the politics of representative government, liberty and equality.

Soon after he completed university, he read Carl Sandburg's monumental, six-volume biography of Abraham Lincoln. The experience was a vivid milestone in the development of his political thinking. To Sandburg, poet and professor, history that endures treats with the heart. His work on Lincoln is lyric in language and ranges through the emotions of exploration, war, fratricide, ambition and evil to define a lofty vision of *homo politicus*. Because Sandburg was a mid-American whose sense of place was with the plains and the Mississippi, his idiom harmonized with Manning's Albertan sensibilities. Sandburg connected with Manning's quest for a mature sense of politics.

Sandburg concluded that without the Civil War, Lincoln might have been a mediocre president. The war defined a playing field that Manning recognized: Manning thought the book to be the classic study of secession and used it to inform his analysis of western alienation and Quebec separatism. More important than that, he learned from Sandburg's book that Lincoln had lead the formation of the Republican Party, in less than a decade, from its origin as an outsiders' grassroots movement in the American West to become the party of the president in 1861 and, with the Democrats, one side of a stable two-party system that has functioned in the United States since the Civil

War. In this respect, the Republicans achieved more than Jennings's Populists and the Canadian prairie third parties ever did. Manning's beacon of confidence that a Canadian Reform Party could form a government before the end of the twentieth century was based on Lincoln's success.

The Civil War, however, commanded Manning's attention first. Sandburg recounted how, in his first inaugural address, March 4, 1861, with the coming war already a dark shadow, Lincoln defined the power of the citizen: "In your hands, my dissatisfied fellow countrymen, and not in mine is the momentous issue of civil war. The government will not assail you. You can have no conflict without being yourselves the aggressors." The new president also said, "No government proper ever had a provision in its organic law for its own termination. The central idea of secession is the essence of anarchy. If a minority will secede rather than acquiesce, they make a precedent which, in turn, will divide and ruin them; for a minority of their own will secede from them." In the 1970s, with the FLQ and Quebec's October Crisis still a fresh memory in Canadian politics, the words burned.

Lincoln's final contribution to Manning's thought was his unswerving commitment to democratic processes. At the end of his first term, Lincoln risked his presidency and the outcome of the war to honour the constitutional requirement for an election. Others in the president's cabinet believed this was a constitutional crisis in 1864: whether to have an election during a civil war. Lincoln believed he had no choice. At his second inaugural address on the evening of November 10, 1864, in torchlight with partisan banners surrounding the north portico of the White House, he said, "It has long been a grave question whether any government not too strong for the liberties of its people can be strong enough to maintain its own existence in great emergencies. We cannot have free government without elections; and if the rebellion could force us to forego, or postpone, a national election, it might fairly claim to have already conquered and ruined us."

When he began to read Thomas Jefferson, Manning "discovered that he gave words to the ideas and conclusions I was reaching about politics in my early consulting years." Manning liked to memorize passages of favourite books, a habit developed when he was learning Scripture as a boy. He loved to recite Jefferson and got his children to memorize him, too. They'd quote the third American president to one another at the dinner table while Sandra rolled her eyes.

Manning's favourite passage from Jefferson came from a letter written when the former president was in his eighties: "I can think of no safer depository for the ultimate powers of society than the people themselves, and if they are not yet fit to exercise self-government with a wholesome discretion, then the remedy is not to take self-government from them but to inform their discretion."

If anybody had a right to be arrogant about his mind being better than others, Jefferson had the right, Manning thought. Jefferson was adept in a dozen fields of scientific and humanistic knowledge. He founded the Library of Congress with his personal collection of books and the University of Virginia as a retirement project. He had been an ambassador to France, secretary of state, vice president and president of the United States. He'd written the constitution of the State of Virginia and co-written the Declaration of Independence. Yet he still believed the will of the people, not the wisdom of experts, ought to govern the new American nation and he battled against the federalists who wanted to restore some of the privilege and élitism of the British parliamentary monarchy to the American Constitution. For Jefferson, political reform remained a process, not a fading memory of the revolution he helped to inspire. "Every man is an instrument of government," Jefferson had written. "And the spirit of resistancy to government is so important that it must always be kept alive."

Ten days before he died, looking back fifty years to the signing of the Declaration of Independence, Jefferson told a friend that the drafters of the Declaration knew they were deciding between "submission and the sword." The price of liberty was revolution, and in his old age, the consolation of that dreadful choice was that "our fellow citizens, after half a century, continue to approve the choice we made. May it be to the world what I believe it will be: the signal arousing men to burst the chains under which monkish ignorance and superstition has persuaded them to bind themselves, and to assume the blessings of self-government." The cadence of these words, as well as the content, worked their way into Manning's political consciousness.

Canadian reform history, however, was the bedrock on which Manning built his movement. In the West, reform starts with the Métis rebellions lead by Louis Riel in 1869 and 1885. Contemporary historians such as Gerald Friesen, who believes that the West's political identity depends on protest, usually date the beginning of regionalism in prairie politics with Riel's desire for provincial government in what is now Manitoba to replace the colonial status of the North-West Territories. Although Métis communities were loosely organized and based on somewhat utopian ideals, Riel's people were schooled well enough in the Canadian Constitution to believe that they could best preserve the Métis culture, which combined Catholicism, the French language, the freedom of aboriginal community government and the anarchical lifestyle of a trapping and trading economy, in a province.

In his frequent business dealings with the Métis of Alberta, Manning learned that the Métis regarded Louis Riel as the first western Reformer. As he circulated his ideas for a new Reform movement in 1986, some Métis leaders told him the Reform Party would be "the third Riel rebellion." The first two were a watershed in the history of the West. The first Riel rebellion affected the terms on which Manitoba came into Confederation in 1870, even though Riel was discredited and exiled to the United States. The Métis thus initiated western third-party opinion. Never would the Conservative or Liberal Parties enjoy more than temporary sufferance on the soil west of the Ontario-Manitoba border.

The frosty autumn day in November, 1885, when Riel was hanged after his second bloody uprising is in the tribal memory of all western dissidents. They hold as a tenet of political faith that democracy, representative government on the prairies, regional self-determination and the battle against the colonial federalism were born of Riel's blood and in the place of his death. The strength and influence of that conviction is evidence that political culture lives not in historical veracity or policy exegesis, but in a people's sense of themselves.

Manning admired Louis Riel's courage and political sagacity. He recognized his importance to western Canadians as the first advocate of responsible, elected government in the North-West Territories. But one hundred years after his death, Riel had been reduced to an archaeological artifact—symbolic but mute, prone to self-interested interpretion by contradictory political causes. Preston was more at home with Frederick Haultain, the father of Alberta and Saskatchewan, as his reference point for the beginning of the Reform movement in the West. And he recognized that the United Farmers and Progressives had quarried the stones after the First World War that he could now directly incorporate into the Reform movement.

Sir Frederick W. G. Haultain is a singular choice for a populist to anchor the history of the Reform movement. One can search in vain in mainstream history texts for his story. His portrait hangs in the Alberta Legislature, and its image was branded into Manning's brain as a young man. In that painting Haultain is formally dressed, but his jacket is unbuttoned and he is holding a lighted cigarette with René Lévesque's careless poise—but Haultain is handsomer and had a better tailor. That picture is part of the living history that Manning absorbed as a student of his father's government. He gained the lore of Haultain from Edward Trowbridge, who was his father's first deputy minister in 1935 and who had been clerk of the North-West Territories government from 1897 to 1905, when Haultain was the premier of the Territories.

Haultain was a country lawyer from Fort Macleod, a dusty, Palliser Triangle hamlet built as a Mounted Police post and expanded for a railway station and one of the first communities in the province to get a boost from the nascent, nineteenth-century natural-gas industry. Haultain was thirty-one years old when he was first elected to the Assembly and thirty-four when he was appointed head of the territorial administration. From 1891 to 1905, he was the most important political figure in the Territories, and he was the region's spokesman during the long, slow fight for political autonomy. The progress from a colony ruled by a single governor to a territory, and then to the admission to Confederation of Alberta and Saskatchewan in 1905 was entirely due to Haultain's relentlessness.

The procrastination of the Canadian Liberal and Conservative governments in giving the colonial West representative government, provincial charters and equality with the other provinces strongly influenced the region's taste for third parties. The impression that the rest of Canada wanted the West as a permanent economic fiefdom indelibly marked federal elective politics and federal-provincial relations for the entire twentieth century. The bitter taste of colonialism was still a political asset for the Reform movement in 1986.

The region was a commercial principality of the Hudson's Bay

Company under royal charter for 197 years. Following Confederation, it was transferred to Canada, and a "temporary" government was established in which a lieutenant-governor was the sole authority receiving direction from the federal cabinet. In 1870, a portion of present-day Manitoba was sliced off and given provincial status. In 1873, Ottawa established a "provisional" government for the rest in which the lieutenant-governor had appointed advisors but a newly created Department of the Interior still called the shots. Between 1875 and 1888, while Ottawa shuffled its seat from Fort Garry to Battleford to Regina to please competing partisan factions, the North-West Council of five was allowed to expand and the lieutenant-governor was invested with legislative power over local affairs.

After 1888, there was an elected Legislative Assembly, and in 1891, the Assembly was given broad legislative powers, but the inequalities were glaring. It could not borrow, did not control natural resources and the head of government was still a lieutenant-governor who was the velvet glove over the iron fist of the Department of the Interior. Haultain's nonpartisan battle between 1891 and 1905 for provincial status made his political reputation.

In the 1970s, in search of a greater understanding of reform politics and for the kind of inspiring ideas he'd found in Jefferson, Manning looked up Haultain's lawyerly, logical speeches to the Assembly at Regina and his memoranda to Prime Minister Laurier. These documents articulated the western demand for equality with the provinces but Haultain's words are not memorable for being quotable: they are dull and dusty. Their passion is in the irrefutable argument that the colonial status of the Territories was unconscionable and Laurier had no excuse to delay provincehood. Delay he did and created in Haultain a gentle and soft-spoken political hero.

Haultain had two objectives. He advocated the creation of a single province with all the rights of the established provinces, including ownership and control of natural resources. And he wanted a nonpartisan legislature with assembly members "who made their main concern the well-being and development of the area they represented, not the interests of a particular party involved in federal politics—spokesmen for all the people in their ridings." Haultain became the West's first twentieth-century victim of Ottawa power politics and its colonial treatment of the region: Laurier broke the region's power by dividing it into Alberta and Saskatchewan. He refused the new provinces control over resources by retaining that right for the federal government. He denied them the constitutional status of nonpartisan legislatures, ensured the Liberal Party was organized to contest elections before the provinces were chartered and named Liberals to the controlling positions in the brief transition from territory to province. Haultain ought to have been designated by Laurier as the first premier of one of the provinces but was passed over because he had always voted Conservative federally.

The western wing of the Farmers' and Progressive movements in the 1920s knew their debt to Haultain. Agrarian prosperity during the First World War gave farmers political clout, ambition and the desire to right some past wrongs. There was little satisfaction, in either Alberta or Saskatchewan, with the Laurier-imposed Liberal premiers. The current of contrarianism ran deeper in Canadian politics than westerners realized. On October, 20, 1919, the descendants of the Upper Canada rebels of 1837 elected a United Farmers government in Ontario. On July 18, 1921, Alberta followed suit and threw the sixteen-year-old Grit government out of office in favour of the farmer iconoclasts who believed they could change the world from their homesteads. (In Saskatchewan, where voters quickly decided that they disliked any political movement from Alberta, third-party politics waited to assert itself until the rise of the socialist Canadian Commonwealth Federation during the Depression.)

The Farmers' movement moved onto the national stage in June 1921, when a by-election in Medicine Hat, Alberta, returned a UFA candidate. Then, in December, the Farmers stormed Parliament Hill, electing sixty-five Progressives. This cast a pall on William Lyon Mackenzie King's newly won leadership of the Liberal Party, which gained 117 seats, one short of a majority. That election was an unsettling experience for Canada's mainstream parties, who saw the results as a balkanization of Canada, with Liberals, Progressive and Conservatives all assembling regionally based caucuses and the CCF making a breakout in Saskatchewan and Manitoba.

The underlying significance of this election result was quickly obfuscated by the canny Mackenzie King. He knew the danger of the West's anger over the National Policy, conceived by Sir John A.

Macdonald, which reduced the Prairies to the status of an economic colony of central Canada. Macdonald had established a tariff system that forced western farmers to purchase high-priced Canadian equipment and goods without access to competing American suppliers, while holding agricultural production captive to Canadian markets and railways. King had no desire to change this policy in 1921. He manoeuvred to maintain control of Parliament and the hapless leader of the Progressives, Thomas Crerar, blinked. Crerar declined Official Opposition status and waived a platform in the House of Commons for his movement. Prime Minister King deflected Progressive anger, and new lore was created in Ottawa: that western discontent could be contained, and its politicians subsumed.

In crystallizing his ideas, Manning passed lightly over two movements. The Social Gospel was an interpretation of Christian social justice that emerged from the Protestant tradition quite gracefully in the 1920s. It did not challenge the authority of the church but drew on the primitive, New Testament tradition of compassion and care of "the poor, widows and orphans." The Social Gospel had a social democratic tinge to it, which Manning wanted to avoid. And its influence was diffuse because its practitioners were in all political parties. The Social Gospel also fell into the political arsenal of Liberal leader and Prime Minister Mackenzie King, who recognized its potential and manipulated it to defuse the power of the Progressives and later the CCF. King, a practising Christian, probably concurred with the sentiments, if not all the prescriptions, of the Social Gospel. He "borrowed" (some critics said "stole") the policies of the Progressives and the CCF for programs such as old-age pensions and national health care, toning down their collectivist rhetoric and implementing them as slowly and cautiously as possible.

Manning also treated the socialist CCF gingerly, although he frequently added it and its leaders, without comment, to his list of prairie movements when he wanted to point out of the depth of western discontent with federalism and the breadth of appeal of third-party populist movements. One obstacle he faced in building his western base was that in the CCF stronghold of Saskatchewan, Reform was thought of as Albertan, and people in Saskatchewan generally dislike Albertan political movements.

To complete his Canadian reform history, Manning turned to the first

This formal portrait in oil of William Aberhart—Manning's political grandfather—painted near the end of his life by the Western Canadian artist Grandmaison shows Aberhart in his home study. It was in this room that he and his young protégé, Ernest Manning, launched the Social Credit Party in the Depression years of 1933 to 1935. PROVINCIAL ARCHIVES OF ALBERTA, HARRY POLLARD COLLECTION (P.5326).

Ernest Charles Manning, Preston Manning's father, in a formal photograph taken in 1943 by the distinguished Harry Pollard, shortly after Manning, at age thirty-four, was sworn in as Alberta's eighth premier. PROVINCIAL ARCHIVES OF ALBERTA, HARRY POLLARD COLLECTION (P-5337).

Muriel Aileen Manning (née Preston), Preston Manning's strikingly beautiful mother, in her early thirties. Muriel and Ernest Manning met when they were both working at Aberhart's Prophetic Bible Institute. PROVINCIAL ARCHIVES OF ALBERTA, PUBLIC AFFAIRS BUREAU COLLECTION (PA 2315/12).

Ernest Manning at the pulpit of the Calgary Prophetic Bible Institute. Muriel, who was the pianist, is seated alone to the left. Above Manning is a canvas chart of world history seen in apocalyptic biblical terms, painted by William Aberhart in his garage. PROVINCIAL ARCHIVES OF ALBERTA, HARRY POLLARD COLLECTION (P.5324).

The Manning family (*left to right:* Ernest, Preston, Muriel and Keith) in their home in Edmonton's Garneau district. Preston is about ten years old in this picture. Muriel was a formally trained concert pianist; singing around the piano was a family activity that Ernest first experienced as a young man boarding in the home of William and Jessie Aberhart. PROVINCIAL ARCHIVES OF ALBERTA, PUBLIC AFFAIRS BUREAU COLLECTION (PA 2315/14).

The Manning home opposite the campus of the University of Alberta in Edmonton's Garneau district, taken in the autumn after the first snow. Preston Manning lived for the first twelve years of his life in this modest, two-storey frame house. PROVINCIAL ARCHIVES OF ALBERTA, PUBLIC AFFAIRS BUREAU COLLECTION (PA 2315/12).

A friend described Preston Manning and Sandra Beavis as "Mr. and Mrs. Perfect" at their wedding in the Fundamental Baptist Church in Edmonton, on March 23, 1967. The reclusive, reserved Mannings and the gregarious, voluble Beavises were a study in contrasts but were nevertheless close friends long before Preston and Sandra fell in love. PHOTO COURTESY OF THE MANNING FAMILY.

Westerlea, the Manning family farm where Preston Manning lived from the age of twelve until the end of his first year at university. Ernest and Muriel scrimped and saved for ten years to build the ranch house on the right. The property extended to the north bank of the North Saskatchewan River, on the left. PROVINCIAL ARCHIVES OF ALBERTA, PUBLIC AFFAIRS BUREAU COLLECTION (PA 2315/15)

The vice-president of Manning Consultants in December 1978. After ten years out of politics, Preston was considering an offer from Progressive Conservative leader Joe Clark to run in the 1979 federal election, a proposition he turned down in favour of eight more years in political exile. PROVINCIAL ARCHIVES OF ALBERTA, *EDMONTON JOURNAL* COLLECTION (J. 4366)

Preston and Sandra Manning on horseback at Casket Mountain near the Alberta-British Columbia border. It is day ten of their annual Rocky Mountain summer trail ride, an outfitter's expedition taken with a close circle of friends. Manning skipped the 1997 edition of the wilderness holiday to study French in Quebec. PHOTO COURTESY OF THE MANNING FAMILY.

Time out on an airport tarmac, during Manning's 1993 election tour of Canada, to toss the Reform Party's lucky football, a black-and-white-striped pigskin with the appropriate brand name of Stealth. The ball became a campaign mascot when Manning carried it into the leaders' television debate. In 1997, the football reappeared on the tour, at the leaders' debate and on election night. PHOTO BY DAVID BURTON.

The leader of the Reform Party of Canada and Ontario young Reformers in a celebratory mood during the 1997 campaign. As it turned out, the celebration was premature, since the party took no seats in the province. PHOTO FROM PETER BREGG/MACLEAN'S.

The leader of the Official Opposition in the thirty-sixth Parliament of Canada. Manning's image had been modified before the 1997 election campaign to shake his bookish, "preacher's kid" public persona. Laser eye surgery, a new hairstyle and a more fashionable wardrobe produced a look that was closer to the tough and assured Preston Manning, the product of a lifetime of political study, experience and experiment. PHOTO FROM PETER BREGG/MACLEAN'S

Reform parties that catapulted Upper and Lower Canada into insurrection in 1837. He viewed William Lyon Mackenzie and Louis Hébert Papineau, who led men in open rebellion, suffered casualties under fire and fled to exile in the United States, as extremists who made life difficult for the real reformers. In the same way, Manning thought the more bombastic twentieth-century reformers in the West, like William Aberhart, were the "wrecking crews" of change. Effective reformers who wanted to build, as his father had built, had to distance themselves from the politics of anger and alienation, and to make it clear that they stood more for solutions than against old grievances. It came as no surprise to Manning that Aberhart identified strongly with the Upper Canada rebels, especially his home-town hero, Colonel Anthony Van Egmond, who died a political martyr's death in a wet and icy cell following the failure of William Lyon Mackenzie's insurrection in December 1837.

Manning saw his interests with the more moderate Upper Canadian Reform Party, led by William and Robert Baldwin, Francis Hincks and Egerton Ryerson. These men tried to talk Mackenzie out of the Montgomery Tavern skirmishes that cost Van Egmond his freedom and life and resulted in the hanging or exile of more than two hundred Upper Canadians.

The Baldwins played a longer card than the rebels. They had been Reform Party members before 1837, when Mackenzie was simply an overblown nuisance who edited and published an inflammatory political tabloid. The Baldwins' objective was to displace colonial rule by an unelected governor with elected, representative assemblies. They were patient, they were conciliatory, they were articulate. While they bore no love for the Family Compact, they believed the British Crown would not wish to lose the Canadas to the same political movement that had cost it the American colonies. In many ways, their relationship resembled that between Ernest and Preston Manning in the last years of Ernest's premiership. Both were father-and-son dynasties in which the father established the basic political ideas and style and the son inherited them.

The Baldwins stayed on their self-imposed high road. Reformers who took to arms were shot in battle, executed after trial or sent on transports to Australia. The Baldwins remained to participate as the united provinces of Canada moved by stages to responsible government, then independence as a Confederation. Robert Baldwin played a pivotal role at the climax by creating the historic English-French coalition with Louis Lafontaine that supported the first Reform government in Canadian history in 1842. The strength of that coalition survived ten years of the vagaries and chaos of the brawling frontier elections and rustic assemblies that met in Kingston to govern the Union of 1841. While it was a pre-Confederation government, Manning knew he could make use of the powerful symbol of a Reform Party in power.

Manning had great admiration for Joseph Howe, the Nova Scotia reformer and architect of responsible government in that colony, who accomplished it constitutionally, without rebellion, loss of life or the intervention of the British government. Howe was the bitter foe of separation from Britain; he overcame the argument that the neighbouring New England states had prospered as a republic and foiled all demagogues simply by the strength and power of his vision for a democratic, parliamentary model government in Atlantic North America.

In 1986, Preston Manning had been influenced by a wide range of historical figures and an equally wide range of political philosophies. It was fundamentally all the same thing, no matter if you called it the common sense of the common people, or third-party politics, or the discontent of westerners who resented Conservative and Liberal treatment, from the colonialism of the North-West Territories to the denial of the CF-18 maintenance contract for Winnipeg. He was personally not a "populist" so much as what Americans in Jefferson's time described as a "whole hog democrat": one who wants politics out of the embrace of establishments, élites, special interests and influences. One who wants government to be representative and responsive to the judgement of the people. Manning saw politics as a tableau in which the key process is to inform the electorate's sensibilities and give it clearly defined choices. Politicians would be obliged to be persuasive, clear, specific and unequivocal. Elections would be events in which a party accepts the endorsement, or rejection, of the people.

He was now quite sure that he could give voters, at least in Western Canada, a choice on the ballot in a new party that would be consistent with their twentieth-century political experience, conform to their values and purposes, and give them a credible alternative to the separatism of the past three years and to the failed Conservative and Liberal politics that had created the anger and alienation in the West.

CHAPTER ELEVEN # The West Wants In

"Let them come, if they dare."

—LIEUTENANT-GOVERNOR SIR FRANCIS BOND HEAD
A warning to the Reformers of Upper Canada, 1834

AFTER PRIME MINISTER Brian Mulroney sent the CF-18 maintenance contract to Montreal instead of Winnipeg, Manning was convinced by the level of political anger and alienation that the West was ready to produce one of its periodic political movements as it had with the Progressives, CCF and Social Credit. In small groups of six or ten, in coffee shops and basements, people were starting to search for and would support a new political option. This was the opportunity to put together a new party to do some of the things he and others had been speaking and writing about—and hoping would come out of the Conservative Party after 1984, but they were now convinced that a Mulroney government would never do.

On October 17, 1986, James Gray, the President of Canadian Hunter Explorations, invited Manning to his 4th Avenue S.W. boardroom in the heart of Calgary's oil patch to meet with a small circle of Alberta opinion leaders. Canadian Hunter was a symbol of what independent exploration companies could still accomplish with a drill bit. Other executives were more interested in mergers and acquisitions; Gray and his partner, geologist John Masters, were finding big natural gas and oil deposits in the Rocky Mountain foothills of Alberta and British Columbia. Masters was a quiet man, with little profile outside the industry. Gray, however, was widely engaged in a score of educational, charitable and business enterprises that had a common theme: excellence and innovation. People who wanted to start something new in Alberta called on Jim Gray, who enjoyed his role as an instigator and catalyst.

Gray also invited Dr. David Elton, a University of Lethbridge political scientist and Canada West Foundation board member; *Alberta Report* publisher Ted Byfield (who was ill and sent his regrets); lawyer Robert Muir, who was a former Dome Petroleum executive, and independent oil financier Douglas Hilland. Muir was a member of the brains trust that had built Dome from a quiet little independent in the 1950s to an international giant in the 1980s. When the company collapsed and was taken over by Amoco Canada Petroleum, Muir found it difficult to find something to do that was as interesting. Hilland and his family were private oil men with superb political connections. Elton and Manning had worked together on several Canada West projects.

Manning proposed four political alternatives for western opinion leaders concerned about the future of the region. The first was to continue to work for western interests inside the system through already-existing interest groups, within the traditional federal parties and with the provincial premiers and intergovernmental affairs ministers. Gray, who supported Calgary's Tory MPs such as Harvie Andre and Barbara Sparrow and would soon join the group of business people, politicians, power brokers and community leaders who backed Ralph Klein's rise to power as Alberta's premier, said he would choose that option. Even if the Tories had made mistakes, Albertans should cut them some slack. There was a powerful western caucus, and the cabinet ministers from the region had enormous power. It would pay off, but they needed time to settle in and figure out the system—after all, they'd been in opposition for thirty years. Elton's position that all the options needed further study effectively put him in Gray's camp.

The second option was to resolve the role of the separatists by ignoring, opposing or encouraging them. Muir and Hilland bitterly noted that some influential members of the oil patch had badly miscalculated by endorsing Western Canada Concept. They had paid a severe price: they were subsequently excluded from the sphere of influence around Peter Lougheed's Alberta provincial government and banned from the circle of movers and shakers who'd backed the election of the huge fifty-eight-member Tory federal caucus in 1984. Manning supported a third option: a new western reform party to run candidates in the next federal election, expected in 1988. All present at the meeting had read the memos he'd written in the summer and early autumn proposing this course of action. Had Byfield been at the meeting, he would have spoken for that option, but Manning detected no great warmth in the room for a new party.

At an impasse, the meeting turned to the last option—a "Parliament of the West" to be convened in 1987 to consider the political future. Manning explained that the assembly could put the region's "discontents" on the table and discuss what it would take to bring the West to equal partnership within the Confederation. The others were, at first, inscrutable. Gray and Elton were unenthusiastic, but perhaps too polite to resist much. Muir and Hilland were quiet. Manning summarized the meeting for the others, suggesting that at the very least, there was no serious objection to a regional convocation.

This was much less than he had expected, but immediately after the meeting, things began to look up. First, Muir and Hilland took him aside. They dismissed Gray and Elton as "talkers" and offered to introduce him to a group of "doers" to whom he should present his proposal to run a slate of reform candidates in the coming election. Manning made his presentation to the Muir-Hilland group on November 13 and got strong endorsement from several participants both for his "Parliament of the West" and to run candidates for a western-based federal reform party in the 1988 election.

Ted Byfield weighed in; he wanted to see Manning to go ahead and organize the party. Byfield offered to help with preparations for the assembly and pledged the editorial resources of *Alberta Report* and *Western Report*. Manning accepted, although he and others among his supporters couldn't fathom whether Ted was still a federalist or wanted to elect MPs who would hold the threat of separation over the federal government to get reform. Then Stan Roberts came to see Manning in Edmonton. He and Francis Winspear had continued to explore political options with Winspear's $50,000 fund and were encouraged by the mood in Manitoba and British Columbia. Yes, he would help organize a big meeting somewhere, and he'd ask Winspear—who had been offering to finance a political alternative—to write the cheque.

Byfield suggested the meeting be held in Vancouver, and started writing promotional material for his magazines and others. His star columnist, Ralph Hedlin, coined the phrase "The West Wants In," which became the theme. Winspear put up another $50,000. Manning and Roberts organized and named the Reform Association of Canada, with a $25 membership fee, to host of the Parliament of the West. Southern Alberta grain farmer Bob Grbavac, a young political activist who was the informal head of an agricultural protest movement that had developed a modest profile, said he'd not only attend the assembly but endorse it and lend his group's support.

Manning ended 1986 with Sandra and the children at Ernest and Muriel's winter home in Arizona. It was a very happy family Christmas, and the last break before the toughest year in his life.

The date for Manning's assembly was set for the weekend of May 29–31, 1987, and a venue selected: Vancouver's Hyatt Regency Hotel. The event was given a ponderous, weighty name: The Western Assembly on Canada's Economic and Political Future. Manning, Muir and Roberts became the steering committee. Speakers accepted invitations, memberships started to flow in and delegate recruiting got under way.

The political establishment reacted with hostility. Prime Minister Mulroney warned his caucus that no Conservative was to attend. Western Tory cabinet ministers and MPs, furious that Manning would not give them the time they said they needed to prove that they could influence national policy, charged that the organizers were extremists. The western provincial premiers ignored the budding movement, the tactic they had successfully applied to the separatist Western Canada Concept and Confederation of Regions movements.

National newsrooms ignored the event. The regional coverage in the West was divided: the Alberta papers treated the assembly as another meeting of the angry and alienated. Political reporters in Manning's home province thought him a dull, plodding economist with a political past in a party that was dead and buried. The preassembly coverage in British Columbia was more courteous, but reserved. The Reform Association was treated as an Alberta-based prairie phenomenon. Byfield's support was hardly a help: by now *Alberta Report* was engaged in a running ideological battle with the major newspaper and electronic media chains over almost every issue on the public agenda.

The steering committee had foreseen the issue of the movement's credibility. New movements attracted the political margin and were vulnerable to being taken over by extremists. To screen attendance, a stiff $200 registration fee and a "pay your own way" policy for delegates were imposed that would turn this into a $1,500 to $2,500 unsubsidized weekend (including air fare) for those from outside Vancouver. They created an "official delegate" status that required a nomination from a grassroots citizens' meeting that would be reviewed by a nominating committee. The organizers wanted sixty official delegates from each of the four western provinces and would themselves select sixty "at large" participants. They wanted a hall full of serious, recognizable people and, they hoped, none of the hard-core, unrepentant western separatists, Ayran racists, anti-French-language bigots and violent militias hanging around the fringe of western Canadian politics, looking for a political vehicle to ride in those turbulent times.

Some hardball-playing political groups on the periphery had just enough members, money and organizing skill to take over Manning's Parliament of the West. The organizers were keenly aware of the radical fringe in western politics, and planned to screen it out. The outcome of the recruiting drive was 58 official delegates from British Columbia, 100 from Alberta, 38 from Saskatchewan and Manitoba combined, 350 hand-picked delegates at large, 23 speakers, presenters and observers (including a handful of independent-minded MPs and provincial MLAs who defied party cautions not to attend) and 100 journalists, supporters who couldn't get official-delegate status and other curious hangers-on. The radical elements that the organizers feared would get through the filtering process were not in evidence during the weekend.

In the process to ensure suitable delegates and screen out those who would damage its credibility, the Reform Association had initiated a tiny breeze that would soon return a whirlwind of criticism. The leadership of this grassroots movement had a degree of control over its assembly that contradicted its aspiration to be a populist movement. The paradox was difficult for sympathetic outsiders to understand, and critics turned it against the Reform Association. Why did the Reform Association not want to hear from all the grassroots? For twenty years Manning had practised solitary politics—reading, thinking and writing. He had arrived at organizational ideas and policy prescriptions to which he'd committed himself, and he did not change his mind easily. When he stepped into the public arena, he demonstrated a propensity for command and control that he explained as a desire to protect his movement's credibility by distancing it from the wrecking crews of political change. It was, however, interpreted by Conservative politicians and most political journalists as Manning's insistence on getting his own way.

In screening the delegates through so fine a filter, the steering committee had screened out some of the creative energy and adrenaline surging through the region. The nominating process produced a room full of affluent political junkies, policy wonks and dropouts from the mainstream parties. These were mostly white, middle-aged men. There was more grey hair and fewer people of colour than in the population at large. No one seemed poor or afflicted. The presentations were eye-glazing in detail; too many numbers and too few flashes of political passion. The coffee-time and meal discussions were subdued. Reporters struggled unsuccessfully to find the zeal and fire that prairie populists were supposed to create. The Alberta MLAs who attended returned home to report that the Reform Association was, in cowboy slang, "all hat and no cattle."

Almost in spite of its dull papers, its stiff formality and the caution of its organizers, the weekend established some momentum for the movement. The assembly achieved the important consensus Manning had hoped for: the old federalist parties were finished in the region. The Liberals and New Democrats were a spent force, surviving in isolated pockets that depended on the shifting allegiances of a tiny group of élites. The Tories had failed to meet high western expectations. Injured by the CF-18 fiasco, they had been further wounded on April 30, a month before the Parliament of the West, when Prime Minister Mulroney pressured the first ministers to sign the Meech Lake Accord. The Accord was a formula to get Quebec's signature on the 1981 Constitution by recognizing its linguistic and cultural distinctiveness and giving it several legal prerogatives not available to other provinces: the right to opt out of national programs with financial compensation, control over immigration as it affected the province, a role in Supreme Court appointments and a constitutional veto. Western anger was building against the special status the Accord would give Quebec, and the fact that the province said it would use its constitutional veto to kill Senate reform.

The fresh anger against the Meech Lake Accord energized the assembly's conviction that the Tories were through in the West. Juxtaposed to the negative verdict on the old parties were assembly resolutions that summed up its motto: The West Wants In. The resolutions provided Manning with the populist premises on which the Reform Association could build. These delegates wanted in on terms of unity that were equitable to all provinces, taking into account the distinctive history and political cultures of all regions, including Quebec and the West.

The assembly format, however, looked and felt like the old, controlling politics of any major party's membership convention: the leadership put the followers through some hoops that were supposed to look to the rest of the world like an open process. But the chemistry of politics took over. At the beginning of the weekend, only three hundred delegates made it to the first session and they hung back as if they'd wished they'd never come. The policy sessions drifted. Then on Saturday afternoon, Manning surprised the room.

He had been a mousy presence during the weekend. His platform skills were rusty; he seemed aloof; he had underwhelmed many participants. The sessions on economic policy indicated that this convention was ideologically conservative, pushing for less government, fewer taxes, less spending, freer trade and markets, less business regulation. However, the specific remedies voted on were unrealistic (a Western Canadian Economic Community) or arcane (tax reform) or were rejected by delegates (entrenching economic rights in the Constitution).

In his most nasal tones, Manning had chastised a social policy session for being too narrow. He was out of step with delegates who were there to raise hell about welfare, unemployment insurance and trade unions. He could not forge a consensus on national unity. The delegates split a vote on the Meech Lake Accord. Only the proposal to support the Triple-E Senate received approbation.

When he stood up to the podium on Saturday afternoon he talked for forty minutes, breathing life into the history of western protest and Canadian reform and offering to expand "the great tradition" established by past protest movements and third parties. In cadences that reminded elderly delegates of Tommy Douglas and William Aberhart, he offered a party that would make the West its priority in a broadly inclusive, positive, visionary program that would move beyond old divisions between left and right. This was not another splinter party, he said, but a voice for populist energies that already existed: "The West is in deep trouble economically, but no existing party makes our needs its number one priority. The West is in need of a new instrument to advance new solutions."

To delegates, weary of a decade of conflict with Ottawa in which the West was always the loser, Manning gave the elixir that always works in politics: he gave them hope. In the next election, barely two years away, they could change things. It was the defining moment of a convention that otherwise would have failed, leaving Manning on the political sidelines for a very long time.

On Sunday morning, 77 per cent of the delegates endorsed the formation of a new political party and agreed to meet again in the autumn to pick a leader and a name, set policy, craft an election platform and organize the financing of a campaign in 1988. The weekend's critics said the outcome of the vote was carefully orchestrated by organizers, but the steering committee had had serious doubts about the outcome even after Manning's speech. Sunday afternoon, six hundred noisy, backslapping delegates and gatecrashers cheered when Manning promised, "What we are doing here this weekend and in the months to come will establish the western fact in Canadian Confederation."

After the assembly, Sandra flew back to Edmonton; the Manning children now faced years of nights without one or both of their parents, and she needed to break the news to them in person. Manning and *Alberta Report* editor Kenneth Whyte spent the evening together watching the Edmonton Oilers win the final game of the 1987 Stanley Cup final against the Philadelphia Flyers. For Manning, an avid Oiler partisan, the 3–2 score and the assembly's endorsement of a new party made the day a double victory.

On June 3, the premiers and the prime minister endorsed the formal constitutional amendment to implement Meech Lake; now it had to be voted on in the provincial legislatures. The angry debate in the West gave a profile to the Reform Association and its issues as it prepared to pick a new leader. Manning confirmed that he would be a candidate for party leadership when it met again in Winnipeg.

In his keynote speech at the Vancouver Assembly, Manning promised a new federalist, nationally based, ideologically balanced party drawing enough support to contest the 1988 election on short notice. It would not just split the Conservative vote. It would harness the western political energy that had rejected the major parties but could not endorse separatism. By October 30, 1987, when the Reform Association convened in the Winnipeg Convention Centre, it was evident to delegates, journalists and observers that it had settled for much less. The vision may have been sound, but the penny-bright optimism about how fast it would happen had been misplaced.

The would-be political party was an Alberta- and British Columbia–dominated organization. Manning knew that three-quarters of his following were disaffected Progressive Conservatives. It had not attracted enough members of less than forty years of age or women. It was almost uniformly white. It had attracted a strong following of neo-conservatives, a new Canadian breed of fiscal conservatives who wanted to reduce the size and role of government, lower its spending, balance its budgets and pay off its accumulated debt. In spite of recruitment and screening efforts to keep the party out of the hands of special-interest groups, powerful lobbies had joined its ranks, including gun-control advocates, victims-of-crime groups and members of the religious right, which planned to take control of the party for causes such as the abolition of legal abortion.

Manning was ambivalent about the trade-off he was being forced to make between an open party and control over fringe elements. He was criticized for measures that filtered members and criticized when supporters expressed extremist sentiments on matters such as immigration and crime. He had not found the means for the Reform Association to be inclusive and to impose discipline on its fringe element, and it was hurting his cause. "Preston was a very likable fellow, but the people he attracted were very scary. You might like his ideas, but his followers gave you the shivers," a professional woman who dropped out of the party early recalled a decade later.

Meanwhile, western Tory MPs and cabinet ministers were winning the argument that the Conservative Party should be given time to prove the Mulroney government could deliver for the region. The West would be the biggest beneficiary of the federal government's free-trade negotiations with the United States. The economy was improving in British Columbia and Alberta. And if the Liberal leader, John Turner, was no Pierre Trudeau in charismatic appeal, he was also quite obviously more western in his outlook and empathies. The Reform Association placed a political alternative on the table, and the West took a last, hard look at the politicians and parties it already had. The movement had already suffered its first defection: farmer Bob Grbavac had quit to seek a federal Liberal nomination.

In retrospect, Manning misjudged the mood of the West in 1987; the anger was not as widespread as it had seemed in the aftermath of the CF-18 debacle. He also misjudged the way in which politics had changed since the halcyon days of prairie populism and pre-Confederation reform. In a pluralistic, urbanized society, the demographics were more complex, the electorate more skeptical and their sense of political identity more ambiguous. A new prairie fire would not sweep out of the West overnight. And he did not yet have at his disposal the kind of talent that could mount a winning political campaign. Manning was leading a pack of neophytes; the limited political experience in the ranks was largely that of cast-offs who had failed to make the cut in the mainstream parties. All of these flaws became apparent over time. At the Winnipeg assembly, however, there was a consensus that Reformers weren't going to change the face of politics yet.

The makeup of the 305 voting delegates registered for the Winnipeg assembly revealed Reform's structural problems. One hundred and forty were from Alberta and 90 from British Columbia. Only 10 came from Saskatchewan. The 65 from Manitoba reflected the much lower costs for local delegates. There were few women (and those present were older and wealthy) and no people of colour or delegates less than 40 years of age. This was a party of grey hair, white skin, long pants and thick wallets.

At Winnipeg, Manning also faced a showdown over his leadership of the party from Stan Roberts, who had the financial backing of Francis Winspear, recognized as the Reform Association's most important patron and patriarch. In the intervening months since Vancouver, Roberts had developed a visceral dislike for Manning and a grave suspicion of the Christian evangelicals whom he accused Manning of preferring as working partners. Winspear also was put off by Manning's strong faith. He was in populist politics because his high school math teacher and guidance counsellor, William Aberhart, had figuratively kicked him in the buttocks until he'd gotten passing grades and developed a responsible attitude to his future. When Winspear became an accountant and made millions in business, he credited Aberhart's mentoring. But he did not share his teacher's religion: Winspear was a professed agnostic who had thoroughly studied the world's great religions and had a strong moral compass but thought religious people were foolish. What he thought of Manning personally Winspear kept to himself, for the time being, but he endorsed Roberts as the able and appropriate leader.

With Winspear's backing in the form of a $25,000 contribution, Roberts produced a relatively polished campaign, with posters, a trademark scarf for his delegates and a well-stocked bar in a hospitality suite. Roberts did not get a great deal of media scrutiny; they were forgiving of his obvious ambition and his plastic, partisan past as an ex-Liberal. He was the opponent, the guy who'd give Manning his comeuppance, so going into the convention the media took Roberts seriously. He was cast as the dark horse and the preference of delegates too polite to tell Manning what they really thought of him.

With the exception of *Alberta Report*, journalists covering the assembly said that they did not, as a rule, much care for Preston Manning. His style was not telegenic; they regarded him as too intense, too certain of himself. He was the politically privileged blue blood; his followers were people who did not like the media and lived by different political and cultural values from those of most journalists.

Regardless of Manning's lip service to the open process by which the party intended to pick its leader, it never occurred to him that he would not win the vote. He had urged Ted Byfield to run for the leadership and was not surprised when Roberts declared. But his real interest in credible candidates was cosmetic. He wanted his leadership to come from a credible race the party, the voters and the media would take seriously. He had no intention of letting an opponent actually beat him.

In the intervening months since Vancouver, Manning had chaired the assembly steering committee that had organized the eighty-eight western federal constituencies and nominated delegates. He had not actively campaigned for the leadership and had left it to a few friends to run a committee for him. He spent only $2,000, most on his personal travel to the convention and some on a plain blue button reading: "Manning: A Voice For The West." However, he had been the leader—not just for the five months it took to organize the Winnipeg assembly but also for the eight months it had taken to put Vancouver together. He was already the *de facto* head of the party.

During the first day of business, when delegates formally passed a resolution to form the party, named it the Reform Party of Canada and approved the constitution, Roberts mingled with the delegates, saw numbers of blue Manning buttons and ascertained his own low delegate count. He was on home ground in Manitoba, so he sent his organizers out to find new delegates; he believed that convention rules were loose enough that this was permitted. But he let his plan slip during the candidates' speeches to the delegates that evening. Manning's supporters, including most of the party executive, feared a deluge of instant memberships; it might not unseat Manning, but it would compromise the party—they'd look like a wheeling and dealing gang of partisans. On Saturday morning, the pro-Manning executive counterattacked with a snap resolution to cut off registration seven and a half hours early. Roberts's overnight recruiting drive had fallen well short of the number of delegates he would have needed to make a showing, but he stormed out of the meeting and did not return for a scheduled afternoon policy session. For the rest of the day, he plotted but could devise no strategy. To the media, he accused Manning of manipulating the assembly and of having a following of cranks and small-minded evangelicals.

On Sunday, cooler and sober, Roberts met with Manning, Bob Muir, Francis Winspear and the party's interim president, Jo Anne Hillier.

She recommended that Manning and Roberts serve as coleaders for a year. Roberts wanted a mail ballot taken in six months. Manning said the assembly had come expecting to pick a leader and should be allowed to do so. No decision was reached, but Stan Roberts went immediately to the convention floor and withdrew his candidacy, stating that the integrity of the Reform movement had been compromised. Ray Speaker happened to be chairing the session that Roberts interrupted for his emotional announcement. Speaker coolly called Manning to the podium and asked for a vote acclaiming him as the new leader of the Reform Party of Canada. (Roberts stayed in the party and unsuccessfully ran for nomination as its 1988 candidate for the Vancouver Island riding of Saanich–Gulf Islands. Two years later, he was diagnosed with brain cancer and died suddenly.)

So the auspiciously named Founding Assembly of the Reform Party of Canada ended badly. The newly elected executive committee—chaired by Diane Ablonczy, a young Calgary lawyer, and Gordon Shaw, a retired Imperial Oil executive living in British Columbia—met briefly. The atmosphere was tense, and everyone was very tired and a bit depressed by the manipulative way in which the leadership issue had been resolved. The new leadership took comfort in knowing that the Reform Party of Canada, with more than three thousand members and money in the bank, had survived its first crisis—bloodied but undeterred. It was now something much bigger than an essay in Preston Manning's ubiquitous briefcase. There was a broad leadership base. There were good people seeking candidacy in the election. A couple of fine speeches, one by Manning and one by University of Calgary economist and former Tory Stephen Harper, had unambiguously defined the party as national in its outlook, populist in its roots, western in its foundation and fiscally conservative, with a social conscience. There could be no doubt where it came from, what it stood for and where it was going.

The bad news was that in the party's first crisis, Manning had failed the test of reconciliation. The showdown with Roberts presaged a period when Reform's problems would be with personalities and the threats would be internal.

CHAPTER TWELVE

Turning Points

This is history; naked and unshaped.

— MICHEL DE MONTAIGNE, "On Books," *Essays*

A FTER WINNIPEG, PRESTON Manning's political life alternated between quixotic hope and the mundane truth that there was no groundswell lifting the Reform Party towards the coming election. The West, the nation, was giving the political devils it knew one last chance. After the Vancouver assembly, there had been euphoria, and otherwise sensible people talked of Reform winning thirty to forty seats in the 1988 election. After Winnipeg, there was realism, the task was too monumental and it was too late to organize the kind of complex, modern political campaign necessary for victory.

In the autumn of 1987, the Mulroney government was languishing; its percentage of popular support was in the low 20s. The opposition

NDP and Liberals stood in the mid to high 30 per cent range, separated only by the polls' margin of error. All the evidence, however, was that Canadians were sorting out what to do with the familiar. The nation wore these three parties like an old sweater. The idea of casting the garment off for something new was unsettling.

Preston wound up Manning Consultants—his father retired—and went to work January 1, 1988, as a full-time political leader. Political passions need accountants, lawyers and photocopiers. As the weeks stretched into months, Manning's leadership consisted of dull administrative detail: mailing lists, executive-meeting agendas, fund raising. The offices of Manning Consultants became the head office of the party. David Berger, a business associate of the consulting company, and Jeanie Clemenger, his secretary, segued into new responsibilities as his staff. In Calgary, Stephen Harper became an unpaid policy chief and Bob Muir took on the legal work for fund raising and for transforming the Reform Association into a national party that complied with the Canada Elections Act. Vancouver businessman Ron Gamble opened a British Columbia office. Manning concentrated on nailing down campaign policy positions and finalizing election strategy.

The party council took on constituency development. The executive recruited candidates. They had rudimentary tools: a brochure, a constituency kit and a newsletter. By spring it was certain the party would have enough nominated candidates—fifty—to qualify as a national party for tax purposes. It expected to have nearly complete slates of candidates in Alberta and British Columbia, but its base would stop at the Saskatchewan border.

The national focus in the campaign would clearly be on the Canada-United States Free Trade Agreement. Reform was not going to oppose that; the West stood to make major economic gains. It had, however, found a regional issue with a federalist connection: Senate reform. For several years there'd been a popular nonpartisan movement to amend the Constitution to create the Triple-E Senate: elected, equal representation of the provinces with new legislative powers to make it effective. In a watery bribe to gain ratification of the Meech Lake Accord: the drafters had given a nod to Senate reform as a sop to western opinion, but it was a matter of record that once it had the Meech amendment to the Constitution, Quebec would block the Triple-E reform.

With the help of Alberta grain farmer Bert Brown, who led the nonpartisan Canadian Committee for a Triple-E Senate, the Reform Party drafted a constitutional amendment for a 108 member Senate (ten senators from each province and four from the two territories) to be elected under provincial supervision and with the power to safeguard and enhance regional interests but not to defeat the government in the House of Commons. On May 18, the morning after this draft was completed in Victoria, British Columbia, Manning jumped on a two-car chartered train, dubbed the Constitutional Express, and chugged up Vancouver Island to the resort town of Parksville to gatecrash the western premiers' annual meeting, which was then in session.

Manning was not invited in by the premiers, but after a picnic lunch and outdoor rally in the warm seaside air, Manning handed a leather briefcase, embossed in gold with the words "Western Constitutional Amendment" to an annual meeting official. It contained copies of the draft for each premier. The briefcase was returned, empty, and Manning got a thank-you letter from the meeting's host, British Columbia Premier Bill Vander Zalm. The other politicians treated him as if he didn't exist. Privately, they thought him presumptuous and interfering because he was an as yet unelected and unproved politician, and they continued the practice of disregarding the leaders of the new parties that the 1980s had produced in the West.

A week later, on Friday, May 26, the party's election campaign was unofficially launched when Manning walked into the Edson, Alberta, recreation centre during the lunch hour. There he announced to a small group of three dozen people that he would run as the party's candidate against External Affairs Minister Joe Clark in Yellowhead, the northern half of the redistributed riding of Rocky Mountain that Clark had taken in 1979, 1980 and 1984. The home-town boy was taking on the home-town boy. In practical political terms, it was a serious blunder that exposed Manning's naiveté.

A Reform poll showed that 65 per cent of the riding had never heard of the party; that should have set off warning signals. But 17 per cent knew Manning's name well enough to say they'd vote for him, and only 23 per cent were as yet committed to Clark. Manning fastened his hope on the 32 per cent undecided and the 30 per cent who could not name their MP. He ignored Joe Clark's huge pluralities in previous elections: in 1984 Clark won by a margin of 30,000 votes. He ignored Clark's high level of name recognition. Manning did not seem to realize that preelection polls have a large component of vote-parking by respondents who usually vote for the same party they did the last time. When people saw Clark's name on their ballot, the outcome would be secured.

Manning's poll was, typically, an amateur one complied by volunteers and without the interpretive skill of a seasoned pollster. Other, more reliable data were telling Reform organizers their best shot was in Alberta seats where the incumbent was not running. Manning had always promised to conduct politics differently. Now instead of selecting a safer riding, in which he was more likely to gain an all-important first seat in the House of Commons, he was going to make a point. The most successful prime ministers had swallowed their pride and run in obscure places to meet their obligation to lead from within the House of Commons. But Manning was going to teach Joe Clark a lesson.

The former prime minister, he said, had lost touch with the riding, hardly visited it and no longer spoke for it on many issues. Clark "epitomizes the kind of politician who moves away from the values of his electors in order to gain stature in the party. By running against him I can bring this issue to the forefront and at least get people to think about it," Manning said.

Clark turned the confrontation by depicting the campaign as an opportunity to show the riding how "Albertans can lead Canada," pitting his track record against Manning's ambition. And so the campaign unfolded. At 10:00 A.M. on October 1, a chill, overcast autumn day in Ottawa, Governor-General Jeanne Sauvé welcomed Brian Mulroney at the crackling hearth of her official home. They exchanged pleasantries and conducted the formalities. The thirty-third Parliament was dissolved and the general election set for November 21.

The Reform Party had candidates in 72 of 89 ridings in the West and twelve hundred members. The only glaring gaps were in Saskatchewan and the Territories. They'd done an official campaign launch in August with a special policy session organized in Calgary by Stephen Harper. Then they hit the ridings. Manning found it an ordeal; the party struggled with the mechanics of campaigning. There was no money to spare, no television advertising, no professional polling. Was the party on its way down or on its way up from the Vancouver assembly just a year and a half earlier?

Manning talked up Senate reform and the Constitution—issues Joe Clark characterized as "on the margins of the national agenda." The rest of the West, the rest of the country, talked about free trade. Liberal leader John Turner turned that into a debate on patriotism and the callousness of the market economy. The resulting examination of ideologies and values proved to be the last time Canadians were satisfied with the alternatives tendered by three national parties that could claim an electoral base across the country.

In British Columbia, Manning had his first battle with the extremists who coveted his party, in the person of cantankerous newspaper columnist Doug Collins, whose reputation for intolerance of immigrants of colour, Jews, and gays was—for all his disingenuous protests to the contrary—perceived as racist and homophobic. Collins thought Preston Manning was a wimp, "a good Sunday school teacher but not tough enough to be a political leader." Collins won the Reform nomination, over the leader's public objection, in the West Vancouver riding of Capilano Sound. Manning refused to sign his nomination papers and effectively booted him out of the party. The clash gave him the first taste of the media's lash: in addition to being caricatured as red-neck for its gun-control and criminal-justice policies, Reform was now being pigeonholed as extremist, racist and nutty.

Manning spent the final weekend of the campaign in Edson; he and Sandra had their sons, David and Nate, with them. They checked into a motel to watch the results. The party polled 275,000 votes and elected no MPs. Manning ran second to Joe Clark, with 29 per cent of the vote. In sports, folks say that statistics are for losers, and Manning took what comfort he could in the numbers. In Alberta, the party got 15 per cent of the vote, running third behind the Tories and NDP. Nine Reformers finished second in their ridings. In British Columbia, Reform had five per cent of the vote; in Saskatchewan and Manitoba, the 22,000 votes split among sixteen candidates were negligible.

Reform's only perceptible impact on the electoral map in the Alberta base was Edmonton East, where they split the Tory vote and New Democrat Ross Harvey was elected. This was the first crack in the Tory Alberta hegemony since 1972. In six British Columbia ridings, angry Conservatives blamed Reform vote-splitting for the election of New Democrats. In the result, the NDP provided the surprise in the West, electing thirty-three of its forty-three-member caucus in the region. But it had no seats east of Ontario. The Liberals had only eight seats in the West, five of those in Manitoba. Manning interpreted the result as the erosion of regionalism doing its quiet work; in 1988 two of the three mainstream parties were finished as national forces. He thought the Reform Party had staying power.

The Tories were gloating at the outcome and sneering at the Reform candidates, but that just seemed to stiffen the resolve of many members. The party's supporters had voted with their wallets, giving $1.6 million, which meant the party finished the campaign and the year in the black. On that score they'd beaten both the Liberals and NDP. And between the election and year end, the membership grew by 25 per cent.

The 1988 campaign had been a stiff workout. It set the tone for the next ten years: nothing was going to come easily. However, the executive, the candidates and a core of several thousand volunteers were sticking around. No one was acting as if they felt whipped, even if some postelection media commentary treated Reform as a one-time thing that had come and gone.

The party had learned some important things about itself. Its natural constituency had two ideological boundaries: the Constitution—Western federalism and Senate reform—had been the draw, but the people who'd come in were a new breed of conservative. Reform was, apparently, the natural home of neoconservatives, Canadians interested solely in balancing budgets and paying off public debt by cutting the role and size of government.

Almost at once, the neoconservative influence—a form of single-issue politics that he wanted to avoid—made the party less inclusive than Manning had originally envisioned it. Because social conservatives and neoconservatives had a symbiotic relationship, the party drew in strong interest groups with an agenda of social-issues reform. The success of one such faction, the victims of crime, gave Reform a criminal-justice agenda of tougher sentences, harsher young offenders' law and a referendum on the restoration of capital punishment. Another faction got it committed on gun control. The religious right was less

successful; the party remained wary of an activist antiabortion commitment, promising only a national referendum to settle that issue as well.

Manning claimed his reform agenda was ideologically neutral. He
was first interested in changing the political process to make it more
populist—through Senate and parliamentary reform—so that laws
would be made to reflect "the common sense of the common people."
He wanted popular opinion, not political élites, including the leadership of the Reform Party, to resolve fiscal and social issues. To maintain
credibility, he fended off extremists like Doug Collins, whose opinions
he found egregious and not reflective of popular opinion, but he
claimed not to control the natural policy-making processes of the party.
He accepted the policy commitments it made as a reflection of its
grassroots. One thing that hadn't caught on in the party was "populism"; Reform Party members were inclined to think of themselves as
Western federalists or neoconservatives, but not citizen democrats.
Manning was the party's only visible self-described populist. There was,
however, tension on policy making within the party because Preston
was the source of its thinking on the dominating areas of constitutional
and fiscal reform. He was accused, from time to time, of manipulating
the party's processes to get endorsements for his views. The problem
was, in those early years, that he was the party.

The 1988 results also delineated a strong geographical profile. The
party's natural base was in British Columbia and Alberta. Saskatchewan
and Manitoba would have to be won on the ground. The preoccupation
with making a breakthrough in Ontario to prove that Reform connected to national history and regional political cultures outside the West
obscured the fact that first of all, Reform had to secure the Prairies.

As 1989 opened, Manning was unexpectedly campaigning again;
this time for a by-election in the Alberta riding of Beaver River. The
MP-elect, John Dahmer, had been hospitalized with cancer during the
fall campaign. He died on November 26, and Prime Minister Brian
Mulroney decided on a by-election earlier rather than later in the six-
month window the law gave him to call one. On January 9, 1989, in
the Ukrainian National Hall at Smoky Lake, a farming community east
of Edmonton, the Reform Party nominated thirty-six-year-old school
teacher Deborah Grey as its candidate. Twelve days later, Mulroney set
March 21 as the voting day.

Beaver River stretched from the edge of Edmonton's urban sprawl to the Saskatchewan border, through small towns, mixed farms and poplar forests. The Ukrainian homesteaders favoured this region of Alberta because it reminded them of the steppes: thick grass, gentle rivers cut deep into the plains and extremes of climate—hot, dry summers and bitter winters. Grey taught school in the town of Dewberry, settled by Scottish homesteaders from Ontario after Alberta became a province. On the flatlands north of town, in precontact time, aboriginal hunters set grass fires to trap the buffalo, and the fields were thick with arrowheads in the spring. Vancouver born and educated, Grey loved the parklands and bush of this region. Several kilometres north of Dewberry, across the Saskatchewan River at Frog Lake, she'd had her first teaching job on the Cree reservation.

She'd been recruited to run in the 1988 campaign by the party's vice chairman, Gordon Shaw, during a casual meeting on an airplane between Calgary and Vancouver. He'd struck up a conversation because he saw she was reading a party brochure, given to her by two women who were the party activists in the Dewberry–Smoky Lake district. Grey had run in the constituency and finished fourth in 1988, and was hooked on politics. Although Manning briefly considered running in the by-election, he realized that Grey had developed a following and might win.

Grey was capable of being brash, and she launched her by-election campaign by working the floor at the Conservative nomination of her rival, Redwater real estate salesman David Broda. She worked the riding by the book; Reform had learned a lot in the hard going of the 1988 campaign. Manning also campaigned several days with her. Grey was articulate, funny and warm; in the close quarters of by-election campaigning, with no national overtones and issues, the force of her personality was proving to be a serious danger to the Tories. By February, Conservative polls revealed Broda's vote was weakening and Grey and "undecided" were gaining.

When Prime Minister Mulroney's government proposed the Goods and Services Tax during postelection budget preparations, Grey seized it as an issue. Then Mulroney gave her a second shot at Broda. There was a vacant Senate seat in the province that had become an odd campaign issue. In the Alberta Speech from the Throne in February,

Premier Don Getty's government promised a Senatorial Selection Act. Under it, Alberta would conduct a plebiscite-style vote to determine the name the premier would give the prime minister before a federal Senate vacancy was filled. Under the terms of the pending Meech Lake constitutional amendment, the prime minister would be bound to consider recommendations from the premier of a province before filling a vacancy from that province.

When Mulroney said he'd reject any Senate candidate elected by Albertans in a plebiscite, the by-election campaign was all but over. Grey would be elected to send a message to Mulroney that the people of Beaver River didn't think much of his attitude to Albertans who wanted to vote on their candidate for the Senate seat. Why Mulroney injected himself into the issue is a puzzle. Shortly after the Throne Speech, Premier Getty called a provincial election for March 20, and the proposed legislation died. Had Mulroney kept silent, the Tories might have held Beaver River.

On March 13, Grey won a landslide with 51 per cent of the vote and a margin of 4,200 votes over Broda. Less than two years after its formation, the Reform Party had its first MP: a young professional woman of modest means who broke the party's wealthy-white-male stereotype. It was Manning's great good fortune that she was the nonpartisan, non-ideological product of a grassroots draft: an authentic populist. There weren't many Manning-style citizen democrats in the party's candidate pool—she just happened to be one of them. The leader was also fortunate that Grey was instinctively pragmatic and a team player. She could sit in Parliament and take the media scrutiny without undermining his leadership and his position as an acclaimed party leader and politician who'd lost the only two elections in which he'd ever run.

There was a celebratory dinner on March 18 in Calgary for Grey, attended by Preston, Sandra, Ernest and Muriel Manning and hosted by Stanley C. Waters, a Winnipeg-born, sixty-eight-year-old retired Canadian Armed Forces general. Waters had battlefield service with a commando unit in Italy and Europe during the Second World War, and had commanded the Canadian Army from 1973 to 1975. He had lived in Calgary for nine years, working as president of the Mannix family's principal enterprise, the Loram Group. Before retiring in 1989, he'd helped Fred Mannix Jr. set up the Bowfort Group, a venture-capital

operation. Waters had joined the Reform Party after becoming disillu-
sioned with the Conservatives, for whom he had been a fund raiser.
His role as the host of the Grey victory dinner marked his rising
influence in the party. He was soon to be Preston Manning's next
political star.

In 1989, Don Getty's year was off to a bad start. His government had
been re-elected, but he'd lost his Edmonton Whitemud seat and been
forced to run in a snap by-election in the rural riding of Stettler. A
revival of the Senatorial Selection Act pleased him on two grounds: it
restored his popular appeal and it let him poke a finger in Brian
Mulroney's eye for the prime minister's brusque repudiation of the idea
in the spring.

The election of Alberta senators was, in fact, solidly entrenched in
provincial Conservative policy. The Triple-E Senate had been endorsed
by the party's annual meeting in 1984, and a select legislative committee on Senate reform recommended it to Premier Peter Lougheed in
1985. Lougheed demurred, but the Canadian Committee for the
Triple-E Senate, whose Alberta membership and funding were largely
Conservative, was formed that year in the village of Kathyrn, north of
Calgary.

When Getty succeeded Lougheed, he made his support of Triple-E
a signature piece of policy to differentiate himself from his predecessor.
Getty had disappointed the Triple-E committee by not trading senate
reform for his signature on the Meech Lake Accord, but he did persuade Mulroney to agree to appoint senators from lists provided by the
premiers. When Ontario and Quebec refused Getty's proposal in
August 1988 to attend a first ministers' conference on Senate reform,
Getty responded by inserting the Senatorial Selection Act into the 1989
Throne Speech and reintroducing it after the election. On August 18,
1989, the Act was proclaimed and Getty called a plebiscite for October
16, the day of municipal voting, to determine his recommendation to
the prime minister for Alberta's Senate vacancy. The Meech Lake
agreement allowed him to send the prime minister a list of recommendations; Getty said his list would have one name—the name voters
picked in October. On August 28, the Reform Party nominated Stan
Waters as its candidate; a few days later, the Reform Party filed its
application to become a provincial party—legally a requirement to

have a candidate on the Senate ballot. The petition carried fifteen thousand names of eligible Alberta voters.

Senate reform had become a Reform Party issue in the 1988 federal election campaign, and Waters was the odds-on favourite. His only serious opponent was Bert Brown, the chairman of the Canadian Committee for a Triple-E Senate and a lifetime Conservative. However, Brown was handicapped by the rising unpopularity of the federal Tories and his connection to Don Getty, whose public support was sliding so badly that the knives were out for him in his own party. The NDP, which advocated the abolition of the Senate, ignored the campaign, and the Liberals appointed lawyer William Code, a party veteran organizer and fund raiser, as their candidate.

As he had with Deborah Grey's by-election, Manning made sure this campaign was run by the book. The party spent $250,000, used television advertising for the first time, blanketed the province's households with a brochure and sent Waters out on a tour that exceeded in intensity and exposure any past premier's campaigns. Waters was well liked by journalists and presented himself effectively on television and in print interviews. Manning also toured, giving stump speeches and introducing Waters at dozens of functions. The Reform Party of Canada was learning how to campaign, use volunteers and raise money; the amateur demeanour of the 1988 federal election was all but forgotten. In the final days, when it was clear that Waters was winning, the campaign captured some of the invigorating presence that autumn brings to Alberta.

On Monday, October 16, Waters polled 620,000 votes, 42 per cent of those cast. He was 120,000 votes ahead of Bill Code and 130,000 ahead of Bert Brown. Early in the evening, Don Getty called to congratulate the victor and invited Waters and Manning to meet him in Edmonton the following day.

The three men compared notes on their respective stratagems to pressure Prime Minister Mulroney to accept the results and appoint Waters to the vacancy. Getty would draft a letter to Mulroney immediately. Waters, Grey and Manning would hold a news conference in Ottawa that week. On Friday, Getty's letter landed on Mulroney's desk. "The people of Alberta have selected Mr. Stanley Charles Waters as the person to represent them in the Canadian Senate. I urge you to appoint

Mr. Waters without delay." Delay he did, until June 11, 1990, 238 days after the senatorial selection ballot. The polite but cool reception that Waters received in Ottawa that Friday afternoon was the first indication that Ottawa insiders anticipated what Mulroney was up to. Waters was philosophical; he had learned how Ottawa worked when he commanded the Canadian Army and organized peace-keeping missions. He called it Fumble on the Rideau. So he went back to Western Canada and established himself as a spokesman for Senate reform and the subtle subtext of the Triple-E Senate movement: national unity based on equality of the regions and provinces.

There is no fairness in politics. Waters, the Reform Party and Preston Manning had won Alberta's first and only senatorial selection ballot. But the victory had been paid for by Bert Brown and Don Getty. Their grace and style contrasted sharply with the mean-spiritedness of Brian Mulroney, who would delay eight months before capitulating to the decision made by Albertans on October 16. As he delayed, the Reform Party felt divided emotions; Mulroney's attitude was destroying his party's voter base in Alberta and contributing to its erosion in British Columbia. Waters was possibly more valuable waiting outside the Senate than he would be inside.

Mulroney had his reasons: Meech Lake was not yet ratified and there was a great deal of hostility in the federal establishment—that well-defined circle of politicians, journalists, political appointees and politically connected public-service employees who lunch during the week within the sound of the Peace Tower carillon—to what audacious Alberta had done. "Alberta, the volcano of extraordinary remedy," the late Bruce Hutchison, one of their own, once wrote. Mulroney was advised that to appoint Waters would create a backlash in Quebec that would undermine Premier Robert Bourassa's tenuous position as coauthor of the Accord. With apocalyptic certainty, the Tories believed that this was "the last chance" to save Canada. Mulroney asked his advisors, why didn't the West seem prepared make the usual sacrifice on behalf of the greater good? It always had in the past.

Many westerners, however, opposed Meech as an intolerable concession to Quebec, which would take the advantages of the Accord, concede nothing in return (least of all Senate reform for the West) and come back for more in what its future premier Jacques Parizeau described in the autumn of the Alberta Senate plebiscite as "the endless trip to the dentist." Mulroney erred twice in judging the western mood when he procrastinated on the Senate appointment to save the Accord. As Manning interpreted these events, Canada's regionalism was destroying the old parties. In the West, the old alienation of more than a century of protest and third-party movements was dying. It was being replaced by a tough, new federalism that offered an ultimatum for constitutional reform—equal provinces and equality of all citizens. The Reform Party was the mouthpiece for that prescription.

CHAPTER THIRTEEN # The Touchstone

Yet come it will, the day decreed by fate.
The day when thou, Imperial Troy, must bend
And see thy warriors fall, thy glories end.

— HOMER, *The Odyssey*

IN THE LATE summer and early autumn of 1989, as Stan
Waters's nomination and campaign for Alberta senatorial
selection were being organized, Manning and his family
moved to Calgary. The Reform Party needed a larger, better organized
headquarters. Calgary was the logical base: a stronger Reform city than
Edmonton with more votes and membership, and financial and logisti-
cal resources. It was easier to fly to Vancouver and Ottawa. Bob Muir
worked in Calgary, as did Cliff Fryers, a rising influence and soon to be
party chairman; Gordon Shaw, a former Calgary-based Imperial Oil
executive who now lived in Vancouver, was frequently in town on personal business. This was Stephen Harper's home, although he was tem-
porarily in Ottawa working in Deborah Grey's office; major financial

and organizational supporters such as Jack and Sheila Mackenzie and Ellen and R. Campbell Todd lived in the city. The media were more sympathetic, and when the 1988 election results were analyzed, it was evident that Manning should run in a Calgary riding in the next election. Independent oil executive Jack Pirie gave Manning office space at Sabre Petroleum, and the Reform Party set up its modest shop in it.

The Mannings sold their acreage in the Sturgeon River Valley and purchased a home in a prosperous southwest Calgary neighbourhood. Shortly afterwards, Ernest and Muriel also sold their home in Edmonton and, after an absence of fifty-three years, returned to the city where they'd met, married and been caught up in politics to spend their last years close to their son's family. Over the next two years, Andrea entered the University of Calgary to study prelaw; Avryll registered at the Mount Royal College nursing program, Mary Joy joined the Calgary Aquabelles synchronized swim team and took classes at Bishop Carroll, a Catholic high school with a flexible class schedule that attracted many of the city's young national and Olympic amateur athletes. The boys attended the Glenmore Christian Academy, a private school. The entire family, including Grandpa Ernest and Grandma Muriel, joined the First Alliance Church, a mainstream Christian and Missionary Alliance evangelical congregation with a reputation for supporting foreign Christian missions. Part of the appeal of this church for Preston and Sandra was the focus, style and content of its program for adolescents. The five Manning children enjoyed the ambience and responded to the influence; First Alliance Church was a factor in the decision of all five to make at least one major summer trip overseas to work with various Christian missionary enterprises.

Sandra took charge of the business of the family's transition. Manning prepared for the party's annual assembly, set to be held in Edmonton two weeks after the Alberta senatorial vote. It was time to consolidate the gains made since the 1988 general election. Manning wanted to cement his position as the leading federalist in Western Canada and chief challenger to the federal status quo.

In the cascade of events since the flash point autumn of 1986 and the catalytic meeting in Jim Gray's office, the Reform Party had grown from a sixteen-page idea in Preston Manning's briefcase to an influential force in western politics. It had, however, more energy than shape. To build a ballot-box coalition strong enough to carry him from where he was—the leader of a curious movement—to where he wanted to be—sitting in the House of Commons as the Official Opposition after the next election—Manning needed a touchstone, a major-league franchise. This meant he must find a single clear defining issue and build from it to articulate and sell a political identity and purpose strong enough to attract votes from politically undecided voters and supporters of traditional parties in addition to his initial base of the angry and the disaffected.

The Reform Party was an expression of frustration: federal politics needed fixing; Ottawa should be torn down and rebuilt. The Party was also an expression of hope: an alternative to western separatism. The things that defined it looked like unconnected seamounts breaking the surface of an ocean—Triple-E Senate reform, a new populist style of conducting politics, gaining fiscal control of government. There was nothing to delineate the size and power of the geological forces below the surface pushing the peaks into view.

The party was antiestablishment. The slogan "The West Wants In" was outsiders' cant. When party members made the case for selecting Stan Waters as Alberta's nominee to the Senate, they used the catch phrase "If you want Ottawa reformed send real Reformers." But that covered a lot of ground. If nothing else, it was counterproductive to Manning's objectives because the lack of clarity was taken by the fringe—from holocaust deniers to violence-advocating antiabortionists—as an invitation to come into the tent.

The Vancouver and Winnipeg founding assemblies had been energized by an ill-defined anger at Ottawa stemming from the National Energy Program and CF-18 decision. The meetings drew support from strong federalists disenchanted with the old parties and also had the endorsement of soft separatists. Fiscal and social conservatives who had specific quarrels with Ottawa attended. So did a large number of neophytes who'd never engaged in politics, but because of a litany of grievances—Meech Lake, criminal justice, gun control, the CF-18s—were now up off the couch and volunteering in the party. Manning and his organizers also fretted over constant rumours of extremists—racist, anti-gay, antifrancophone, and the like—who wanted to hijack the party for various causes, although the unsavoury fringe seldom showed its face.

What drew and held these diverse interests together from 1987 to 1989 was the party's antiestablishmentarianism. When political scientists put pen to paper on the subject of Reform, they cited it as an example of the West's history of protest and alienation. The founding of Reform did not draw support from the centre or left. The left had its party of protest: the NDP. People who were middle-of-the-road on economic and social policy continued to support the mainstream parties. They viewed Manning as an outsider. In the West, with its history of splinter politics, outsiders were treated by the established parties, especially the premiers, as unstable and unpredictable.

The Alberta senatorial selection ballot gave Manning a wedge issue—the Triple-E Senate—that enabled voters to grasp the difference between Reform and older parties. Its candidate won because a majority of voters understood that Waters's appointment would put the West's voice in the enemy camp and provide a platform for the West's prescription for constitutional change. Westerners saw Senate reform as the other side of a constitutional package acceptable to Quebec—a counterweight to the concentration of federal political power in the two central Canadian provinces.

When 1,000 Reformers gathered in Edmonton during the last weekend in October for the assembly, the party had grown to 30,000 members (17,000 in Alberta, 10,000 in British Columbia and 3,000 in Saskatchewan and Manitoba). It had raised $3 million in two years and was closing 1989 with $200,000 in the bank. It had been seasoned in a federal election in which it had run 72 candidates. It had the Beaver River by-election and senatorial selection plebiscite victories under its belt. A December Angus Reid poll reported that in Alberta, Reform stood first in popularity among the four federal parties with 25 per cent support; the NDP second at 19, Liberals third at 18 and the Tories last at 17 per cent.

The country was rife with speculation that weekend that the Meech Lake Accord would fail to get the approval of all ten provincial legislatures before the mid-1990 deadline. Prime Minister Mulroney and the premiers of the ten provinces had signed the Accord back on June 3, 1987, with the understanding the premiers would get it ratified by their legislatures quickly. But nearly two years had passed, and there were still three holdouts: the New Brunswick, Manitoba and Newfoundland legislatures, all crucial because new governments and new premiers had been elected since the Accord was first signed. The impending constitutional crisis promoted further speculation that Quebec Premier Robert Bourassa would be destroyed politically by the rejection of Meech, which contained terms for Quebec's concurrence with the 1981 Constitution Act that amounted to special status for Quebec. With Bourassa gone, his province could fall, again, into the hands of separatists.

Opposition to Meech in the West had several threads. The Accord was élitist, created behind closed doors, without any national debate or groundwork. Although in its preamble the Accord paid lip service to equality of the provinces, its rigid constitutional amending formula guaranteed that Quebec would veto Senate reform in perpetuity while gaining five points of constitutional empowerment—acknowledging its special status over other provinces, Reform critics said.

Opinion in the country was running against the Accord. Even in Quebec, more people rejected than accepted it. In the West, opposition ran above 60 per cent in the polls. Meanwhile, Mulroney was delaying a decision on the vacant Alberta Senate seat, though polls taken at the end of 1989 and early in 1990 showed half of all Canadians, including between 55 and 60 per cent in Ontario and British Columbia and two-thirds in the Prairies, supported Senate reform.

Edmonton's Convention Centre is perched on the top of the escarpment above the North Saskatchewan River and commands a breathtaking view of the city's southern urbanscape. Here, with that inspiring view to lift it above the ordinary, the national crosscurrents and the conflicting pressures within the party met with the intensity and excitement of an open convention floor, the place where political parties mark their milestones. On the last weekend in October 1989, in the company of the one thousand registered delegates to the party's oversold fourth assembly, Manning found his franchise: preserving national unity with a new federalism from the West.

Reform was at the crossroads of a decision on expanding into provincial politics. Two election victories in Alberta created a tempting possibility that the party could organize to run in the next Alberta election. It had taken 42 per cent of the vote in the senatorial selection ballot, and polls showed that Reform led all the provincial parties in support. Don Getty was a weak premier. Conventional wisdom held that parties have a better chance federally if they have provincial premiers, caucuses and organizational machines.

Manning demurred. The party owed Getty a debt for going ahead with the Senatorial Selection Act over objections within the Conservative party; to run against him would be needlessly ruthless and tasteless. More than that, Waters wasn't in the Senate yet; Reform needed Getty's pressure on Mulroney to make that decision. The Alberta premier was an ally, not an enemy. Manning also needed Alberta Conservatives in the coalition he was building for the next election. The West, with its history of third-party provincial governments, had several generations of voters who voted for the provincial grassroots parties—Social Credit, CCF or NDP—and Liberal or Conservative federally. Manning planned in 1990 to court Liberal and NDP supporters as well as the Tories. Starting a provincial party would preempt tactical efforts to create greater inclusiveness.

The party existed to form a federal government and had set itself a deadline of the year 2000 by inserting a sunset clause into its constitution that required a future plebiscite of the members to continue past that year. In spite of the right-wing orientation of Reform's core supporters, it would have to move to the centre to win enough seats in the House of Commons to reach its goal. Until the party was more mature, better positioned in the centre and more experienced at dealing with the inevitable internal ideological conflicts that mainstream parties face, provincial politics was a potential trap. Manning and his inner circle crafted a clever stratagem, one that kept the options open and offended no one. The assembly ordered the leadership to form an Alberta Task Force on the Reform of Provincial Politics to investigate the costs, benefits and mechanisms for future engagement in provincial affairs. The delegates also rejected a resolution that the party remain a western regional organization and reaffirmed the mandate to organize a national party for the next election.

On Saturday night, Manning gave the assembly the most important speech of his young political career. It defined his political purpose and identity and set the course of the party. Sandra has often said of her husband that he arrives at his ideas carefully and once committed does not change his mind. In preparing his notes, he'd gone back to Carl

Sandburg's great biographical work on Lincoln, revisiting the story of the rise of the American Republican Party in 1858 as a prescription for the divisions that eventually led the Union into civil war. The Republicans were a regional party formed in the West, the states of Jefferson's Louisiana purchase. The Republicans had the new ideas and new energy in American politics, and by 1861 had won a national following and elected America's first western president—Lincoln. It was Lincoln's destiny to preserve the Union in its great secessionist crisis; Sandburg believed that no president from the North could have done so in face of the insurrection in the South.

Manning recounted for the delegates twenty-five years of Liberal and Conservative policies and decisions to address relations between Quebec and the rest of Canada. The underlying assumption of centralist prime ministers had been that Ottawa, not the Quebec National Assembly, protected "the French fact in Canada."

> Has this approach produced a more united, less divided Canada? No, it has not. Has this approach produced a more contented Quebec? No, it has not. Has this approach reduced the use of Quebec separatism as a threat to wring more concessions out of the rest of Canada? No, it has not. Has this approach engendered in Quebec politicians an emotional as well as economic commitment to Canada? No, it has not. Has this approach produced in Canadians a new sense of national identity, pride and purpose sufficient to guide us into the 21st Century? No, it has not.
>
> As a great reformer [Lincoln] once said long ago, "a house divided against itself cannot stand." . . . Leadership demands that we rise to our feet in the federal political arena, and say at least three things on behalf of Western Canadians.
>
> First: We do not want to live, nor do our children want to live, in a house divided against itself, particularly one divided along racial and linguistic lines.
>
> Second: We do not want nor do we intend to leave this house ourselves, even though we have spent most of our constitutional lives on the back porch. We will, however, insist that it cease to be divided.
>
> Third: Either all Canadians, including the people of Quebec,

make a clear commitment to Canada as one nation, or Quebec and the rest of Canada had better explore whether there exists a better but more separate relationship between the two.

In short we say that living in one Canada united on certain principles, or living with a greater constitutional separation between Quebec and the rest of Canada, is preferable to living in a "house divided."

Our preference is for a united Canada in which Quebec is prosperous and culturally secure. The loss of Quebec will diminish Canada. If, however, we continue to make unacceptable constitutional, economic and linguistic concessions to Quebec at the expense of the rest of Canada, it is those concessions themselves which will tear the country apart and poison French-English relations beyond remedy.

If Canada is to be maintained as one undivided house, the government of Canada must ask the people of Quebec to commit themselves to three foundational principles of Confederation:

That the demands and aspirations of all regions of the country are entitled to equal status in constitutional and political negotiations.

That freedom of expression is fully accepted as the basis of any language policy.

That every citizen is entitled to equality of treatment by governments, without regard to race, language, or culture.

If these principles are rejected by Quebec . . . Quebec and the rest of Canada should openly examine the feasibility of establishing a better but more separate relationship on equitable and mutually acceptable terms.

From the West's perspective, such terms will be judged satisfactory if they are fair and advantageous, if the new relationship with Quebec can be established and maintained without violence, and if the terms are approved by a majority both in Quebec and the rest of Canada.

This was Manning's answer to the failing Meech Lake Accord. It was also his natural issue. Everything in his background—his training and experience, his bloodline, his political exposure, his self-image as a conciliator, his sense of history and timing, his internal values—prepared him to redefine the future of Canada from the West with a definition informed by western ideas and history, and animated by western optimism and energy.

After Edmonton Manning was still considered by the political establishment—the national media, the federal government and the opposition parties—to be an outsider and an intruder. His views were marginal to the debate. The premiers ignored him; the federal Conservatives dismissed him when asked about his significance. "The Reform Party is on the margin of the national debate," former prime minister Joe Clark said repeatedly. His exposure in the media was sporadic. He had no voice outside the West because he did not yet travel beyond its bounds. He had no access, through language, geography or experience, to the ear of Quebec. As the Conservatives began to plot election strategy for the next trip to the polls, they calculated that he had already flared and would now fade. When he was discussed in the Conservative Party, on television news panels or in print, Manning inspired not respect but contempt—this squeaky, eccentric little parson, this overpuffed oddball, this son of a funny-money politician. Who was he to say how it should be? *Maclean's* and *Financial Post* columnist Allan Fotheringham contemptuously dubbed him "Parson Manning" and "Presto." Editorial cartoonists portrayed him as Howdy Doody. Stand-up comics turned Reform's policy of "deficit elimination" into a toilet joke.

Unperturbed by these obstacles, Manning quietly gathered his personal and political resources for the next stage of the Reform Party of Canada's development. He sensed the momentum and judged that circumstances were in his favour. He believed he had the political vehicle, the issues and ideas to open a new era in Canadian politics. All he needed was time and patience. He consolidated his position and began probing for his opponents' weaknesses.

He had concluded that the old parties and their old strategies and ideas were failing and he based his strategy on that. The country was in a fiscal crisis because of government debts and deficits. The nation was coming apart, and the cure offered by Ottawa was as bad as the disease. It was now clear that if the Meech Lake constitutional amendment was enacted, it could destroy the country in terms of the West. British Columbia certainly and Alberta probably were just one charismatic leader away from a secessionist movement, Manning began to tell others.

He believed the new ideas, energy, and political will to reform the federation were all coming from the West. He thought the region's economic power and expanding population, translated into seats in the House of Commons, could give it enough muscle to make the difference in the coming political debate on the future of government, of the country and of the political system.

The party drew its strength from outside the political establishment and was now using the tools of populist, bottom-up development to expand its base. It was positioning itself as the federal voice of these new ideas and the political means to move them onto the national agenda. It owned what it considered the three best new ideas in Canadian politics: fiscal responsibility, expressed in balanced budgets and debt repayment; constitutional reform, expressed in its alternative to Meech Lake; and parliamentary reform, expressed by its senator-in-waiting. Manning prepared to travel extensively in 1990 to bring his strength in British Columbia up to Alberta levels, to fan the Prairie fire in relatively unreceptive Saskatchewan and Manitoba and to cross the Manitoba border into Ontario, a prospect that Reformers viewed with an almost military bloodthirstiness.

Through the late winter and early spring of 1990, Manning intensified his pressure on Don Getty to reject the Meech Lake Accord unless the prime minister put Waters in the Senate. Getty squeezed Mulroney. Trying vainly to keep the Accord alive in the trauma room, Mulroney relented. Waters entered the Red Chamber on June 11. In wishing Waters well in Ottawa, Manning reminded him of the oratorical and ferocious Cato the Elder, who for years during the Punic Wars campaigned for the invasion of the city of Carthage. He ended each speech in the Roman Senate, no matter what the topic, by declaring, "*Delenda est Carthago.*" (Carthage must be blotted out.) Waters adopted this and ended all his Senate of Canada speeches, until his untimely death from cancer, by declaring, "The Senate must be reformed." As a consequence of the Senate-appointment delay, the party awarded Mulroney its Reformer of the Year award for the person contributing most to its rising popularity, surging membership and swelling bank account.

The party's task force on Alberta provincial politics kept the pressure on Getty through the spring. It held eleven town-hall meetings, at which it heard, and the media reported, that Albertans did not believe the Tories would ever regain their confidence, leaving a void that Reform could fill. The task force recommended staying out of the arena until a decision of a future general assembly, effectively holding a sword over Getty's head until the outcome of the Meech Lake Accord was determined.

At the end of May, Manning wrote a memorandum to the three hold-out premiers, Clyde Wells of Newfoundland, Frank McKenna of New Brunswick and Gary Filmon of Manitoba, to warn them that the politicians who supported Meech would be discredited by history as "defenders of a dying constitutional order." In contrast, "politicians who reject Meech and seize the positive possibilities beyond it, will go down in history as the fathers of the new Confederation." Such correspondence seemed presumptuous coming from an unelected politician leading a neophyte party with a very tenuous presence in federal politics. Not only was it dismissed by its recipients, it fed a media line on Manning that he didn't know his place and was due for a comeuppance.

Still unperturbed, Manning started to develop his base outside the West, travelling in March to Ontario and the Maritimes. By the fall, Reform had its first Ontario constituencies organized and Manning had a steady stream of speaking engagements and private dinners with the illuminati of Ontario business and politics. This drew an angry response from soft separatists in the party; Manning was delighted to shuck off the malcontents who'd drifted in from Western Canada Concept and Confederation of Regions (two anti-Quebec, separatist movements). He was now actively working to exfoliate the party's fringe. Gordon Shaw, who had been instrumental in the shake-out of Doug Collins in 1988, was commissioned to quietly deal with extremists as they were identified.

Some of the orthodox right-wing conservatives noticed that Manning was going out of his way to talk about politically neutral populism and reform. "We are neither left nor right," Manning frequently said. This bothered some of the founding members, such as Ron Gamble, a key organizer and staff member in British Columbia, who thought Manning was trading principles for power and saying "left-wing things" because he wanted to be prime minister more than he wanted to be a true Reformer. However, by the summer membership had risen by 14,000 to 44,000, and the growth now included 1,000 from Ontario and the Maritimes, a near doubling of support in Saskatchewan and Manitoba and balanced gains in Alberta and British Columbia.

On June 23, 1990, the Meech Lake Accord collapsed when the Newfoundland Assembly refused to ratify it. *Alberta Report* described the outcome as a moral and political victory in the West for Reform. That was an uncritical opinion, and though the political establishment might not have appreciated Manning's overeager incursion into what it regarded as a problem for first ministers, it was beginning to realize that Manning was someone to reckoned with.

Now, as the federal politicians went back to the drawing board, Reform was pressed to clarify its unity message. This put Manning on the road almost continuously. He found that he was encountering an increasingly hostile media, but he'd anticipated that and hired Calgary radio news director Ron Wood, who for the next three years was to be his constant travelling companion.

The two men were well matched as much by their differences as by their common interest in politics. The gregarious, sociable Wood knew the sophistry and vindictiveness of the media, knew how to play their game by their rules and took nothing at face value; the quiet, shy Manning took journalists at face value, was too inclined to trust them and had scant regard for the polish and style he needed to be telegenic.

Manning and Wood met in late 1989 almost by accident when Wood substituted for a sick reporter in what was to have been a four-minute interview. Wood had worked in Ottawa, had a sense of western history and a grounding in western political issues and irritants. The interview ran to twenty-four minutes, and Wood later recounted that he was taken by Manning's self-evident honesty and integrity. This was the first politician he had interviewed who answered a question, "I don't know." Wood was not argumentative, just tough, and Manning was tough in return. Wood asked solid questions and got back reasonable answers.

The whole interview was aired over the noon hour, and the station's phones lit up. Wood observed that many young people called to ask for more information. He ran a promotion during the afternoon to talk up a rebroadcast, which drew more calls. In Calgary Manning was good for ratings, so the interview ran again on a Sunday week-in-review show. Wood visited his dad and said, "I think I'll vote for him." His dad replied, "I thought you'd see the light." It surprised Wood that his father thus indicated he'd vote for Manning; he never thought his father would support a protest party.

In February, when Manning decided he needed a media aide, he hired Wood. He asked him, "What plan do you have in mind for me?" "You are a box of cereal on the bottom shelf at the supermarket," replied Wood. "My job is to move you to eye level. Your job is to be prepared so people will take you off the shelf."

CHAPTER FOURTEEN # The National Stage

Udum et molle lutum est, nunc properandus et acri fingendus
sine fine rota. [The clay is damp and soft, let us hasten and
shape it on the keen, revolving wheel.]

—PERSIUS, *The Satires*

N O ONE HAD organized a modern, national third
political party in Canada since the Depression,
when the Social Credit Party and Canadian
Commonwealth Federation expanded out of the West. At that, the
Socreds and the CCF, later the NDP, had not succeeded in gaining the
pan-national representation that the Liberals and Progressive Conservatives could claim. Manning had no textbook or template, no experts to
call on. He didn't even have the support of all Reformers; many
wanted to remain a movement in the West. His organizational plan was
simple: get on a plane, go places, meet people. His deadline: the next
election, expected sometime in 1992 or 1993.

He said that you couldn't buy a populist movement, that it

depended on the opinion of the people. He had a short time frame to win the base of support needed to achieve the party's first ambition of becoming the voice of the West in national politics. His own ambition went beyond that: he wanted to lead the Official Opposition after the next election, then form the government before the end of the century. Reform Party Chairman Cliff Fryers advised him that he doubted the momentum and organization could be sustained for more than a couple of elections. And there was the sunset clause in the party's constitution that required a plebiscite of membership to carry on past the year 2000.

Manning was the party's campaigner on the road, its principal idea machine and he also maintained executive control of its operations. He had a small but reliable team to work with: a strong executive and seven-member council covering the West and ensuring that constituency organization continued, and day-to-day-support from Gordon Shaw, R. Campbell and Ellen Todd in British Columbia; Cliff Fryers, Bob Muir, Jack Pirie and Diane Ablonczy in Calgary; Marshall Copithorne working on the problem of provincial parties; Elwin Hermaston in Manitoba; Reginald Gosse in Ontario, and Stephen Harper helping Deborah Grey in Ottawa. Although he had physical endurance, worked very long hours, and was criticized by some party staff and members of trying to micromanage all the details, he could no longer personally supervise all the party's business. His adopted an executive management style, concentrating on a short list of priorities and delegating the rest to the trusted inner circle, particularly Fryers, Wood, Ablonczy, Harper and Grey. His leadership style had toughened in the months since the founding Vancouver assembly. He dealt firmly and quietly with the petty organizational squabbles to which the party's start-up seemed prone. Gone was the uncertainty and hesitation that had been part of his political style when he was overshadowed by his father in the days of the Whiz Kids, and again when he was looking for the opening to launch Reform in the early 1980s.

To consolidate and expand the Reform Party's base, to get a reading on the grassroots issues for the next election and to test out his ideas, he and Ron Wood went on a ten-month road trip. He went to constituency meetings, encouraged prospective candidates, made speeches, answered questions, asked questions, took media interviews, attended church basement dinners, coffee parties, power lunches and quiet dinners with opinion makers and financial backers. He wrote letters, policy memos, speeches, strategies. He shifted his message from the party's founding theme, "The West Wants In," to "Building the New Canada." The change reflected that Reform aspired to be more than just an expression of regional anger, alienation and protest—Manning intended to position it as the West's constructive alternative to the federalism of the Tory and Grit establishment that produced the failed Meech Lake Accord.

He worked long hours on a recruitment process designed to attract electable candidates and screen out possible embarrassments. Prospective Reform MPs were asked to submit to a review of their credentials and backgrounds that was the most demanding—some said invasive— of any party. In addition to answering a questionnaire on their business or professional résumés, prospective candidates were expected to provide basic information on their personal lives, such as marital status. They were also asked to confirm their support for the party's policies. Local constituencies, not the party, elected candidates, and most nominations were contested; however Manning wanted to ensure that the members knew who they were supporting. This, he and his party officials hoped, would weed out what they called the "loonies." Their trepidation was well-founded: one of the embarrassments they faced was that Mark Waters, son of the Reform senator, joined the Alliance Party, an Alberta soft-separatist group of ex- Western Canada Concept and Confederation of Regions members merged with some of the religious right from the Christian Heritage Party. Waters touted Alliance as a proxy provincial wing for Reform, and while nothing came of this initiative, the Reform executive expended time and energy monitoring this threat to its credibility.

In the summer of 1990, Manning travelled in thirty British Columbia ridings, speaking forty-five times to a total of eight thousand people. In the autumn, he concentrated on the Prairies and slipped in and out of Ontario when he could. He took a trip to visit his daughters Andrea and Avryll in Australia, where they were working in Sydney, and visited that country's Triple-E Senate. Then, he came home for Christmas with the rest of his family. The party gained momentum. Through the summer of 1990, membership grew by two hundred per day. By the end of the year, fifty constituency organizations had been founded in Ontario. Reform was climbing into third place in national polls in British Columbia, Alberta and Ontario, behind the Liberals and NDP but ahead of the Conservatives. By the end of the year, Manning had a quarter of the decided vote in three regions of the country: Ontario, the Prairies and the Pacific. From the Atlantic provinces there was a trickle of invitations to speak and requests for constituency-organizing kits.

In the new year, he went back to Ontario, then into Quebec for the first time. He intended the trip as a reconnaissance on the future of the constitutional issue in the province. In Montreal, Ron Wood had lined up meetings with every influential newspaper and television news organization in the province. To his surprise, Manning found he was something of a media celebrity for a few days and was being scrutinized rather than being able to scrutinize. While he learned less than he taught, he left the province convinced that while the Reform Party and the recently created Bloc Québécois were both born of frustration with the status quo of federalism, they were miles apart on the solution: the West wanted in; Quebec wanted out, and did not have a realistic concept of the terms of separation to which the rest of the country might agree.

In March, he and Sandra took a Hawaiian vacation; they'd not seen much of each other for several months and went into virtual seclusion. While they were away, he gathered his thoughts and wrote his speeches for the 1991 annual assembly in Saskatoon, Saskatchewan. Manning, the executive leadership and the council of the party wanted a clear intellectual decision and an equally clear emotional commitment from the membership for Reform to organize nationally. There were strong, influential members who disagreed with the leadership on the direction it should take.

The party was under pressure from a significant number of members in Alberta and British Columbia to form provincial wings. There was actually a seven-year-old provincial charter for a Reform Party of British Columbia—unrelated to the federal party—that had an executive that was considering reviving its activities. (To forestall this elsewhere, Manning's lawyers reserved the name in the other provinces.) The strongest backing for "going provincial" came from the same people who wanted the federal party to stay in the West. Their strategy was to build a political monolith in the four provinces and a parliamentary caucus with which future federal governments would have to trade.

On its own momentum, Reform had burst the boundaries of the West. But that could be sabotaged. Many conflicting voices claimed to speak for its grassroots membership. Manning intended to resolve the differences in the balloting at the assembly. The membership would also be asked to revise the policy book—the Blue Book—that would contain the platform for the next general election. The speeches, administrative decisions and policy positions taken would, collectively, mark the beginning of the campaign.

The 1,400 registrants (832 voting delegates, 450 nonvoting members) who milled in the hospitality suites or mingled with the 130 accredited observers from other parties and journalists—the assembly prompted the national media's and the Parliamentary Press Gallery's first intensive scrutiny of the party—on the night of Thursday, April 4, now represented a membership of 62,000, including a small number of members in Atlantic Canada and 6,000 in Ontario.

The decision on national expansion came to the floor of the convention on Saturday afternoon. The leaders presented the facts: Ontario was organizing and Atlantic members wanted to get up and running. Some delegates, however, expressed fear that moving without the approval of the entire membership would fracture the party. So delegates approved a mail referendum of members from the West asking them to formally authorize political organization east of the Manitoba-Ontario border, except Quebec, where the party's unilingual leadership faced a serious language barrier. Later that day in a straw poll, 96 per cent of the delegates voted for expansion, and the referendum bore out the consensus of the assembly to get the show on the road. Eight days later, 55,000 ballots went into the mail; on June 3, the results came in: expansion was approved by 92 per cent of the 42 per cent of the Reform Party members who voted.

There were casualties within the party. Ron Gamble, who'd played a key role organizing British Columbia, quit after the Saskatoon assembly. He wanted the party to stay in the West; he said Manning's ambitions would cost the party its populist innocence. Gamble went on to help the Reform Party of British Columbia organize and enter provincial politics.

The Tories were quick to attack the flaw in the Reform expansion strategy. The day after the assembly wound up, Manning's 1988 election campaign rival, Joe Clark, said, "The decision by the Reform Party to expand its operations into some regions beyond Western Canada but not to present candidates in Quebec seems to me to constitute in effect an invitation to Quebec to separate. I think this is a very dangerous, unfortunate position for any national party to take." Even the less-partisan interpretation of events by *Globe and Mail* reporter Miro Cernetig reflected the weakness of Manning's position, when he described the party's decision to organize nationally as "a mandate to campaign across the country as the voice of English-speaking Canada."

Nonetheless, the editorial writers of Cernetig's newspaper identified the strength of Manning's position. The Reform Party is gathering momentum, they said in an editorial during the assembly, because it is a political vehicle that expresses the views of Canadians who see the national political parties as "inaccessible." They asked:

> Who in Parliament will stand up and suggest we revisit national policies on multiculturalism and bilingualism? Who in Parliament argues consistently and forcefully for parliamentary reform? Who in Parliament is willing to raise any substantial questions about the structure of medicare and social programs? None of the three major parties has any desire, or perhaps latitude, to reconsider these issues in a meaningful way.
>
> Who will become the party of Canadian nationalism outside Quebec, whether or not Quebec remains in the country? Many New Democrats believe they are destined to emerge as English-speaking Canada's party of choice, but the growth of the Reform Party suggests there will be a contest from the centre-right for that mantle and those rewards.

After the assembly, the *Globe and Mail*'s editorial team weighed in again with an assessment of Manning's and Reform's prospects:

> Whether the party wins a larger audience will depend in large part on what Canadians think of Reform's stands on Senate reform, welfare, medicare, official bilingualism and the like. It will also depend

on whether Preston Manning makes his presence felt as a new leader on the national scene.

The party may stub its toe, however, on its refusal to consider any special status for Quebec. It is realistic, not arrogant, for Quebec to note that it constitutes a distinct society within Canada . . . but the Reform Party is having none of the idea, and that will handicap its efforts to hold Canada together.

The weekend's proceedings did, however, put paid to the notion that many people have that Reform is some kind of haven for the lunatic fringe; it was not hijacked by racists and rednecks.

The newspaper's distinguished political columnist and author, Jeffrey Simpson, who was at Saskatoon, made his contribution to the *Globe and Mail*'s scrutiny of the Reform Party in a lengthy article based on many interviews with party members and series of four columns in the week following the assembly. Simpson was an opinion leader in the Parliamentary Press Gallery, and his conclusions became a reference point that influenced other journalists' understanding and coverage of Manning and Reform in the following months.

Simpson identified federal fiscal control and Quebec as the two linchpins of Reform's policy. He tuned into the blending of protest against the status quo and new policy prescriptions that Manning had successfully cultivated in tandem to drive his political movement along. Simpson, however, was deeply disturbed by both the party and its leader. On the constitutional ferment, he said Manning had "unwittingly" trapped himself in a paradox by insisting, on one hand, that "the Old Canada as defined as an equal partnership between two founding races, languages and cultures, the English and the French—is dying," and on the other hand suggesting that the "New Canada . . . get its constitutional act together, then sit down with the New Quebec to decide whether an accommodation can be reached to keep Canada united."

Seldom has a political leader articulated more forcefully, if inadvertently, the two-nations theory of Canada, the very theory Mr. Manning so urgently rejects. . . . He is counting on Canadians thinking of themselves as two nations or peoples, so that his Reform

Party can become the vehicle for English-speaking Canadians to articulate their vision of themselves and to defend their interests, all the while denouncing the two-nations theory of Canada.

What Mr. Manning wants for New Canada is so antithetical to anything remotely acceptable to the New Quebec—and visa versa—that without ever stating it directly, he is positioning himself to be a major player in, or perhaps the leader of, the Canadian delegation for the secession of Quebec from Canada, the divorce of the two nations he denies even exist.

Simpson next depicted Manning as a man blending his politics with his religion. He offered as evidence the fact that, as the assembly ended, Manning asked riding executive members to stand. Simpson went on to describe the scene:

"I charge you this day in the presence of the delegates to this assembly," [Manning] intoned, "to go out and find the very best candidates you can discover to carry the Reform Party's banner in the next election" . . . in the church, to be charged is to be given a mission, to be infused with a higher calling.

No other Canadian political leader would dream of using "charge" in this manner, infusing politics with religious language or framing a political statement in the trappings of a religious ceremony. Other leaders would find it too corny and awkward, for most of them have accepted the conventional assumption that religion and politics belong in separate spheres of public life.

The cadences of his oratory, the religiously inspired phraseology, the frequent references to Abraham Lincoln, whose own oratory was so influenced by the Bible: These all bear witness to the blending of religion and politics.

Turning to a profile of the delegates at the assembly, he described them as having an "intensity and sense of mission equalled only when New Democrats gather in convention." Reformers were older people of modest means and less representative of the country than the Liberal, Conservative and NDP parties. Most had British names, there were no francophone Quebeckers, few people of colour, not enough women.

They were people at the margins of social influence who distrusted the power they were seeking.

> Power is somehow corrupting, compromising, a force that stands in the way of the clear expression of the people's will. The powerful have brought Canada to its knees, now the time has come to bring the powerful to their knees so Canada can stand tall again.
>
> If only the exercise of power could be shaped by hard-working people like themselves, Reformers say to themselves, Quebec would be put in its place as a province like the others, the deficit would shrink because people instead of interest groups would rule, the federation would be "balanced," and we would all be Canadians. Canada, in other words, would be more like us.

Simpson concluded his probative analysis by balancing the Reform Party's "challenge to conventional thinking" against the weakness of its position on important issues that it raised in its Blue Book of principles and policies. He noted that Reform opposed the Goods and Services Tax created by the Mulroney government to replace a manufacturing tax. Scrapping the GST, said Simpson, would create a $25-billion federal revenue shortfall. Yet Manning had nothing but "bromides" to offer to make up for the shortfall. And the delegates, having no answer to the problem, referred it for study. The same evasiveness played on other difficult policy questions. "If the party intends to play in the political big leagues, it will have to answer questions from which it now shies," Simpson admonished. Then, with a well-educated prescience, Jeffrey Simpson put his finger on the dynamics of the 1993 federal election:

> The Reform Party is the first protest group from Western Canada that has not called for a substantial transfer of power from Ottawa to the provinces. It's the first of any consequence in two decades to attack bilingualism. It's the first, before an election, to promise to do away with large swaths of government activity. It's the first to call for a massive overhaul of parliamentary democracy.
>
> The Reform Party . . . is trying to transform itself from a western protest party into a national protest party, directing the people's hurts not so much at one region (Central Canada) as at the institutions

of government, which have been unduly influenced by Quebec's agenda.

Publicly, the leaders of the mainline parties scoff at the Reformers. They are whistling past the graveyard. Nobody yet knows just how powerful the Reform Party will be outside parts of Western Canada but, in private chats, representatives of the mainline parties are deeply worried and quite perplexed.

Simpson's series grated on Manning's sensibilities; he thought the pieces were caricatures of him and the party. They also provoked an angry reaction from Ted Byfield, who had skipped Saskatoon and now wished he hadn't done so. Byfield had been distancing himself from the party, but he saw Simpson's series as condescending and dismissive of Reform's purpose, development and support. He wrote a diatribe for *Alberta Report* in which he warned Simpson that the West would no longer be told to "shut up" and submit to whatever the political establishment, including the media, told it to think and do. In spite of Manning's annoyance and Byfield's anger, the major parties and journalists now paid Reform the compliment of taking it seriously and regarding it as a legitimate vehicle of western opinion, more so as the fortunes of the Mulroney government deteriorated.

After Saskatoon, the Reform Party steamrolled towards the election. In May 1991, the initial campaign organization was formed and a strategy mapped out. The pillars of the campaign would be fiscal reform through a balanced federal budget achieved by spending cuts and a reduced role for government; parliamentary reform including the Triple-E Senate, referendums and allowing MPs more opportunity to vote freely in Parliament without party discipline, and constitutional reform based on the equality of the provinces.

The troubled Conservative government postponed the election until the end of its five-year legal mandate, and there were twenty-nine months of work between the Saskatoon assembly in April 1991 and voting day in October 1993. That was fortunate for the Reformers because they had a monumental task to complete in order to be ready. The 1988 campaign had given them a taste for federal elections but could hardly be called serious experience. Across the country, constituencies recruited and screened candidates, memberships were sold and a financial war chest collected. Large provincial rallies were organized to keep up morale and set a media profile.

Manning was constantly on the road with Ron Wood, and put in nearly three years of unabated travel, speeches, interviews and hundreds of thousands of miles of flying and driving. They slept on the rear seats of automobiles or in cold motel rooms in small towns. Retired Calgary businessman Barry McDonald, in a conversation with Gordon Shaw, heard what Manning was enduring to get to the small towns of the West's vast hinterland. Although McDonald was not a Reformer and not particularly political, he was an avid amateur pilot and he offered to be Manning's air chauffeur as often as possible "west of the Manitoba-Ontario border."

Through the winter of 1991 into the spring of 1992, the affairs of the party prospered. It now had a $100,000-a-month revenue stream, and the membership was rising (it peaked at 133,000 during the 1992 campaign against the Charlottetown Accord and plateaued at 110,000 during the 1993 election campaign). There was a growing contingent of political professionals on the payroll and on contract: strategic consultants, pollsters, copy writers, accountants, graphic designers. The party had steady support, as measured by the polls—between 12 and 16 per cent nationally and 20 to 24 per cent in Alberta and British Columbia. Manning's approval rating hung in the 30 to 35 per cent range.

The Mulroney government was foundering and the prime minister was preparing to resign. The Conservatives thought a new leader would improve their standing in the polls—which was below 20 per cent. The Tories' problems, however, were more fundamental. From August to October 1992, the Charlottetown constitutional accord dominated national life—an attempt by Prime Minister Mulroney to revive the underlying substance of Meech in a package that would be politically acceptable to all regions of the country. When the first ministers announced the new constitutional agreement on August 22, the prime minister also disclosed a national referendum would be held on October 26 to approve or reject the new proposal. The Reform Party was elated with the decision to conduct the referendum; this application of direct democracy gave greater legitimacy to its proposals for parliamentary reform.

The referendum campaign, in which Manning opposed the Charlottetown Accord as "the Mulroney deal," produced mixed results for the Reform Party. During the campaign, Manning was treated for the first time as a national leader, participating in the television debate, September 8, between the party leaders. His intervention was widely regarded in Ottawa as his first major national success. The Liberal and Conservative strategists, preparing for the election, paid him a great deal more attention. The defeat of the Accord on October 26 showed that the party's policies on New Canada were in sync with the views of a large number of Canadians. The Charlottetown Accord campaign documented the fracturing of the country and decline of the old parties, the old establishment. This was all to Manning's strategic advantage, but did not deliver hard political gains in the polls. However, during the referendum campaign, the party's organization and fund raising faltered. Manning found the core of voter antipathy to Reform as well as the broad outlines of the support he could count on in the election of 1993.

CHAPTER FIFTEEN # The Breakout

The evil that men do lives after them;
The good is oft interred with their bones;
So let it be with Caesar.

— WILLIAM SHAKESPEARE, *Julius Caesar*

THROUGHOUT THE LONG winter of 1992–1993, the
Progressive Conservative government wrestled with
its future. It had won two of the most commanding
electoral majorities in Canadian history. In 1984, it swept into power
with 211 of the 282 seats in the House of Commons and 50 per cent of
the popular vote. In 1988, it captured 169 of 295 seats and 43 per cent
of the electorate. Consequently, the Tories had been ambitious. Prime
Minister Brian Mulroney had concluded the U.S. and North American
Free Trade Agreements; launched the Meech Lake and Charlottetown
Accords to bring Quebec into what he called "the Canadian constitutional family"; initiated tax reform, replacing the arcane, nineteenth-
century manufacturers' sales tax with the Goods and Services Tax;

brought down several budgets that attempted to reduce the deficit and wean the government off its Liberal spending habits. The results were awful. The constitutional crisis remained unabated; the national debt had doubled from $200 billion when he took office to $400 billion; the GST was hated, the free trade agreements were vilified by nationalists. Lord Bertrand Russell's dictum that "democracy is the process by which people choose the man who gets the blame" was particularly apt, for the party and its leader now had less than 20 per cent popular support in the polls—far behind the Liberals' standing of 45 per cent. Mulroney was battered by criticism and discouraged that the attacks in the media and by opposition parties extended to his wife and family. He and Mila were sending their children to school out of the country to shield them from the rising tide of anger directed against him.

He and his cabinet had hoped for a turnaround, but it was clear he had to resign and the party had to select a new leader. There was, how- ever, a problem of strategic timing. Canadian constitutional law gave the party up to five years in power, and after November 21, 1992, the clock was ticking down on the final year. Prime ministers usually pick a time when things are going well in the final eighteen months of their mandate for an election. Mulroney had run out of flexibility. On February 24, he announced his resignation. Backed into a corner, the party set a leadership convention for June, 1993—planning for a post- convention rise in popularity to set the stage for an autumn election.

The other major parties, however, were already in a campaign mode—with plans, key people, many candidates and platforms more or less in place—by the end of the summer of 1992. The result was a leisurely year-long progress towards election day for the opposition par- ties and a constant political crisis for the governing Conservatives. Preston Manning and the Reform Party did not plan to run against the incumbent government. Instead they intended to run for their own ideas, contained in the Blue Book of policies adopted at Saskatoon in 1991 and now field-tested against popular opinion by Manning during a year on the road. The fact of the matter, which the Progressive Conservatives recognized, was that a major issue in the 1993 election was to determine which of the two—Tory or Reform—would speak for conservative Canadians.

Oddly, Manning—who planned to cast himself as the outsider, the newcomer—would be the only major party head in the coming campaign who had led his team in 1988. The New Democrats had replaced Manitoba MP Ed Broadbent with Yukon's Audrey McLaughlin in 1989. Jean Chrétien had been selected in the summer of 1990 to succeed John Turner as Liberal leader. Following the Liberal leadership decision a group of Quebec MPs who had supported Montreal shipping magnate and MP Paul Martin's candidacy bolted from the party to join Conservative defector and one-time Mulroney friend and confidante, Lucien Bouchard. These disaffected Quebec Grits and Tories now made up the core of the separatist, social-democratic Bloc Québécois, led by Bouchard.

Reform, which nominated 207 candidates outside Quebec for the 1993 election, and the Bloc, which ran 75 candidates in Quebec, were casting themselves as regional parties. The Liberals, Conservatives and NDP, who ran candidates in all ridings, regarded themselves as the only truly national parties. This pre-election positioning was to prove very significant. The dissatisfaction with the traditional parties ran deep that year. Eleven minor parties, including Edmonton-based publisher Mel Hurtig's National Party of Canada with 171 candidates, contested the 1993 campaign, and 151 individuals ran as independent or unaffiliated candidates. Of the 2,155 candidates registered in the country's 295 ridings, 1,271 came from other than the three traditional parties (Conservative, Liberal and NDP) and 989 from other than the five major parties (including the Bloc and Reform).

Manning had an arsenal of policy positions on which to campaign. He could press hot buttons on deficit reduction—$35.5 billion in spending cuts; tax reform—less spending would mean reduced taxes; immigration—a colour-blind system based on the qualifications of the applicant; the role of government—less of it, costing less; criminal justice—constitutional recognition of victims' rights and overhaul of parole including lifetime parole for any crime of violence; the GST—eliminate it; Quebec—opposition to the principles of the Meech Lake and Charlottetown Accords and equal treatment of all provinces; free trade agreements—negotiate and sign them.

The sweep of Reform's platform, however, made it vulnerable in several areas. Its spending reductions were so far-reaching and fast-paced that liberal economists feared they would slow down the economy. The cuts included old-age pension claw backs for seniors with incomes of more than $54,000 per year and medicare reform permitting user fees and extra billing for many specialized services. After the new year, as the other parties began to evaluate Reform's ideas and to attack them, the party's standing in the polls sagged from above 12 per cent to 8 per cent. Factoring out Quebec, the results indicated Manning would win some seats in the West but his tough conservatism was shutting him out of the more liberal Ontario and Atlantic Canada.

The Reform campaign needed a focus. It honed in on three central themes: constitutional peace, democratic reform of the political process and Parliament and a healthy economy kick started by reducing federal deficits, debts and taxes. As the campaign progressed, Manning narrowed this to deficit reduction and a new constitutional model replacing the old formulation of a Canada composed of two founding nations—French and English—with a federal state composed of equal provinces, each with power to protect its cultural and linguistic singularity. Manning said that his Canada "includes Quebec, but without special status." Before the Charlottetown Accord and referendum, his instinct had been to stay away from national unity—to concentrate on the fiscal and social issues. Among other advantages, this strategy made it easier to live with the fact Reform had no candidates in Quebec. He promised, repeatedly through 1993, that there would be Reform candidates in every province "next time."

It turned out that his pre-Charlottetown instinct to focus on economics and social policy was timely on his home ground of Alberta because it synchronized with developments in provincial politics. When Environment Minister Ralph Klein won the leadership of the Alberta Conservative Party in December 1992, and succeeded Don Getty as premier, he had to move hard and fast to define an issue on which he could win reelection in 1993. Klein—an informal populist whose politics were based on popular trust and rapport and his sounding of opinion—fastened on attacking his government's debt and deficit, winning reelection in June 1993 against what had seemed impossible odds. He won on a defining Reform principle: governments should be fiscally responsible, and that meant eliminating deficits. His campaign meshed well with the Reform Party's early spring attack on the final budget of the Mulroney years, which contained a half-hearted attack on the deficit. Manning went around the country making a well-illustrated presentation on the budget that should have been, based on the Reform platform of eliminating the annual federal deficit in three years. Klein was campaigning in Alberta with his own flip charts that showed how he could salvage the province's precarious finances by slashing the budgets of all government activities.

The energy from Klein's whirlwind through Alberta transferred easily into Manning's federal campaign. In Alberta, three-quarters of the Reform Party's members were provincial Conservatives who that year worked on both campaigns. As the federal spokesman for the new genre of neoconservatism—fiscal probity in government through the elimination of deficits and debts—Manning gained momentum from Klein's June electoral sweep. Both men struck the same chord of public confidence and opinion, and did so at the same time. Manning, like Klein, was from outside the political establishment, and people in Alberta that year trusted outsiders. Manning needed a little luck, and the unexpected synergy with Klein provided that serendipity.

Manning also faced the issue of credibility, unspoken of by the party but a nagging concern. To do well, Reform had to shake its image as a party of "loonies"—racists, religious cranks, antiabortionists and homophobes. It didn't need another episode like the 1988 showdown with British Columbia journalist Doug Collins, which ended when Manning refused to sign Collins's nomination papers because of his apparently anti-Semitic attitude to the holocaust. In the recruiting process for 1993's contingent of Reform candidates, Manning screened the party's candidate field as carefully as he could through the *Reform Party Candidate's Questionnaire*. Although the questionnaire was "voluntary," prospective nominees were expected to provide their constituency's nominating committee with answers to the questions, but could control how much information the committee released to the rest of the riding membership.

Although Manning touted the document as a helpful way for the candidate and his or her family to make up their minds about running for the party, the information would warn the local nominating committee of an undesirable candidate—and was accessible to the leader and the national executive. The level of information it acquired from a party member interested in a nomination would flag serious problems that might—in the heat of the campaign and under the scrutiny of the opposing parties and the media—prove embarrassing. The information requested included a personal résumé, a personal and family financial assessment, shareholdings, contracts, business dealings with the government and potential conflicts of interest as an MP. The candidate was asked to provide details of lawsuits, past bankruptcies, previous criminal charges, tax disputes and to give permission for the party to check credit, criminal records and security clearance (mandatory for any future cabinet appointment). The candidate was quizzed on political values, motives for running, commitment to the Reform platform, experience and skills that could contribute to the party, familiarity with and experience in the riding association—and to disclose political vulnerability, including previous involvement with racist or other controversial extremist groups.

At the same time the Alberta provincial election got underway, the federal Conservatives were engaged in a leadership race. The party was dispirited, and many potential successors to Mulroney anticipated that it could not recover enough popularity to overcome a Liberal return to power. Most senior ministers and the more experienced MPs—including many western cabinet ministers—announced they would not seek reelection and, by inference, did not prize the leader's mantle. Only two significant candidates stepped forward. Vancouver MP and former Justice and then Defence Minister Kim Campbell and Sherbrooke, Quebec, MP and Environment Minister Jean Charest. Campbell had the backing of the party machine and most of the Mulroney establishment. Charest entered the race late and reluctantly—at first as a service to the party and then, when he recognized Campbell's inexperience, because he saw the opportunity to become the leader. Campbell, however, emerged as the new prime minister after a lacklustre nominating convention and spent the summer preparing for a fall election.

Initially, Campbell fared well. She embodied freshness and change. She was spontaneous, frank and open—a striking contrast to the well-scripted, superficial Mulroney. She was youthful, she was a woman and she was from the West—three demographic pluses that Conservative organizers felt would play well against the aging Chrétien. They did not consider Manning a major factor in strategic planning, because they felt most secure on his home ground—Alberta—which they had dominated for a fifty-year hegemony, holding all seats since 1974. The polls gave them a juicy postconvention bump. At the end of June, the Tories stood at 35 per cent, within five points of the sagging Liberals, and Campbell had momentum in the shift of opinion.

Beneath Campbell's feet, however, was a badly fractured, disorganized political apparatus. It would not sustain her long, nor did she have the experience and strength, as she later wrote, to control the campaign or the party and capitalize on the recovery. She maintained her popular appeal until after she called the election—but in the gruelling campaign, the Tory election machine disintegrated while the Liberals, Bloc and Reform all campaigned well. In the six weeks of the campaign, Campbell's and the Tories' vote collapsed—on election eve, they had only 17 per cent popular support compared to 43 per cent for the Liberals and Jean Chrétien, whose thirty years in federal politics gave him the savvy and the confidence to take advantage of Campbell's precipitous decline.

The outcome of the 1993 federal election campaign for the Reform Party was decided long before Kim Campbell dropped the writ in September. The well-organized, well-financed and now focussed campaign provided Reformers in the West with a joyous four-month summer season of political barbeques, town-hall rallies and buoyant hours spent in crowded campaign headquarters effusive with optimism. It's fun to play on the winning team, and in those blithe days from July to October the party was on its way to a political breakthrough. At the campaign events and in the store-front riding offices of Alberta and British Columbia it was impossible, by August, to find many volunteers or candidates who were worried about Chrétien's long lead in the polls. Reform's numbers were climbing, too. From a low of 8 per cent when Campbell was selected as the Conservative leader, Reform's popularity climbed steadily to 11 per cent by the end of August, peaking at 19 per cent in the first week in October and plateauing at 17 per cent—tied with the Tories—on election eve. What Reformers pointed out was that none of their support, but some of the Conservative numbers, came from Quebec; in the West, Reform was running second to the Liberals.

Manning's credibility, however, was dogged by extremism on the fringe of the party. Halfway through the campaign, John Beck—Reform's candidate in the Toronto-area riding of York Centre, said in a news interview that each immigrant who obtained work in Canada "takes a job from one of us gentiles." Manning was furious and humiliated. He kicked Beck out of the party, revoked his nomination and promised to find out how Beck slipped through the party's screening process. He tried to defend Reform's immigration policy, but his explanation of it was too complex—with its subtle distinction between qualified and unqualified immigrants—to be effective. And it came just a year after he had removed self-described white-supremacist Wolfgang Droege as the party's policy chairman in Ontario. The Conservatives, who by now were being routed from the campaign, promised a concerted hunt to find more "bigots" among Reform candidates, and the NDP, Liberals and media generated a two-week flow of speeches and stories about the intolerance of Reformers. At least for this election campaign, Manning could not shake off—especially in Ontario and in urban ridings in the West—the party's reputation as a safe and friendly haven for extremists.

Even with the Beck crisis, however, as the election wound down the party was certain of its success with conservative Canadians. In a *Globe and Mail* column during the final week of the campaign, Giles Gherson wrote:

> Twenty-six years ago, Preston Manning and his father, Ernest, then Alberta's Social Credit premier, published a provocative political tract called *Political Realignment*. Its thesis: a merger of staunchly free-enterprise Social Credit and the wishy-washy middle-of-the-road Progressive Conservatives could create a vigorous, crusading national party of the right.
>
> Well, it's taken a while but after next Monday's vote, Preston Manning won't be talking about merging with the disintegrating Tories. He'll be talking about replacing them altogether.
>
> "If we become the official opposition this time, we'll be well placed to form a government before the end of this decade. It'll take two jumps," Mr. Manning told me this week as his bus cruised toward Pickering, Ont., and Reform's biggest rally yet of the campaign.
>
> To a lot of Reformers, many of whom are lapsed Conservatives,

Reform is already the new Tory party. Look at the regular folks streaming into Reform rallies across the West and in Eastern and Southern Ontario. By and large, these are not wackos or political eccentrics. They're Main Street, middle-class, silent-majority conservatives who feel exploited and bullied by a Montreal-Toronto-Ottawa elite that for the past 30 years has controlled the political levers of power and has, over the heads of ordinary Canadians, defined the nation's political orthodoxy.

As conservatives, they're saying they are fed up with a PC party that left its ideological moorings and drifted steadily leftward in its bid to replace the Grits as a national majoritarian governing party.

Mr Manning agrees that Reform is poised to replace the Tories as the party of free markets and fiscal conservatism. But [he] believes Reform is far more than hard-core Toryism. "Reform is a grassroots movement. It is bottom up. A lot of old-style Conservatives have a distaste for populism and won't join us.

"We are advocating far-reaching, systemic change. We are asking people: Are you a traditionalist who believes in the old order, the old approach to economic and social policy, and the Constitution, or are you a system changer?"

When the votes were tallied on October 26, 1993, the Reform Party had swept the Conservatives out of the West and taken 52 seats in the House of Commons. Alberta and British Columbia each supplied 22 MPs, 6 were from Saskatchewan and 1 each from Manitoba and Ontario. Reform had become the ideological conservative party of the West, and the Tories were all but destroyed—holding only Jean Charest's Quebec riding and 1 in New Brunswick. The Liberals had regained their customary twentieth century place as the governing party on the strength of a stranglehold over Atlantic Canada (31 of 32 seats) and Ontario (98 of 99 seats). Jean Chrétien, relieved that he had 21 seats in Quebec and 16 in the West, allowing him to claim a national caucus, celebrated the culmination of a long and successful political career. But Reform had preempted the Grits as the alternative in the West to the Tories and the failed policies of the Mulroney government. Kim Campbell had been the prime minister for only 132 days. Mulroney stayed out of sight, but not out of mind, as Campbell's closest advisors pondered whether she'd been set up to take his fall. She might have stayed to mend her tired, fractured party, but Charest was responsible for the minuscule caucus in the House of Commons and wanted her to go, so she did. Audrey McLaughlin's brief career as leader of the NDP was also finished—her party had dropped from 43 seats in 1988 to a rump of 9.

However, history had played a trick on the Reform Party: in Quebec, the Bloc Québécois had taken 54 seats and would form the Official Opposition. The corrosive forces of change, looking for an alternative to status quo federalism in Canada, had delivered two strong regional parties and eaten away the familiar political geography. Now the landscape was dominated by Reform in the West, the Bloc in Quebec and the Liberals in Ontario. Thirty years of a Parliament made up of alternating Grit and Tory governments—with a socialist-democrat conscience— had come to an end. In his 1995 book, *The Canadian Revolution,* Peter C. Newman said, "The country's three largest regions voted for self-interest in three different political directions. The election wrote an epitaph for Canada's existing two-party state. The party leaders who most visibly changed the status quo with their own dark agendas, Preston Manning and Lucien Bouchard, were rewarded with major gains."

Manning was somewhat dismayed by the paucity of seats in Manitoba and frustrated by what he considered a near-miss in Ontario, where the party had finished second in more than forty ridings and was within a few hundred votes of the winning Liberal in a dozen seats. But he was elated by the breakout from the West. He had a strong mandate to speak in Parliament for two of the nation's strongest, fastest-growing provinces: Alberta and British Columbia. It was an indisputable victory and the party was euphoric. Reformers partied long into the October night.

CHAPTER SIXTEEN

Trial by Fire

He felt no need to pepper his discourse with the annoying edge
of impatient righteousness exhibited by Preston Manning and
the Reformers.

— PETER C. NEWMAN, *The Canadian Revolution*

THE FIRST REFORM Party of Canada caucus trickled
into Ottawa over the last weekend in October and
the first week in November 1993 to find apartments,
set up offices and learn the administrative details of being members of
Parliament. It was a grand and glorious time, rather like being on vacation,
and most were a little overwhelmed with the change in their lives. In the
chilly dusk one late autumn afternoon, Preston and Sandra Manning
strolled on a photo opportunity walkabout, hand in hand down the Sparks
Street Mall and up Wellington Street to Parliament Hill, trailed by television cameras and photographers. There was a feeling of get-even among
these westerners, and over dinner one night, some of the prairie members recalled 1935, when unemployed men from Vancouver started the

On To Ottawa trek to confront the government. That time, the protest from the West ended in bloodshed in Regina, when Prime Minister R. B. Bennett ordered the RCMP to break the heads of the demonstrators. Sixty years later, "the unrest in the colonies," as Ted Byfield called it, had produced an unstoppable gang that would sit in the House of Commons across from newly elected Prime Minister Jean Chrétien.

In short order, Manning established a certain notoriety for thumbing his nose at convention. He conducted a photo opportunity in which he handed Ian Todd the keys of the modest car provided to him as the leader of an opposition party and instructed Todd to return it to the government. He encouraged caucus members to turn down the MP pension plan, and most did so. Some said they'd donate 10 per cent of their salary to charity. When they realized the high cost of living in Ottawa while maintaining a home back in their constituencies, not all followed through on the pledge.

There was a theatrical quality to many of the upstart things Manning did to stake out Reform's turf for the new Parliament. He held one of his first Parliament Hill press conferences after the election at the statues of Robert Baldwin and Louis Lafontaine to show that Reformers had been around long before him and his band. Only two reporters attended, both from western publications, leading Manning to conclude he'd been too unconventional with that gambit. In January, before Parliament was recalled, the Reform caucus hosted a stampede-style pancake breakfast and invited the Bloc Québécois MPs, most of whom, somewhat quizzically, accepted. The Reformers did it to demonstrate their self-described role as national conciliators. It rankled old Liberal hands, who were back in command and expected opposition parties to speak when spoken to and let the government set the agenda.

Manning continued to shake things up. Instead of appointing critics to shadow individual ministers, he set up four policy-analysis cluster groups—economics, social affairs, resources and a catch-all for everything else—and announced he would not take the customary opposition front-bench seat in the House of Commons but instead would sit in the centre of his caucus. Making the best of the fact that the Bloc had the platform, leverage and perks of Official Opposition, Manning said he planned to be "Her Majesty's Constructive Alternative."

For a time, old Ottawa hands stared, bemused, eyebrows arched, at this gang of philistines who did not know the proper way to behave. They had not paid Manning much attention up to now, thinking that Reform was a passing fancy in the West that would have no electoral success. The Bloc and its leader, Lucien Bouchard, were a known enemy. Slowly it sank in that Preston Manning and the Reform Party of Canada were a threat. The authors of conventional Ottawa wisdom now realized that the formerly quiescent country beyond Parliament Hill had become unfamiliar and unfriendly. It had sent barbarians to Parliament, Reform and the Bloc, who did not know that the five hundred people who populated the House of Commons and the Senate, their two thousand or so aides and retainers and the twenty thousand-odd public servants who had some clout were all just on stand-by. The country was run at any one time by maybe one hundred people in the Prime Minister's Office, the Privy Council and the press gallery. Everyone else was supposed to get with the program until pension time. Manning had ceased to be a curiosity. He had serious enemies and could expect to taste the reactionary lash.

The media relationship soured first. Since 1989, Ron Wood had done well, getting Manning news coverage when he was in Ottawa to visit Deborah Grey and Stan Waters. Manning was comfortable in the scrums, the one-on-ones and the occasional news conference. The Parliamentary Press Gallery had given him the customary honeymoon, treating him comparatively gently and helping to establish him as a national figure as journalists sized up his character and ideas, and developed a Reform story line with which to frame their coverage of him. Now Manning had a platform that commanded tougher media scrutiny.

Although Manning was colour blind in his selection of friends and clients, he came with baggage on race issues. Reform had attracted fringe elements and in two successive election campaigns had been forced to discard candidates perceived as racist: Doug Collins in 1988 and John Beck in 1993. This connected with the historic anti-Semitism of some of the members of the Social Credit Party. In 1937, Social Credit whip Joe Unwin and party aide George Powell were convicted of criminal libel and counselling to murder for a virulent Social Credit League pamphlet called *The Banker's Toadies*, which described nine Alberta bankers, lawyers and politicians, some of whom were Jews, as "creepy-crawly," "treacherous and poisonous things" and called for their "extermination." Although the reference in the crudely produced two-page sheet was ostensibly rhetorical, referring to political extermination, it was so offensive that it permanently tarnished the Socreds' reputation. Despite Ernest Manning's efforts to expunge anti-Semitism from the party after the war (the principal reason B'nai Brith gave him its National Humanitarian Award in 1982) the stain remained. Preston Manning inherited the identification with Unwin and Powell.

Journalists were on the watch for confirmation that Reform and its leader were racist. The party had not yet attracted many candidates or prominent organizers from minority groups. Many journalists gave no credibility to the party's statement of principles, which advocated equality and the protection of minority interests. Nor did they acknowledge the screening process that required prospective candidates to answer the question "Have you ever been identified with organizations that promote separatism or discrimination against people on the basis of race, language, colour, religion or culture?" Immigration and multicultural policies were given failing grades. The party was opposed to state-sponsored multiculturalism and proposed an immigration system based on the fit between the qualifications of the immigrant and the needs of Canada. These positions were interpreted to be code for "whites only."

Ron Wood felt the digs as early as 1990. "Gee, Woody," old friends from the press gallery said, "why did you go to work for this guy? I didn't know you were a racist." Manning ran into the problem personally at the Saskatoon assembly, where author William Gairdner appeared to speak. Statements on immigration in his book *The Trouble with Canada* are regarded by some, including the Liberal and New Democratic Parties, as racist. For inviting Gairdner to speak, Manning was called a racist in a subsequent media scrum in Ontario. Opposition politicians fed the perception; Deputy Prime Minister Sheila Copps accused Manning of being "Aryan" and Reform of advocating a racially homogeneous society. Manning was bruised by the accusations and did not want to dignify them with a response, but this was interpreted as ducking the issue.

Manning thought the media applied a double standard to him. On a Team Canada international business development tour in 1995, Prime Minister Chrétien was overheard at a photo opportunity, saying "I like my black people with me for these things." Journalists laughed it off as a bit of clumsy humour. "If I had said that, I'd have been crucified," Manning said. He also thought it unreasonable to tie William Aberhart's anti-Semite connections to Reform, just as it would be unfair to burden the present Liberal Party with Prime Ministers Wilfrid Laurier's and Mackenzie King's racist treatment of Chinese and Sikh immigrants in Western Canada. (The Chinese were forced to pay immigration head taxes and not allowed to bring their wives to Canada; the Sikhs were for many years simply refused entry.)

When Parliament convened in mid-January, Manning did not perform well as a parliamentarian. He erred in not taking a front-bench seat; it made him look weak. He did not look relaxed or comfortable in the dark suits that became his wardrobe in the House. During Question Period, he came across as zealous and hectoring. The prime minister and cabinet had years of experience and masterfully stonewalled him. They counterattacked with sophisticated intensity, going after him personally rather than his ideas.

During Question Period and in debate, Manning's ideas seemed harsh and judgemental because he showed no interest in negotiating—in a legislative forum that prided itself on compromise—on matters such as concessions to Quebec and criminal justice. There developed an intense personal animosity between him and Prime Minister Jean Chrétien that contradicted the image of conciliator that Manning wanted to develop.

During the federal budget debate in February, Manning had to endure the frustration of seeing his election-winning idea—deficit reduction—at work in Alberta, where Premier Ralph Klein, in the late winter of 1994, produced a tough package of deep spending cuts and government downsizing. Saskatchewan's recently elected Premier Roy Romanow soon followed a similar path (he got to a balanced budget before Klein, but also shaved taxes and kept core social programs more intact). Reform did not want to be the party of stolen ideas and was in danger of becoming what western third parties had always been: a goad to change, and the source of the ideas that created change, but never in power.

The spring brought further disarray. In the House of Commons, under pressure, inexperienced Reform MPs were turning into a rowdy mob. Outside, Stephen Harper disclosed that the parsimonious Manning was getting an annual $31,000 expense allowance from the party. This was not an unusual practice in other parties but contradicted

Manning's message of frugality in government. From that time on, Harper was marked by the media as a potential successor to Manning, although he coyly brushed off the suggestion.

In the autumn, the Parti Québécois won the Quebec provincial election, returning separatism to the top of the national agenda. The new premier, Jacques Parizeau, promised a quick referendum on sovereignty. On that issue, Manning spoke for the West and many federalists in the rest of the country. The Liberal government was disturbingly unconcerned; Manning pushed them for a game plan to defend federalism, but they didn't offer one of substance. He reinforced the Reform caucus in Parliament. MPs got professional coaching on Question Period tactics, and Manning established a conventional system of shadow critics—individual MPs assigned to monitor a minister and ask him or her questions in the House of Commons. As the Bloc defaulted on its role as Official Opposition, Reform had an issue and looked and performed more like the real opposition in Parliament.

As the government prepared to bring down its second budget, Reform put it on notice that it must cut spending, reduce the size of government and offer a plan for balancing its annual budget, or face a tax revolt in the West. This level of rhetoric once again inflamed Manning's critics, who said it was irresponsible for an MP and a federal party leader to threaten to be "the command post" of a tax revolt. Finance Minister Paul Martin brought down a budget that financial markets and western business thought made credible progress on the federal deficit, and Manning lost the issue.

Then, as the sovereignty referendum campaign escalated, he insisted that Chrétien was sleepwalking into a major disaster for federalism. Chrétien said the Reform Party wanted the separatists to win the referendum. In October, when the referendum failed to give Parizeau a mandate to secede, by a margin of only 50,000 votes and less than one-tenth of a percent, Chrétien told the House of Commons that Manning was as disappointed as Bloc Official Opposition leader Lucien Bouchard. In the final days of the referendum campaign, Canadians outside Quebec had finally realized there was a real threat and organized a huge rally in Montreal of Canadians from across the country. Manning, seen as a liability, was given no role and had little access to the media to voice his opinion that frankly discussing the consequences of separation with Quebeckers, which Chrétien refused to do, could dissuade them from it.

He regained some leverage after the referendum. First, he declared that Chrétien should be impeached for failing to mount an effective campaign on behalf of federalism. When the prime minister cobbled together a scheme that involved Parliament's passing a resolution recognizing Quebec as a "distinct society," Manning moved an amendment in the House of Commons that specified the resolution would not confer any new legislative or executive power to the provincial government of Quebec that other provinces did not have, that it did not diminish the rights of language minorities in the province and that it did not deny that "Canada constitutes one nation."

By the end of the year, however, Manning realized that Parliament was not the platform in which he could wage the campaign that would win Reform Official Opposition status in the next election. He went back on the road, on the endless tour of small towns and local constituency associations where he could speak directly to voters in small groups, and hear their questions and assess their opinions. He preferred to be out of Ottawa, where he could get a hearing from the local weekly newspapers and small television stations, sidestepping the adversarial coverage he was getting from the press gallery.

As the life of the government reached midterm, Manning was having great difficulty with political attacks on him and several other Christian members of his caucus for their faith. Although leading federal politicians in several parties were practising Christians and members of a prominent multiparty prayer group, Reform was being singled out. Manning was the only party leader who was well known to be a practising evangelical Christian. Most leading western protest politicians in the twentieth century were evangelicals or fundamentalists, but a religious connection was part of Reform's identity in a way that was no longer the case, for example, with the clearly secular NDP. Reform was compared to the Moral Majority and Christian Coalition in U.S. politics and accused of having a "hidden agenda" that included anti-abortion and antigay legislation. (Some critics, such as Sheila Copps, went further to insist that Reform wanted to construct a Puritan theocracy along the lines of John Calvin's seventeenth-century Geneva.)

The Reform Party was neutral on abortion, advocating that it—like all "moral" issues such as euthanasia and capital punishment—be determined by plebiscite that would bind MPs, regardless of their personal views. But antiabortion activists had tried to take control of the nominating process in some Reform ridings to get their single-issue candidates on the ballot. Manning believed that the unborn required certain legal and constitutional protections that amounted to strict limits on the use by doctors of the abortion procedure. (He was, in this respect, not a pro-choice but a some-choice advocate.) The party's position was ambivalent enough that, put to the test, it might limit the availability of medicare funds for abortions. Nevertheless, Manning's and the party's stance resulted in it losing membership to the Christian Heritage Party, which was unambiguously antiabortion.

Manning found it ironic that he often came in for gossip about his evangelical faith inside his own party. And it bothered him when other Christians rode him hard to keep his faith and his politics separate. In November 1995, Lloyd Mackey, who had followed the development of Manning's career since their 1986 *Alberta Report* meetings on the founding of the party, wrote a sympathetic cover story profiling Manning and his family in *The Canadian Baptist,* the house organ of the Baptist Union of Ontario and Quebec and the Baptist Union of Western Canada. In the article, entitled "Preston Manning & A Gospel of Reconciliation," Mackey wrote, "Preston Manning agrees that God has placed him in an 'utterly secular place,' where the mindset of the major decision makers is relatively devoid of 'spiritual dimension' solutions."

Canadian Baptist editor Larry Matthews was flooded with mail accusing him of bad judgement, partisan favouritism and mixing religion and faith. In the February 1996 issue of his magazine, Matthews apologized for selecting a former Reform activist to write the story, for the prominence he gave it and for the pro-Manning headlines above it. Then "as a Canadian and a Christian" he attacked Manning for his "disheartening and disappointing rhetoric" in the parliamentary debates following the Quebec referendum.

Manning made no apology for his spiritual dimension. He prayed and read the Bible daily; most Sunday mornings, even when travelling in strange communities, he could be found worshipping in church, and he was a prominent participant in events such as the National Prayer Breakfast.

He was, however, annoyed by the caricature of his faith in the media and by the reluctance of important religious leaders to join a public discussion of the role of faith in political leadership and the strict Protestant commitment to separation of church and state. He knew it would take more than his efforts to throw a bright light on the fact that the Reform caucus was made up of people who held many faiths or no faith at all, and that candidates were coming forward for the next election from other religions such as Islam, Judaism and Buddhism.

In February, 1996, Ernest Manning died. Too many familiar faces in Manning's long political odyssey were gone now. His father, Stan Waters, Stan Roberts, Francis Winspear, Bob Muir, R. Campbell Todd. Ottawa was a lonely place. Sandra's real estate practice was busy, making heavy demands on her time. David and Nate were still in high school and living at home, but they had busy lives too, and he'd often come off the road or back from Ottawa to an empty house.

In the spring of 1996, Justice Minister Allan Rock introduced Bill C-33 to amend the Canadian Human Rights Act, the law that prohibited discrimination based on sex, marital status and disability. Rock proposed banning discrimination based on sexual orientation in the federal public service, administrative agencies and federally regulated companies. The debate exposed the vulnerability of Reform's social conservatives, who on religious grounds were adversarial to gays. The stance was not one some MPs cared to hide because they represented communities, particularly in rural Alberta and the interior of British Columbia, that were unfriendly to gays. Journalists, gay activists and MPs in other parties probed the weakness.

The break came in a *Vancouver Sun* interview with Bob Ringma, the Reform MP for Nanaimo-Cowichan, a sixty-seven-year-old retired military officer and the party's parliamentary whip. In answer to a question, Ringma said it would be okay to fire or "move to the back of the shop" an employee who was homosexual or who was a member of an ethnic minority if that offended bigoted customers. A few days later, a second MP, David Chatters of Alberta, defended Ringma, who was engulfed in a firestorm of criticism.

Two weeks later, Manning suspended both men from the caucus, the first of several disciplinary actions he had to take to get his caucus out of trouble. But the damage was done. During the two months following the controversy, Reform's standing in the polls cratered from 16 per cent to 11 per cent and stayed there for a year.

In the summer, Manning travelled to Asia on a party-financed tour to raise his profile on trade and foreign policy. Sandra met him in Hawaii, also travelling at party expense. The executive, which approved the expenditure, was trying to do something for the couple because Manning was campaigning all the time and was seldom at home. The party membership, however, raised a storm of protest, faxing and phoning his office—and buttonholing executive members to take them to task for the expenditure, which appeared to contradict Manning's pledge to be frugal. Thus, 1996 became the nadir of Manning's leadership. A wide spectrum of his supporters, including close friends who could not say it to his face, began to discuss the future of the party after Manning.

The intense media campaign against Manning was unlike anything in the experience of more-objective old Ottawa hands for its virulence, its intensity and its closed-mindedness. It was based on a one-sided depiction of Manning. He was portrayed as dangerous, a threat to the ordered establishment. He broke rules and mocked the traditions. His persona was not fixable: he was too zealous, too certain. He might love his country, but he seemed to be unemotional about its people. When he spoke, he hectored and preached. He grated on moderate, nonpartisan people, especially women. Ron Wood had a disturbing meeting with an Ottawa newspaper editor who admitted his paper's treatment of Manning was bordering on the unethical, but shrugged that off. "If he [Manning] survives, it will be an indictment of the political media, most of whom will have neither seen it coming, nor want to see it coming," Wood said. Writing in his monthly newsletter, *Ottawa Report,* lobbyist Jamie Deacey told his corporate clients he'd never seen a politician treated so badly by the press gallery.

Because other connections between Manning and his friends in the West were severed by his distance from home and the demands on his time, the stories that his leadership was vulnerable and that people like Stephen Harper wanted to replace him began to stick. No one challenged it, certainly not Manning. In his intense, head-down, loner's style, he just relentlessly did his job. In July, 1996, when Manning was in Asia, Sandra attended the family wedding of one of the party's officials in Calgary. She was warmly received and at the reception she did her effervescent best to liven the party. She left early to see Muriel, who was not very well that night. After she'd gone, some of the guests looked at each other with resignation and one said, "It's too bad about Preston, isn't it." The Judas kiss.

For the New Year, Manning and Sandra went to Arizona to spend some time with his mother. When he arrived back in Calgary at the end of the first week in January, a friend meeting him at the Calgary airport was struck by the change. His hair had been redone—that had happened before Parliament adjourned for Christmas and was a major year-end news story. Now the trademark glasses were gone, and with them the owlish, academic cast of his face. He'd had laser eye surgery in Calgary over the holidays. It was as if a mask had dropped. His face, with its middle-aged fullness, was more open, transparent, accessible, less hunted. The style changes had been crafted with the help of experts, well ahead of the election campaign expected at the end of 1997 or early in 1998. But the new look also reflected the maturity he'd acquired in nearly ten years at the head of the party he helped to found.

As Parliament returned, the outcome of the 1997 election campaign was already decided in the minds of many analysts. Reform was in disarray. It had many flaws and problems and was stuck dangerously close to single digits in the polls. Strong MPs like Stephen Harper were not seeking reelection. In the minds of both friends and critics, Manning's political career was as good as over.

Even Ted Byfield had distanced himself from the political creature he'd helped create. In a February column, Byfield favourably reviewed a magazine article by ex-Reformers Stephen Harper and Tom Flanagan that dismissed Reform as the political vehicle to merge fiscal neoconservatives and social theoconservatives into a political alternative to permanent Liberal government. Byfield was privately talking about supporting the Christian Heritage Party in the next provincial election and was now publicly looking elsewhere for a political home—possibly to a Reform-Tory merger.

By the end of February, the country was on an early election watch. The prime minister planned to bring down a noncontroversial, good-news budget, then call an election. Manning was better prepared than Byfield or Chrétien expected.

CHAPTER SEVENTEEN

Terms of Unity

We have been a kind of manufactured country all along, put together by political deals and compromises, and I thought what [the 1997 election] said was, "the deal's off!"

— CRAIG OLIVER, CTV News, *Canada AM*, June 3, 1997

IN APRIL, AS spring reluctantly crept across the country, the Reform Party's prospects thawed. The polls, which showed Reform stuck in the mid-teens in popular support, quivered ever so slightly and showed signs of improving. With the country now on day-to-day election watch, the other opposition parties and the prime minister attracted their share of each others' and the media's bile and scorn. The most important factor in the improvement: Manning had stolen a march on the other parties, crisscrossing the country relentlessly for nearly two years of proselytizing for Reform. Ignored by the national media, he'd gotten over the heads of the political establishment and directly to thousands of voters. He had three campaign objectives: to elect more Reform MPs, to make a breakthrough in Ontario with some of those seats and to become the Official Opposition.

Three of his four opponents were new leaders of their parties—Gilles Duceppe of the Bloc Québécois, Jean Charest of the Progressive Conservatives and Alexa McDonough of the NDP. He and Liberal Prime Minister Jean Chrétien were implacable opponents—representing a well-defined choice between federal politics as it had been done for half a century and a new kind of Canada. In the West, where the NDP held all nine of its seats in the House of Commons, the choice between Manning and McDonough was simply between right and left. Charest was his adversary for the same ground. Although the Tories held only two seats, one in New Brunswick and Charest's in Quebec, this election would determine who spoke for the conservative side of Canadian federal politics.

In Calgary, a tightly knit, centralized working team had been carefully unwrapping the formal Reform campaign, beginning with the release of *A Fresh Start*, a plain newsprint twenty-four-page brochure with simple desktop publishing layout and graphics that presented an old-style campaign platform of six planks "to build a brighter future together." Although the political professionals in the other parties scoffed at its amateurish look, it pressed all the right policy buttons to retain the 1993 voter coalition; it was the "West wants in," "build the New Canada," "govern differently" and "fiscal responsibility." The six planks were:

> We'll reduce the size of government to create more and better jobs—a balanced budget by March 31, 1999.
>
> We'll give you tax relief—saving $15 billion a year in spending and lower average family taxes by $2,000 by the year 2000, cut capital gains.
>
> We'll make families a priority—a child care tax deduction of $5,000, legislation against family violence, child pornography and delinquent child support.
>
> We'll make our streets safe again—victims' rights, a reformed parole system, a capital punishment referendum, two-strike legislation with mandatory life sentences for repeat violent offenders and replacing gun control with tougher gun-crime sentences.

We'll repair the social safety net—add $4 billion to health care and education, reform unemployment insurance, reform pensions.

We'll end the uncertainty caused by the national unity crisis— equality of all citizens and provinces, rules for secession referendum, decentralization of constitutional powers and a more limited role for the federal government.

The platform concluded with a guarantee for political accountability through legislation to allow a constituency to recall (fire) its MP, more votes in Parliament free of the party line, an elected Senate, the right for voters to request referendums and citizens' initiatives on policies of their chosing, more say in the Constitution through citizens' assemblies, parliamentary scrutiny of public appointments to end patronage and the termination of "gold-plated" MP's pensions. This was Manning's populism defined in clear, concise terms.

The Calgary campaign headquarters arranged distribution of 400,000 copies of the platform and the delivery of 1 million summaries to homes during the second week of April. Television advertising was being readied with the same messages. Each week in the campaign would concentrate on one point. News conferences during the campaign would be staged in front of display boards with *Fresh Start* slogans, and these would be changed from day to day. The objective was to stay on the *Fresh Start* messages, and repeat them at every opportunity.

There was money; the campaign was well organized. There were between twelve thousand and fifteen thousand volunteers across the country. There were candidates in every province, including a sprinkling in Quebec. The screening had been touchy because the party held back from parachuting candidates or endorsing them. They'd managed, however, to keep out the kind of controversial candidate who'd caused so much grief in the past. If there was an obvious weakness, it was the lack of passion, of the intensity that had ignited the 1993 campaign.

The campaign team was a marriage of the old gurus and veterans of the party to a vanguard of young neoconservative candidates called the Snack Pack, and more candidates of colour, linguistic diversity and women than any of the other parties. The old guard, however, made up the tight inner circle. Lawyer Cliff Fryers, party chairman Harry

Meyers, converted Grit and Ottawa insider Rick Anderson and Manning's personal aide, Ian Todd, had all been around in 1993. Ray Speaker was not seeking reelection; he took on the task of keeping the candidates in line. That helped Gordon Shaw safeguard the flank from the nuts. Ellen Todd flew in from Vancouver to manage the leader's tour.

When she arrived in Calgary, she found a well-prepared team in high spirits and a steady flow of good news from the constituencies. This did not correspond to the rumours she'd heard from party members and read in news stories that Manning would not survive a campaign in which his party would be reduced to its proper, insignificant place in political life as the Tories, without Mulroney and Kim Campbell dragging them down, came back as Parliament's natural opposition party.

"We just want to get into the campaign and get face to face with Charest and Chrétien," Ron Wood was telling the journalists who called. "There are wedge issues to distinguish us from the others: gun control, taxes, distinct society and unity, apprehension about the justice system, the economy. Deb Grey and others, in the run up to the election, have successfully blurred several of those issues into one of discontent with Liberal performance, conveying that Prime Minister Chrétien doesn't have answers, doesn't care, that he's lost it."

The practical operating tactics were focussed on Manning; in many parts of the country, even in bedrock Reform regions, the campaign didn't exist fifty feet away from his tour. By the time the writ was dropped, Manning had travelled to more than two hundred ridings, visiting virtually every constituency outside Quebec, and some within it as well. He had done hundreds of interviews with the weekly newspapers and small radio and television stations. He had stood in front of scores of meetings with two hundred to three hundred people per meeting.

In those small meetings, Manning was at his best. At a distance, through the television camera lens, he seemed self-sufficient. He was not inclined to show weakness, and people want their politicans to be a little vulnerable. It was his honesty and directness that made him seem aloof, as if all that mattered were the facts. He didn't operate on the gut; he wanted to see the numbers, hear the argument. When he got excited about his ideas, he tensed and seemed too zealous.

But he loved to persuade people. He wanted to loaf around in sweaters and open collars. When he got close and talked, he was persuasive and warm. He'd say, "We need all the help we can get." And people wanted to help him when they heard that. Manning didn't care about party labels, and that made it easier for him to work the rooms in the small towns where everyone goes to everyone's political functions.

On the road, he made time for small talk—the dogs, the crops, the way you'd redone your house. He was intensely disciplined and had unusual physical stamina. Only once in three years on the road together had Ron Wood ever seen him drop off to sleep on a plane. He focussed and worked constantly while campaigning. When he was being driven, he'd say, "I have some work to do, I hope you don't mind if we don't talk." He'd delve into the paperwork, writing letters, developing pamphlets, writing speeches and a four-hour drive would go by without a sound. Eighteen- and nineteen-hour days were nothing to him. Long after his staff were asleep, he'd still be working, would slip notes under their hotel room doors. A physical guy with a passion for fishing; a horseman; a pick-up hockey, basketball and touch-football player, he found there wasn't a lot of time for these things, but remained fit through the long months of hard travelling.

Many politicians come into politics because they have a hole somewhere inside them that they think can be filled by power, perks and privileges. But when politics goes away, they still have the big hole. Manning didn't have the hole: his faith had filled it and given him a solid foundation. On the endless road to reform that winter, he had carried himself with an impressive serenity.

There were weaknesses. He was not easy to work with; he could be unpredictable and erratic in his supervision of details. Many who worked with him found him autocratic and insular. He did not seek out the ideas of others. He isolated himself for long periods to prepare for speeches and meetings. After one unsuccessful trial, he didn't bother with speech writers.

He was far too guarded. Once, after an interview lasting several hours, author and columnist Peter C. Newman was leaving the hotel where the two men had talked and he saw Preston and Sandra Manning in the coffee shop, eating decadently mountainous slices of lemon cream pie topped with meringue. Newman gave them a friendly wave, thinking that it was endearing to see the two snatching a moment together, and was startled to see that Manning was embarrassed to be caught in that private moment. "This was like he'd been caught with his pants down and this was his greatest sin, eating meringue," Newman chuckled.

Manning displayed little conventional political ego but he took his role as leader seriously. He ran a tight ship; he was folksy but not soft. When people worked with him they quickly learned Reform had one leader. The 1997 campaign was his to win or lose; it was his career that was on the line.

As the window for the election call narrowed in the second week in April, Edmonton-based Southam columnist Lorne Gunter wrote, "Reports of the Reform Party's demise have been greatly overstated. Reformers have made plenty of bone-headed moves since being elected in strength to the House of Commons in 1993. As a result, the party's standing has roller-coasted in the polls for most of the past three years—15 per cent one month, 11 per cent the next." But, said Gunter, Reform's polls were improving going into the vote. The party had enviable financial and volunteer support at the grassroots. The quality of its candidates had improved. "Moreover, if his performances during the Charlottetown referendum campaign and 1993 general election are indicators, Manning is a more effective campaigner than parliamentarian. Reform may not win the coming election, but it will hardly disappear."

By the third week in April it was apparent that Prime Minister Chrétien would call the election for early June, after only three and a half years of a five-year mandate. This was an unusual decision for strong majority government. The Liberal poll numbers were declining and could drift lower during the campaign. Usually one doesn't go into an election not knowing how far down the polls will go before finding bottom. The Reform campaign team decided this was their first break: the prime minister was in trouble.

Chrétien then made his second mistake. He got himself locked into an election call for the first half of June when record levels of flood waters were moving down the Red River towards Manitoba. Winnipeg and a score of small communities would be fighting the flood during the campaign. Hundreds of farms would be under water. It was as if it didn't matter to the Liberals, because Manitoba was in the West. Manning asked the prime minister to hold off until October, a date that the Grits had considered as an alternative to June. On Sunday, April 27, in the bright, warm eastern Ontario summer sun, the prime minister drove into Ottawa from his official summer residence at Harrington Lake and asked his old friend, former cabinet colleague and now the governor-general, Romeo Leblanc, to dissolve Parliament and set the election for June 2. Vancouver media personality and former Social Credit cabinet minister Rafe Mair said in a *Vancouver Courier* column: "Something's wrong here, folks. The polls have Preston Manning's Reform Party dead in the water. The official polls are wrong as hell and will be proved so."

In Toronto, where the Liberals and the media had, incredibly, started the campaign by trying to discredit Reform candidate Janice Lim, a young Chinese-Canadian woman, as a racist, Manning warned eight hundred cheering supporters, "As the Liberals lose support in this election, they will resort to every dirty device known to man to stop the slide. They will pin the racist label on us because we do not accept their immigration and aboriginal policies, they will brand us as homophobic because we defend the traditional family. But on the streets of Canada people are getting sick and tired of this Liberal-imposed, Liberal-promoted political correctness that points the finger at everyone else but never at itself."

After the flurry of the campaign launch, politics disappeared from sight for a week of apparent national lack of interest, until late in the afternoon of Monday, April 28, when an anonymous caller, probably a worker involved in the production of the Liberal campaign platform Red Book, *Securing Our Future Together,* reached Cliff Fryers by phone and a few minutes later faxed a copy of the document to the Reform headquarters. By Monday night, Manning had a fax copy in his hotel in St. John's, Newfoundland. Overnight, while campaign policy analysts prepared a digest for Manning, another party official obtained a red-bound original of the platform and personally flew with it to Fredericton, New Brunswick, to give it to the leader. Manning read it on the jet en route to Quebec City. There, on the promenade between the old city and the Plains of Abraham, high above the St. Lawrence River, Manning held up the leaked Liberal game plan, which had $6.5 billion in spending promises, and said, "Good-bye, Red Book; hello, cheque book."

Within a few hours, the campaign had a second scoop to embarrass the Liberals: a Reform researcher produced an analysis of election law that could permit Chief Electoral Officer Jean-Pierre Kingsley to postpone voting in the Manitoba ridings affected by the flood. Although he didn't, Manning and his team had become the ginger group of a campaign that was as much fun as 1993's had been.

In the second week, Manning seized the substantive side of the agenda, in spite of solemn pronouncements by the usual array of pundits that he would turn off voters who were weary of constitutional wrangling and predisposed to think of Reform as just a bunch of angry rednecks from the West. What gave Reform control was the final commitment in the six-point *Fresh Start* brochure, to "end the uncertainty caused by the national unity crisis." The words that animated the issue were "equality of citizens and the provinces." This was as powerful a constitutional message as Mackenzie King's sound bite "Conscription if necessary but not necessarily conscription," which dominated the divisive April 27, 1942, national plebiscite endorsing a military draft.

Manning elaborated his position. A new Canada could endure as a federal state, he said, only if it was reconstituted as a relationship between equal citizens and equal provinces. Two centuries of concentrating authority with the central government would be replaced with a radical devolution of social responsibility and taxing authority to the provinces. As to the chronic threat of separatism, Quebec would be told in advance, firmly, the cost of sovereignty. The rest of Canada would expect it to assume a proportionate share of the national debt and surrender the privileges of Canadian citizenship, including passports. Final terms and conditions of a secession agreement would be subject to a national referendum: this would not be a deal cut between Quebec sovereignists in their National Assembly and Quebec federalists in Ottawa.

The outraged response of the political establishment made it the defining issue of the campaign. In Vancouver, NDP leader Alexa McDonough said, "I think it is absolutely clear where Preston Manning's policies would lead us in this country is straight into civil war." The prime minister contributed this: "Manning is obsessed with scenarios for breaking up the country. The Reform Party pushes all the hot buttons, they use all the code words and they appeal all the time to what divides Canadians, not what unites them."

The Reform Party's support, as registered in the polls, started to move up. The party stayed ahead of its leader, but both numbers improved. Manning had defenders. In a lead editorial May 22, the *Edmonton Journal* said,

> Reform Leader Preston Manning has committed the cardinal sin of Canadian politics: he has failed to toe the national unity line of successive federal governments and opposition parties.
>
> What has he done to foment such strife? He has dismissed distinct society as "empty rhetoric" and said it is not an answer to the country's unity problem.
>
> In response to the misconception of many Quebec voters that in an independent Quebec they would still enjoy many of the perks and privileges of Canadian citizenship, such as keeping their Canadian passports, Reform takes an unequivocal, unyielding stand to the contrary.
>
> These are not the divisive rantings of someone bent on destroying the country. Indeed, they are not unlike the view of many Canadians. It is not disloyal to express views on the future of the country that differ from the failed unity policies of the past 30 years. It contributes to a civil debate, not a civil war.

The dramatic focus of Canadian federal campaigns since 1984 has been the leaders' English and French television debates. Manning downplayed the 1997 editions: "These defining moments have often turned into phoney defining moments." Nevertheless, the setting, in the political heart of Ottawa, dramatized the conundrum created by his midelection momentum. The polls showed, by the night of the first debate, that he would be elected leader of the Official Opposition. The outsider was soon to be a member, at least on paper, of the political establishment.

The debates were held in Ottawa's cavernous converted railway passenger station, now the National Conference Centre, on Wellington Street. The location seethed with Canadian history and politics. The massive grey building brooded over the Rideau Canal; on the opposite bank squatted the National Arts Centre. Beyond that, in the centre of a great traffic circle, was the country's magnificent war memorial.

North, across Wellington Street, the Chateau Laurier was poised above the Rideau Canal and the Ottawa River. The great hotel's walls are the keepers of the secrets of a thousand political trysts; a century of deals made and dishonoured and, more rarely, pacts sealed and kept. A brisk, uphill walk over the Canal bridge led to the low stone wall and wrought-iron rails that encircled the Parliament Buildings.

A bronzed Sir Wilfrid Laurier gazed back across the street to the Conference Centre entrance and to the extravagantly dressed buskers and street vendors who hawked their wares beneath its shadow. Behind Laurier rose the Mecca of Manning's political ambition, the Parliament Buildings. Closest was the East Block, where prime ministers from Sir John A. Macdonald to Pierre Trudeau kept office hours, until vanity, convenience and the heightened need for personal security moved them a few hundred feet further west to the Centre Block, beneath the lofty Peace Tower and in front of the venerable Parliamentary Library. Hidden away, off the beaten path, was the monument of Reformers Robert Baldwin and Louis Lafontaine, frozen in a permanent conversation. They once were the politicians of the New Canada.

As one circled beneath the window of the prime minister's present office, past the West Block and the Confederation Building (with their warrens of offices for ministers of the Crown and MPs) and back along Wellington Street to the Conference Centre, one passed the National Press Building, the Embassy of the United States of America and the Langevin Block, a pompously Edwardian pile of rock, and the working offices of the prime minister's sprawling staff and other senior worthies of government, the Privy Council, who preferred to keep out of the limelight.

The Conference Centre evoked its own cornucopia of recent political memory. Here country's premiers were hijacked into the infamous Meech Lake Accord when Brian Mulroney trapped them into a week of negotiations that ended with the ill-fated agreement, while the national media with their cameras and coils of microphone wire ran ambushes on their brow-furrowed sources. On the night of the English-language debate, many of the same reporters were back again. Now they were hemmed in by jovial partisans, sporting tee-shirts bedecked with slogans, waving signs and sending cheers for their respective leaders into the warm evening air. The heat of the day, a premature taste of summer after an unusually harsh winter, seeped towards the sunset, and the breeze off the canal was a balm for the sticky perspiration of the day.

The leaders, four men wearing indistinguishable dark suits and ties and Alexa McDonough in a navy blue suit with a light blue and grey silk handkerchief, took turns making celebrity entrances past the cameras. In the postcard dusk, Manning arrived holding Sandra's hand. His yellow tie and fresh haircut drew the spectators' attention to his pale, tense face. The hard work was finally beginning to show. In the crook of his arm, he carried the black football, the good-luck charm of the 1993 campaign. He was flanked by Cliff Fryers, Ian Todd and Ron Wood. As he threaded his way through the scrum, smiling and nodding to reporters and the cameras, the voice of one journalist came over his right shoulder, "What do you hope to accomplish, tonight?" He turned back and laughed. "I want to win."

With five party leaders in the fray and an inflexible, two-hour format based on questions from a panel of journalists and a hand-picked audience, it was not in any conventional sense a debate that could be won or lost. What it lacked in conflict, however, it made up for in opportunity to deliver clear statements—electronic sound bites—on issues, and for that reason Manning fared well because that was the strategy of his entire campaign. On national unity he said, "Give each province a bundle of rights and allow them to develop the distinct features of their economy and their society"; on job creation, "after the budget is balanced, a personal income-tax cut to put $2 billion back into the pockets of consumers"; on health care and welfare, "Increase transfer payments (from the federal treasury) but give the provinces greater authority over how to spend the money." He told the prime minister that in dealing with the Quebec sovereignty referendum the previous year, "You almost blew it sir. If you do that again you will really blow it, and you do not deserve a second chance unless you have a fresh vision." He differentiated himself from Tory leader Jean Charest: "Why would people believe you could deliver a tax cut now when you didn't do it during nine years in office."

The following night, during the French-language debate, he was unable to participate in the give and take due to his limited French, but with the benefit of a translator was able to convey his key message to Quebec, that Reform was proposing a *troisième voie*—a third option—

in place of separatism or the status quo—constitutional reform grant-
ing equality of the provinces, which would permit Quebec to protect
and develop its unique character but also permit other provinces to do
the same.

He had done a workmanlike job in the debates, staying in character
and on message. Quite remarkably, given the attacks on his constitutional policy earlier in the campaign, he had not been singled out for
attack—the other leaders had concentrated on the prime minister. But
Manning had not sparkled; Jean Charest's rhetoric on national unity
had been emotionally charged and telegenic. He had declaimed the
sound bite of the night: "If there is one commitment I made to my
children, it is that I will pass on to them the country I received from
my parents." In the final stretch of the campaign, Charest had the
momentum that could stop Manning in Ontario.

CHAPTER EIGHTEEN A

Season of Transition

The win of the Farmers creates a serious outlook for the Liberal Party whilst it spells complete ruin to the old Tory Party.

—WILLIAM LYON MACKENZIE KING
Diary entry, October 1919

REFORM'S CAMPAIGN HAD one more hurdle to clear, and in the fourth week of the campaign Manning dealt with it by escalating the stakes on the unity issue. Because of his effective presentation in the leaders' debates, Charest's support was rising in Ontario. There was a risk that Charest could preempt Reform's Ontario breakthrough. A television ad was prepared at the London, Ontario, advertising agency of Thomas, Crncich and Partners to recapitulate Reform's unity prescription of equality for citizens and provinces. The narrator asked for a "voice for all Canadians not just Quebec." On screen, pictures of Prime Minister Chrétien, Tory leader Charest, Quebec Premier Lucien Bouchard and Bloc Québécois' leader Gilles Duceppe came up and a red circle with a bar diagonally across it—the international sign for "no"—was stamped on their faces with a metal-on-metal slamming sound.

Chrétien was furious with the content of the ad. "It's to make people believe we're all separatists in Quebec," he said in Saskatoon. "That's the very clear indicated intention. It's pretty insulting for someone like me who has fought for Canada for thirty-four years. I have a lot of scars back home because I've always fought for Canada." Charest called Manning a "bigot." Alexa McDonough's response was more measured. She said unemployment, not unity, was the issue in the campaign and that the other three leaders had lost sight of what concerned Canadians most—jobs and a secure future.

Manning responded in Winnipeg. "There's a lot of yelping from the other camp about this ad, but that's because the message is resonating with large numbers of Canadians. It just says: 'Not just Quebec political leaders' and that's exactly right." The ad, said its developer Bryan Thomas, "emphasizes that all Canadians deserve a voice in the national unity debate. It's not just about what Quebec politicians think, its about what all Canadians think." Overnight, Reform's polling numbers in Ontario started to rise and continued to climb, rising more than ten points up to election day. "Manning bombed Charest's bridges at the Ontario-Quebec border," said *Ottawa Report* in its election update to its clients.

The final days of the campaign—at thirty-six days, the shortest in Canadian history—brought Manning and his campaign team a surge of adrenaline and a sense of certainty that they would achieve their three goals: more seats in the House of Commons, Official Opposition status and a breakthrough in Ontario. The numbers indicated a solid lead—possibly a sweep—on the home ground of Alberta and British Columbia, with gains in Saskatchewan and Manitoba. In Ontario, Reform's second-half gains were holding.

As the end of May approached and the campaign wound down, Sandra travelled constantly with Manning on the campaign jet. The two were frequently seen and photographed, travelling between events with their arms around each other's waists in a private, honeymoon bubble that added a softness to the positive emotional ambience of the tour. In the middle of the final week, the tour went to Vancouver and Edmonton for enormous rallies.

On the final Wednesday morning of the campaign, Manning invited journalists to the steps of Garneau school. In a damp early summer fog, he talked for a few minutes about growing up and playing pick-up football in the schoolyard, then led a walking tour across the High Level Bridge, retracing the boyhood steps he followed to meet his father at the Alberta Legislature. Manning and Sandra spent most of the walk alone, hand in hand, with the reporters holding back to give them privacy and to let the cameramen capture an intimate tableaux, rather unusual for button-downed, carefully scripted Canadian photo opportunities in which the relationship between leaders and spouses is not normally portrayed with quite so much intensity.

Then the campaign flew to Ontario for a final four-day push, with rallies in a belt from the southwest peninsula cities of Kitchener-Waterloo and Windsor to the central heartland of Collingwood, Orillia and Parry Sound. Manning stopped in Toronto, but his main goal was ridings outside the metropolitan area in which he could not crack the liberal veneer of the sophisticated, affluent urban establishment whose response to Reform had always been, and would be on election day, to sneer and jeer and rebuff.

For the other parties, Manning was the target in the final week of the campaign. Chrétien had trailed him west and matched him, rally for rally, in Calgary and Edmonton. Now Charest was working Ontario in similar southwest and central communities on the fringe of Manning's itinerary. On *Canada AM*, Charest said Reform's TV commercials "appealed to the worst part of human nature—to bigotry." In Tillsonburg, he said Manning was an anti-French "bigot" and that the Reform campaign had set a new low in Canadian electioneering. In Montreal, the prime minister said Reform had appealed to the dark side of humanity and this would have utterly perverse effects on Canadian politics. "He preaches policies that appeal to division and intolerance. He scrutinizes the racial origins of candidates to measure their ability to lead."

Manning was sanguine about the attacks. He knew that Charest and Chrétien were now offending the voters who agreed with Reform's message and were planning to vote for it. He had developed a pretty thick skin; for four years, the Conservatives and Liberals had routinely vilified him. After four years of travelling and speaking in Ontario, he knew that many people agreed with him, and he was prepared to take his chances with a message that gave voice to their frustrations.

In Forest, Ontario, near Sarnia, he said, "We believe a big green wave of Reform is going to roll across the West into Ontario and beyond. I don't want to be in Parliament as some lone wolf and I don't want to be there with just MPs from the West." On Saturday, the jet turned towards home. It had done five round trips across the country; its passengers had driven 32,000 more kilometres in Manning's fleet of blue and green campaign buses. It stopped one last time in Winnipeg, where Manning spoke a final time, and on Sunday, June 1, flew into Calgary.

There he stood on one final platform: one final cheering, seat-thumping, flag-waving crowd—this time the people from his constituency and the city that he'd made the party's national headquarters. The Stampede Corral, an aging hockey rink on the Exhibition and Stampede grounds, has seen a long and stellar history of junior hockey and senior politics. It has hosted every major Canadian political leader since Mackenzie King. Every Alberta political party has used it for conventions and nominating meetings; it is to Calgary political junkies what the Civic Centre in Ottawa is to their Ontario comrades-in-arms.

On Sunday night, 2,500 Reformers stormed the Corral. There were fireworks, and the floor rumbled with high-volume rock music. There was one last long applause, interrupted occasionally by Manning's speech. To the north, in the gathering night, the Edmonton candidates in Alberta's toughest-fought ridings made phone calls, knocked on doors, handed over brochures until the lights in the houses began to flicker out and the people opening the doors were dressed in their night clothes.

Outside the Metropolitan Centre in Calgary, an upscale meeting and convention facility in a renovated cinema in the heart of downtown, the television location trucks rolled up onto the sidewalks. This was the Reform Party's election central. Police threw traffic barricades around the trucks. Inside, in the main auditorium, technicians worked through the night installing risers and furniture for the media, banks of television monitors, rows of computer terminals, TV cameras and microphones.

In the ghostly predawn of Monday, June 2, 1997, as the voting began on the eastern shore of Newfoundland, a light drizzle moved in from the foothills across Calgary's western edge, then relented. The voting would start early—at 7:30 A.M. in Alberta—to accommodate the staggered polling hours that even out the time differences across the country. Returning officers for the remotest polling stations in Alberta, located in damp community halls in the western high country and the north, were up as early as 3:30 A.M. and on the road in their pick-up trucks by 4:00 A.M. to get the coffee on and the doors opened on time. The early summer sun broke through across southern Alberta and heated up the day to a pleasant 20°C in Manning's home town. There was a bomb scare at one school in northwest Calgary, and for an hour at noon, people uncommonly cheery in spite of the circumstances cast their ballots in the parking lot while police cleared the building. In the ridings, constituency workers made telephone calls offering to baby-sit while mothers voted or to drive the elderly to the polls.

Manning read the papers, did some work, made a few calls, voted and began to prepare for the evening. At the Metropolitan Centre, volunteers were putting up Reform posters and bunting while the technicians ran hundreds of yards of electronic cable and tested satellite transmission dishes. Upstairs, the catering crew began to arrange the comfortable room in which the Mannings would wait for the election results. The RCMP went over the details of Manning's walkabouts and photo opportunities. Ron Wood's cellular phone began to ring, and would keep ringing through the afternoon, as journalists checked in to get the schedule and set up interviews for the evening. Across the country, 12,644,078 Canadians cast ballots on that day, and in that paper flood was the verdict on the television ads, the speeches and brochures and strategies.

To control the crowd at the Metropolitan Centre, Reform officials had distributed numbered blue-on-grey invitations, and by 6:30 P.M., an hour before the polls closed, a well-dressed, ebullient throng had gathered on the street outside the doors. People were reluctant to file in because it was a perfect summer evening, and even with the air conditioning inside, it was warm. The cash bars in the lobby were doing a brisk trade, and folks gathered around large bowls of snack food. When Manning and Sandra arrived, they went straight to the second-floor hospitality room to watch the television coverage of the returns, which began at 7:30 P.M.

As the crowd thickened around the TV monitors in the main hall, the artificial drama of election night unfolded. It was soon evident that the Liberals were in serious trouble. Atlantic Canada fractured three ways—with the Conservatives' 13 seats and NDP's 8 breaking the Grit stronghold. The Liberals were shut out of Nova Scotia and held onto 11 seats in the region. There was some disappointment on the floor: Reform had had some good rallies in New Brunswick. There was also a bit of restlessness at the Conservatives' success, which intensified when Charest picked up 5 seats in Quebec. However, the Bloc took Quebec with 44 seats, and that was double good news. Not enough seats to threaten Reform's shot at Official Opposition status and enough so that the Liberals obtained only 26. People began to murmur, "minority government."

Then came the tantalizing tease: Reform was leading in some Ontario seats in the early count; followed by the brutal disappointment: no Reform seats were won in the coveted province. The cameras in the hospitality suite captured Manning's crushed expression. He smiled, but it was frozen to his face for a few minutes. Sandra coolly rubbed his hand and gave the camera her best careless grin. Down in the hall, people enviously looked at the 2 ridings posted on the monitors that Charest managed to wrestle away from the Liberals, who swept the other 101.

The election was determined, however, in Reform country. The Prairies and the Pacific coast returned 60 Reformers, 8 more than in 1993 and enough to form the Official Opposition. The region also grudgingly gave the Liberals a slim majority from 15 seats concentrated in Vancouver and Manitoba. The New Democrats surprised the Reform Party but not themselves with 12 seats, finishing third among the federalist parties with a total of 21, evenly distributed everywhere but Quebec and relegating the Tories to fourth, cornered in Atlantic Canada. (The Bloc finished third among all parties but was badly weakened by internal strife and overshadowed by Quebec Premier Lucien Bouchard, its former leader. "The Bloc members will be in the House of Commons to accumulate pension eligibility," Manning said caustically.)

The election had produced a regionalized House of Commons in which the Liberals would govern with a slim five-seat majority.

Reform was now anchored to the West, the Liberals grounded in Ontario, the Bloc in Quebec and the Tories in Atlantic Canada. The NDP had nothing in Quebec, but held its position in the West and picked up eight seats Atlantic Canada. The underlying text, however, was that only the NDP and Reform had expanded their regional base: the New Democrats on the east coast and Reform in Saskatchewan and Manitoba. The crowd in the Metropolitan Centre buzzed over the unexpected results. It was for Manning to define for his party what the outcome meant.

His advisors kept an eye on the clock to see if they could juggle things so that Manning made his televised speech after the other leaders. They had to fake out the other campaigns and the television producers, who were all monitoring each other and whispering into cell phones from Halifax to Calgary. Reform's most important audience would be in the Central, Mountain and Pacific time zones, so Manning could outwait the others and still speak to his prime audience at a decent hour. It would be a bonus to keep Ontario voters, in the Eastern time zone, at their television sets, but on that score Manning would do no worse than the others. At 9:30 P.M., Manning's mother and several of his children and some party officials came down from the hospitality room and were seated near the stage. Manning and Sandra held back. At 9:45 P.M. Mountain time, Alexa McDonough in Halifax stepped up to the cameras; she was followed in brisk sequence by Gilles Duceppe, Jean Charest and a weary Jean Chrétien, who were in their home ridings scattered around Quebec.

Cliff Fryers took command of the stage, calling up the Manning children and Muriel Manning, Harry Meyers, the chairman of the party, and Rick Anderson and Ian Todd from the campaign committee. In his hands he carried the black football—appropriately, its brand name was "Stealth"—that travelled with the campaign and had been under Manning's arm when he entered the first leaders' debate—was that three weeks ago or three hundred years?

"I can tell you that Manning is on his way. And we will hand to him when he arrives the ceremonial football. For those of you who don't know the story, in 1993, when we were preparing for the leaders' debate in our first major election, this football was purchased as a method of keeping morale up and easing tension. At the start of this campaign it was handed back to the tour team and it went with them all across the country. We played football with it at various airport tarmacs, outside buses and in various community halls and took it into the leaders' debate again. This football is our lucky football and all I can say is our luck is still with us." The crowd exploded, and Fryers grinned a face-splitting grin as he began to toss the football with Rick Anderson.

Finally, the partisan ritual; the set piece of Canadian political victories: the leader entered the hall with his phalanx of security guards. He was dressed in a dark, conservative suit and he held Sandra's hand as if he had not let it go since last publicly seen at the voting station earlier in the day. Sandra was wearing a simple black business skirt and jacket. They were surrounded by microphone booms and flash guns and videocams, but with their free hands they grasped the extended hands of well-wishers. The hall reverberated with the indecipherable throb of rock music. The crowd roared, "Pres-ton, Pres-ton, Pres-ton." The music changed to a campaign theme: "Taking care of business." A young girl near the stage sagged back, almost fainting in the heat but not wanting to give up her place. The people around her made some space, and in a near-Biblical miracle a young man produced a glass of water for her.

When Manning finally stood to the microphone, he turned back to Sandra. "Ladies and gentlemen, let Sandra have the first word." She stepped in quickly. "Wasn't this one incredible thirty-six days?" she asked. "Ten years later, and now the Official Opposition." The one thousand people at her feet and in the lobby roared back their approval, with some relief. Yes, this was a victory. Not all that had been expected, but enough.

Then it was Manning's turn. He thanked the crowd, the candidates, several people on the stage who'd played important roles in the campaign. Following protocol, he spoke of the prime minister and the other party leaders: "We are opponents yet we congratulate them on their individual victories." Then he turned to the results:

By tomorrow everyone else will have commented, so I'd like to get my licks in first. The reduced support for the government is surely a warning that you can't break your promises, can't go through an election with nothing to say on the big issues like jobs and unity. I trust the government got the message.

The surprising renewal of the NDP creates a vote-splitting opportunity on the left, and we are not discouraged by the prospect. The failure of the PCs to renew themselves as a national party is a sign that the old political landscape is changing and will be shaped by new forces and new ideas. The removal of the Bloc from the position of Official Opposition is a development welcomed everywhere by federalists, including federalists in Quebec.

The emergence of Reform as the national alternative to the Liberals—as Her Majesty's Official Opposition—shows that we've come a long, long way because we are the only third party from outside the traditional parties to have ever made it to being the Official Opposition in the Parliament of Canada.

Some will say this is a house divided. But I see it this way: with the election of this Parliament, Canada has entered into a season of transition, a period in which old ideas and old forces are dying and new ideas and new forces are being born. This is a season of transition and it is one to be welcomed rather that to be feared.

Because of the weakness of the varied representation of this Parliament, it will be a challenge to make this Parliament work. Reform is committed to making it work and one of the keys is to implement that free voting system that Reform has so long advocated and whose time is now right for implementation.

To the Prime Minister and to the other leaders I say, it is the people of Canada who have sent to this Parliament the varied representations of all the major options for the future. Let us therefore resolve to make this Parliament the transition Parliament that will guide the way to the new Canada of the 21st Century.

June 2, 1997, passed by stages across Canada's five time zones into June 3. As night turned to morning, the political wakes and celebrations wound down; the winners and losers, the drunk and the sober, the elated and the inconsolable departed to their separate homes. The last journalist at the last laptop modemed the last wrap-up story back to the newsroom, and editors turned their energies to the next day's stories. In the pattern of results in successive elections, one could read the progression of the Reform Party. It secured Alberta in 1988 and 1989, British Columbia in 1993, and Saskatchewan, with a breakthrough in Manitoba, in 1997. Each time Reform established new footholds, and the voters did not turn back.

In 1993, Manning led fifty-two Reform MPs to Ottawa on a wave of idealism and hope. Four years later, bruised by the pounding of public life, he had survived political extinction. He had overcome the solitary inner-directed man in himself and developed an engaging public persona that the polls indicated people trusted. Now he could claim the legitimacy to speak for the West. After a lifetime of political study, he was eminently qualified to lead but he had not persuaded voters outside his region to let Reform change the way Ottawa worked. His cachet as an earnest prairie populist was tarnished by hard usage. To many, he was an ambitious westerner who needed to be broken on Ottawa's wheel. His vision of federalism, however, would change Canada if he ever held the levers of power. Once a man named John Diefenbaker, another outsider, loner and iconoclast, came out of the West after a long political career that began with a string of electoral failures. By sheer determination, he overcame defeat, forced his way to the top and became prime minister of Canada. Preston Manning's future on that morning of June 3, 1997, depended on his persistence and determination.

EPILOGUE

If you know others and know yourself, you will not be imperilled
in a hundred battles; if you do not know others
but know yourself, you will win one and lose one;
if you do not know others and do not know yourself,
you will be imperilled in every single battle.

—SUN TZU, *The Art of War*

LESS THAN TWO hours after Manning finished his upbeat
speech at the Metropolitan Centre, he sat in a
comfortable chair in front of a CTV-News camera in
Calgary to talk with Valerie Pringle, *Canada AM*'s cohost in Toronto.
With the two-hour time difference between the cities, for him it was a
predawn interview, and his face was puffy from lack of sleep. But the
impatient process of electronic politics was already illuminating the
course for the next Parliament.

Pringle asked him, "Why does it make any difference that you are
the Official Opposition?" He said, "It does give us a different position
and platform in the House of Commons from which to communicate

our ideas. It's a lot easier to do the job we want to do from that position than from the third-party position."

"Now you call this a transition parliament, a transition to what?" Pringle asked. Manning grinned and settled in his chair:

I think you see some old ideas, Valerie, that have been around for a long time in Ottawa and are starting to fade away. Ideas like you can overtax and overspend with impunity; the idea that you can unify the country through special status for Quebec or distinct society. I think that's on its last legs. This idea that you can run things from the top down, that you can break promises and be unaccountable, I think those things are going out the window and being replaced by alternative views.

"You mean your views," Pringle interjected. He smiled:

Yes, but they are broader than Reform. The concept of democratic accountability, of equality of citizens and the provinces, the concept that you have to be fiscally responsible no matter what your political stripe is. These are ideas whose time has come and are going to emerge more strongly in this Parliament that in any in the past.

"You talk about the emergence of Reform as a national alternative; that's what you said, but you didn't have the success you were looking for in Ontario. What happened? Why didn't they buy it this time?" Pringle probed. Manning shrugged:

Well that discouraged . . . disappointed us, but on the positive side we do have this new platform of Official Opposition from which to advocate the ideas we think ultimately Ontario will buy. I think Ontario was hung up halfway between supporting the old ideas or the new ideas and a lot of people voted for the new ideas but not enough to elect members. We think that is going to improve in the future, particularly when they see the futility of the old ideas as advocated by the government.

Pringle arched an eyebrow. "Well, you know the Tories still tied you, pretty much, in popular support in the country." Manning leaned forward:

> Yes, but you know the Progressive Conservatives got a real difficult problem because the majority of their members are from Atlantic Canada. It's going to be extremely difficult for them to represent themselves as a national party from that base.

Pringle prepared to wrap up the interview. "Do you feel basically that you are still the voice of the West?" Manning's face brightened:

> Oh yes. I mean we got a mandate from the West, but what the rest of the country should understand about the West is it is no longer just advocating answers to its own regional concerns and problems. The West has come of age in Confederation. The West is advancing ideas and solutions to national problems. And you are going to hear an awful lot about that, and I don't think the West is to be denied in this next Parliament.

Pringle picked up one last point. "Do you see this as a victory at all for the Liberals? Winning back to back majorities?" He replied:

> I see the Liberals as declining. I think they got through by the skin of their teeth and they'd better look after the health of their members because they've got an awful thin majority.

In the next segment of the show, in the *Canada AM* studio in Toronto, Valerie Pringle sat down with a much gloomier guest, her network's bureau chief in Ottawa, Craig Oliver. "What kind of House of Commons will this be? Raucous? Ugly? Or something that's more real and actually more representative of what's going on on the ground out there and is going to have to be dealt with?"
Oliver shook his head and frowned:

> It's not very good. I mean the country spoke with a divided voice and you hear five different voices with no consensus of what kind of country we want to have any more. And you know when you think

about it, we have been a kind of manufactured country all along, put together by political deals and compromises, and I thought that what last night said was, "The deal's off!" And what you have to understand about Mr. Manning and the Reform Party, they are a no-compromise bunch of people. I spent a lot of time in this campaign in the West. It reminded me of that anchor, Peter Finch, in the movie *Network* who said, "I'm mad as hell, and I'm not going to take it any more." That's what westerners are saying.

Pringle mused. "You hear Sheila Copps and Alexa McDonough and the Tories saying how scary they find Reform, and Reform saying, you are all the old parties with old ideas. That's a huge rift. You wonder about the animosity between the traditional parties and Reform." Oliver's eyes narrowed:

This election exposed all the fissures and cleavages on the Canadian body politic, and what you have to understand about the westerners who elected Mr. Manning is that the idea of Canada without Quebec to them is not unthinkable, as it is to the people in Central Canada. So they are saying, Quebec make up your mind and let's end what Parizeau once called the endless trip to the dentist, and if that's the way it's going to be, then let's get on with building what is left.

"Let's get on with building." In so many words, Oliver said that Preston Manning's long political apprenticeship was over. The son and political heir to a premier, Ernest Manning, who'd earned a reputation as a political builder, had started erecting a structure of his own: it remains to be seen if he can finish it.

In a news conference in Calgary later that morning, Manning described himself and his new role in the federation as "a warm western wind," borrowing an analogy describing Western radicals as a great prairie wind, created by John Dafoe, a Liberal Winnipeg newspaper editor and nationalist who in the first half of the twentieth century wrote about the Progressives, the CCF and Social Credit. Manning was, however, more like a fire in the western sky than a benign wind. Prairie fire is an uneasy, powerful force for fear and flight, as well as for the renewal of the grassy landscape in the inevitable and welcome cycles of nature.

On the hot summer nights of every grassland in the world, from the pampas of Argentina and the steppes of Asia to North America's Great Plains, the crack of lightning produces a glow on the horizon that, once seen, is never forgotten. The wind whips the fire below at great speed across the bosom of the earth and all living things are stirred. Only the wisest and most experienced can face the threat, manage it with firebreaks and backfires and outlive it to see the life it brings when lush vegetation springs up from seeds released by the flame and fed on the nutrients concealed in the ash. Time will tell whether Manning can turn the energy of his wind and fire into a force to build something enduring for all Canada. If he rides his fire into the prime minister's office, what will he create? What kind of Canada will he lead? If he fails, what will become of the energies that fuelled the uncompromising rise and run of the Reform Party?

CHAPTER NOTES

SOURCES

The selected bibliography that follows these notes lists forty-two of the books and publications consulted during the writing of this biography. These provided both information for all chapters and a check on the consistency and accuracy of facts from all sources. Interviews with participants in the events narrated were a fundamental source of information, and specific aural sources are cited in the notes when these sources provided important contributions to the text. Other published works and material that is unpublished or has limited circulation are referenced in the Chapter Notes. The author was present in his capacity as a journalist at many of the political events in the period from 1967 to 1997, and this also is noted. When direct quotes are made of the opinions of print columnists or from transcripts made by the author of electronic reporting, these are referenced and dated in the text. Other news sources are cited the notes below.

PROLOGUE

Preston Manning provided the text of his funeral address, *Tribute to Ernest Charles Manning*. Other facts came from an interview with Ron Wood and coverage of Ernest Manning's funeral by *City Light News: Calgary's Christian Newspaper*, March 1996, *Alberta Report*, March 4, 1996, and the *Calgary Herald*, February 20 and 22, 1996.

CHAPTER ONE: BLOODLINES

Material on East Anglia, Oliver Cromwell, the English Civil War, the Restoration and the Protestant Reformation is drawn from *Freedom's Own Island* by Arthur Bryant and *World Progress* by Willis Mason West, the Canadian Edition prepared by Mack Eastman (Allyn and Bacon, 1924). This was a text used by Ernest Manning's public school class. Muriel Manning and the late Eva Reid gave interviews on the Aberharts' family life.

CHAPTER TWO: A VERY POLITICAL HOUSEHOLD

Principal sources: interviews with Preston, Sandra and Muriel Manning, and the author's research notes and script for the 1973 CBC Radio *Ideas* documentary *The Summer of 1934: William Aberhart and the Something for Nothing Gang.*

CHAPTER THREE: THE YOUNGER SON

Principal sources: interviews with Preston, Sandra and Muriel Manning and Ron Wood. Friends of the Manning family also provided recollections. The Charles W. Comfort painting *Skyline of the North* was published by The House of Seagram in the *Cities of Canada*, 1953. Materials on the history of the university in the archive of the University of Alberta and on the history of Garneau in the Edmonton Public Library and the City of Edmonton archives were consulted.

CHAPTER FOUR: WESTERLEA

Principal sources: interviews with Preston, Sandra and Muriel Manning. Friends of the family also shared their recollections. The author consulted *Alberta: A Natural History*, edited by W. G. Hardy (Hurtig, 1967) on the topography, climate, flora and fauna of the region. Former Social Credit MLA and minister of public works Albert Ludwig supplied notes and comments.

CHAPTER FIVE: RITES OF PASSAGE

Principal sources: interviews with Preston, Sandra and Muriel Manning. The Blair archive at the University of Alberta, friends of the late Sidney Blair who worked at the Bechtel Corporation, and the History Room at the Calgary Public Library provided useful information. The author was involved in the Inter Varsity Christian Fellowship organization in Ontario at the time of these events and followed many of the principal participants and events.

CHAPTER SIX: EXPERIMENT AND EXPERIENCE

Principal sources: interviews with Preston and Sandra Manning and friends of the Manning family. The Provincial Archive of Alberta contains information on Preston Manning's candidacy in the 1965 federal election. Coverage of the 1967 Canadian Centennial inauguration at the Alberta Legislature by the *Edmonton Journal* and the *Calgary Herald* was consulted.

CHAPTER SEVEN: THE WHIZ KIDS

Principal sources: interviews with Preston and Sandra Manning, friends of the Manning family and those who were Manning's professional colleagues at the time. *The Lougheed Legacy* by David G. Wood (Key Porter Books, 1985) was invaluable. The White Paper on Human Resources is a 1967 publication of the Government of Alberta and Ernest

Manning is frequently cited as its author. Information on TRW Inc. and Dr. Simon Ramo was obtained from various internet web sites. The author consulted the *Edmonton Journal*'s and *Calgary Herald*'s coverage of the release of *Political Realignment* by Ernest Manning (McClelland & Stewart, 1967) and the 1969 Edmonton Strathcona by-election. The author covered the 1968 Social Credit leadership convention and the 1971 Alberta provincial election, retaining notes and files from these events.

CHAPTER EIGHT: THE CONTENTED EXILE

Principal sources: interviews with Preston and Sandra Manning, Sandra Manning's sister, Marian Stuffco, friends of the Manning family and Manning's professional colleagues. *A Third Testament* by Malcolm Muggeridge (Ballantine Books, 1976) was consulted. The author covered the 1972 and 1979 federal elections, the 1976 Conservative leadership convention for various media and worked in Ottawa in 1974–1975 as a senatorial aide, retaining notes and files from these events.

CHAPTER NINE: THE FIRE IN THE WESTERN SKY

Principal sources: interviews with Preston and Sandra Manning and Manning's professional and political colleagues. The author covered all of the political and oil industry events, in particular the implementation and economic impacts of the National Energy Program, for several magazines, including *Oilweek*, *Alberta Report* and *Calgary Magazine*.

CHAPTER TEN: THE ROOTS OF REFORM

Principal sources: interview with Preston Manning, the books Manning read and the papers he wrote, including those for the Canada West Foundation. The Glenbow Library, the Calgary Public Library and the author's personal library provided several out-of-print texts on Frederick Haultain, the government of the North-West Territories, the 1837 Rebellion of Upper Canada, Colonel Anthony Van Egmond, the Baldwin-Lafontaine coalition and the history of the Progressives, the United Farmers of Alberta and the CCF. The Casper Public Library and the Goodstein Foundation Library at Casper College provided extensive sources for Thomas Jefferson and Abraham Lincoln.

CHAPTER ELEVEN: THE WEST WANTS IN

Principal sources: extensive interviews with numerous Reform Party of Canada organizers and members, journalists and political opponents of the party, interviews with Preston and Sandra Manning, and Reform Party of Canada publications and speeches from the Vancouver and Winnipeg assemblies. Of particular help in this and the following two chapters were notes and recollections of many hours spent in the office of the late R. Campbell Todd in the early 1980s. The author consulted coverage of these events in the *Alberta Report*, *Globe and Mail*, the *Edmonton Journal* and the *Calgary Herald*.

CHAPTER TWELVE: TURNING POINTS

Principal sources: extensive interviews with numerous Reform Party of Canada organizers and members, journalists and political opponents of the party, interviews with

Preston and Sandra Manning, and Reform Party of Canada publications from the 1988 election, 1989 Beaver River by-election and 1989 senatorial selection plebiscite. The author covered the 1988 federal election and the 1989 Alberta senatorial selection plebiscite and also consulted coverage of these events in the *Alberta Report*, *Globe and Mail*, the *Edmonton Journal* and the *Calgary Herald*.

CHAPTER THIRTEEN: THE TOUCHSTONE

Principal sources: extensive interviews with numerous Reform Party of Canada organizers and members, journalists and political opponents of the party, interviews with Preston and Sandra Manning, and Reform Party of Canada publications and speeches from the Edmonton assembly. Of particular importance was a 1989 interview with the late Stan Waters. The author also consulted coverage of these events in the *Alberta Report*, *Globe and Mail*, the *Edmonton Journal* and the *Calgary Herald*.

CHAPTER FOURTEEN: THE NATIONAL STAGE

Principal sources: extensive interviews with numerous Reform Party of Canada organizers and members, journalists and political opponents of the party, interviews with Preston and Sandra Manning, and Reform Party of Canada publications and speeches from the Saskatoon assembly. Of particular importance was a 1997 interview with Ron Wood. The author also consulted coverage of these events in the *Alberta Report*, *Globe and Mail*, the *Edmonton Journal* and the *Calgary Herald*. The *Globe and Mail*'s coverage of the Saskatoon assembly includes "Reform Party New-Look Populists Gird for March to East" by Miro Cernetig, April 6, 1991, and the editorials "The Widening Appeal of the Reform Party," April 5, 1991, and "A Weekend in Politics," April 8, 1991. Of particular interest are a long report and four columns by Jeffrey Simpson, "What the Reformers Really Have in Mind," April 8, 1991, "The Two-Nations Paradox at the Heart of Mr. Manning's Reform Party," April 9, 1991, "Preston Manning Infuses His Politics with Religious Spirit, April 10, 1991, "What Distinguishes Reform Party Delegates from Those Other Parties," April 11, 1991, and "The Reform Party Has Yet to Answer a Few Important Questions," April 12, 1991, which provide a detailed, definitive assessment of Preston Manning and the Reform Party from an impeccable source outside Western Canada.

CHAPTER FIFTEEN: THE BREAKOUT

Principal sources: extensive interviews with numerous Reform Party of Canada organizers and members, journalists and political opponents of the party, interviews with Preston and Sandra Manning, and Reform Party of Canada publications and speeches for the 1993 federal election. Kim Campbell's autobiography, *Time and Chance* (1994), was illuminating. Beginning in the summer of 1993, the author contributed a monthly assessment of Prairie politics to *Ottawa Report*, a private newsletter for corporate clients published by Association House, and maintained a continuous, detailed watching brief, including interviews, files and notes, on the Reform Party for that purpose. The author also consulted coverage of these events in the *Alberta Report*, the *Edmonton*

Journal, the *Calgary Herald* and the *Globe and Mail*, in particular Giles Gherson's column "Main Street, Middle Class, Silent Majority Conservatives on the March," October 21, 1993.

CHAPTER SIXTEEN: TRIAL BY FIRE

Principal sources: extensive interviews with numerous Reform Party of Canada organizers and members, journalists and political opponents of the party, interviews with Preston and Sandra Manning, and Reform Party of Canada publications and speeches and the author's files for *Ottawa Report*. The author also consulted coverage of these events in the *Alberta Report*, *Globe and Mail*, the *Edmonton Journal* and the *Calgary Herald*.

CHAPTER SEVENTEEN: TERMS OF UNITY

Principal sources: postelection interview with Preston Manning and extensive interviews with numerous Reform Party of Canada organizers and members, journalists and political opponents of the party, and Reform Party of Canada publications and speeches for the 1997 federal election campaign. The author covered many campaign events and made use of his *Ottawa Report* files. During the campaign, the author complied an exhaustive file of media coverage from *Alberta Report*, *Globe and Mail*, *Financial Post*, *Red Deer Advocate*, the *Edmonton Journal* and the *Calgary Herald*, as well as keeping transcripts from television coverage including CBC's *Newsworld* and CTV's *Canada AM*.

CHAPTER EIGHTEEN: A SEASON OF TRANSITION

Principal sources: postelection interview with Preston Manning and extensive interviews with numerous Reform Party of Canada organizers and members, journalists and political opponents of the party, and Reform Party of Canada publications and speeches for the 1997 federal election campaign. The author covered many campaign events and made use of his *Ottawa Report* files. During the campaign, the author complied an exhaustive file of media coverage from *Alberta Report*, *Globe and Mail*, *Financial Post*, *Red Deer Advocate*, the *Edmonton Journal* and the *Calgary Herald*, as well as keeping transcripts of television coverage, including CBC's *Newsworld* and CTV's *Canada AM* and a live tape recording of events at the Reform Party of Canada's election-night headquarters.

EPILOGUE

The author monitored and prepared a written transcript from CTV's *Canada AM* broadcast of June 3, 1997.

SELECTED BIBLIOGRAPHY

CANADIAN HISTORICAL REFERENCES

Allen, Ralph. *Ordeal by Fire: Canada, 1910–1945.* New York: Doubleday, 1961.

Brown, Craig. *The Illustrated History of Canada.* Toronto: Lester Publishing Limited, 1987, 1991.

Careless, J. M. S. *Canada: A Story of Challenge.* Toronto: Macmillan, 1953, 1970.

Francis, R. Douglas, and Donald B. Smith. *Origins: Canadian History to Confederation.* Toronto: Holt, Rinehart and Winston of Canada, 1988.

Francis, R. Douglas, and Donald B. Smith. *Readings in Canadian History: Pre-Confederation.* Toronto: Holt, Rinehart and Winston of Canada, 1986.

Francis, R. Douglas, and Donald B. Smith. *Readings in Canadian History: Post-Confederation.* Toronto: Holt, Rinehart and Winston of Canada, 1982.

Hardy, W. G. *From Sea unto Sea: The Road to Nationhood 1850–1910.* New York: Doubleday, 1960.

MacGregor, James G. *History of Alberta.* Edmonton: Hurtig, 1972.

Morton, W. L. *The Kingdom of Canada.* Toronto: McClelland & Stewart, 1963, 1969.

Palmer, Howard, with Tamara Palmer. *Alberta: A New History.* Edmonton: Hurtig, 1990.

CANADIAN REFORM POLITICS

Beck, J. Murray. *Joseph Howe, Anti-Confederate.* Ottawa: The Canadian Historical Association, Booklet No. 17, 1965.

Byfield, Ted. *The Deplorable Unrest in the Colonies.* Edmonton: Alberta Report, 1983.

Byrne, T.C. *Alberta's Revolutionary Leaders.* Calgary: Detselig Enterprises, 1991.

Cornell, P. G. *The Great Coalition.* Ottawa: The Canadian Historical Association, Booklet No. 19, 1966.

Dunham, Aileen. *Political Unrest in Upper Canada 1815–1836.* Toronto: McClelland & Stewart, 1963.

Irvine, William. *The Farmers in Politics.* Toronto: McClelland & Stewart, 1920, 1976.

Lingard, C. Cecil. *Territorial Government in Canada.* Toronto: University of Toronto Press, 1946.

MacMechan, Archibald. *The Winning of Popular Government*. Toronto: Glasgow, Brook & Company, 1916.

Melnyk, George, ed. *Riel to Reform: A History of Protest in Western Canada*. Saskatoon: Fifth House Publishers, 1992.

Morton, W. L. *The Progressive Party in Canada*. Toronto: University of Toronto Press, 1950.

Ouellet, Fernand. *Louis Joseph Papineau: A Divided Soul*. Ottawa: The Canadian Historical Association, Booklet No. 11, 1964.

Thomas, Lewis Herbert. *The Struggle for Responsible Government in the North West Territories 1870–97*. Toronto: University of Toronto Press, 1956, 1978.

Underhill, F. H. *Canadian Political Parties*. Ottawa: The Canadian Historial Association, Booklet No. 8, 1968.

WILLIAM ABERHART AND ERNEST MANNING

Barr, John J. *The Dynasty: The Rise and Fall of Social Credit*. Toronto: McClelland & Stewart, 1974.

Colbourne, Maurice. *War and Unemployment*. London: Figurehead, 1932.

Elliott, David, and Iris Miller. *Bible Bill: A Biography of William Aberhart*. Edmonton: Reidmore, 1987.

Hanson, Erik. *The Dynamic Decade*. Toronto: McClelland & Stewart, 1958.

Irving, John A. *The Social Credit Movement in Alberta*. Toronto: University of Toronto Press, 1959.

Johnson, L. P. V., and O. J. MacNutt. *Aberhart of Alberta*. Edmonton: Cooperative Press, 1970.

Macpherson, C. B. *Democracy in Alberta: Social Credit and the Party System*. Toronto: University of Toronto Press, 1953.

Manning, Ernest C. *Political Realignment: A Challenge to Thoughtful Canadians*. Toronto: McClelland & Stewart, 1967.

Morton, W. L. *Social Credit in Alberta*. Toronto: University of Toronto Press, 1959.

Watkins, Ernest. *The Golden Province: A Political History of Alberta*. Calgary: Sandstone Publishing Ltd., 1980.

PRESTON MANNING

Byfield, Ted, ed. *Act of Faith*. Vancouver: British Columbia Report, 1991.

Deacey, Jamie, ed. *Ottawa Report*. Ottawa: Association House. Issues from May 1993 to June 1997.

Dobbin, Murray. *Preston Manning and the Reform Party of Canada*. Toronto: James Lorimer, 1991.

Durant, William, and Ariel Durant. *The Story of Civilization*. New York: Simon and Schuster, 1939, 1969.

Harrison, Trevor. *Of Passionate Intensity: Right-Wing Populism and the Reform Party of Canada*. Toronto: University of Toronto Press, 1995.

Mackey, Lloyd. *Like Father, Like Son: Ernest Manning and Preston Manning*. Toronto: ECW Press, 1997.

Manning, Preston. *The New Canada*. Toronto: Macmillan Canada, 1992.

Padover, Saul. *Jefferson*. New York: Harcourt, Brace, 1942.

Sandburg, Carl. *Abraham Lincoln: The Prairie Years*. 2 vols. New York: Harcourt, Brace & Company, 1929.

Sandburg, Carl. *Abraham Lincoln: The War Years*. 4 vols. New York: Harcourt, Brace & Company, 1940.

Sharpe, Sydney, and Don Braid. *Storming Babylon: Preston Manning and the Rise of the Reform Party*. Toronto: Key Porter Books, 1992.

INDEX